HARDPRESS.NET
HOME OF HARD-TO-FIND BOOKS

The Red River Country
by Alexander Jamieson Russell

Address:
HardPress
8345 NW 66TH ST #2561
MIAMI FL 33166-2626
USA
Email: info@hardpress.net

THE

RED RIVER COUNTRY,

HUDSON'S BAY & NORTH-WEST

TERRITORIES,

CONSIDERED

IN RELATION TO CANADA,

WITH THE LAST REPORT OF S. J. DAWSON, ESQUIRE, C. E., ON THE LINE OF ROUTE
BETWEEN LAKE SUPERIOR AND THE RED RIVER SETTLEMENT.

ILLUSTRATED BY A MAP.

BY ALEX. J. RUSSELL, C. E.,
INSPECTOR OF CROWN TIMBER AGENCIES, CANADA EAST AND WEST.

OTTAWA:
PUBLISHED BY G. E. DESBARATS.
1869.

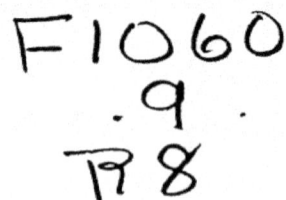

PRINTED BY THE
GLOBE PRINTING COMPANY,
TORONTO.

PREFACE.

————

THIS Pamphlet is intended to present such a summary of the information, given by different writers, respecting the Red River, Hudson's Bay and North-West Territories, arranged under their natural geographical divisions, as may be sufficient to give a general view of their character and comparative value to Canada.

It will be seen by the Table of Contents that I have endeavoured to present a practical view of the reasons why we require these Territories, or part of them; also, of our means of maintaining communication with them, and of the comparative superiority of the routes through our own Territory as highways for the future commerce of the interior, and for communication with the Pacific Provinces.

A. J. RUSSELL.

OTTAWA, 1868.

CONTENTS.

CHAPTER IV.

NORTH HUDSON'S BAY TERRITORY, OR BARREN GROUND.

CHAPTER V.

NORTH M'KENZIE RIVER COUNTRY.

CHAPTER VI.

PELLY RIVER AND MOUNTAIN COUNTRY.

CHAPTER VII.

CENTRAL PRAIRIE COUNTRY, OR RED RIVER, SASKATCHEWAN AND PEACE RIVER TERRITORY.

CHAPTER VIII.

CENTRAL PRAIRIE COUNTRY CONTINUED—LAKE AND RIVER WINNIPEG, LAKE OF THE WOODS, RED RIVER, AND COUNTRY BETWEEN THEM.

CHAPTER IX.

CENTRAL PRAIRIE COUNTRY CONTINUED—RIVER ASSINIBOINE—INFERTILE REGION ON ITS BRANCHES, THE SOURIS AND QU'APPELLE.

CHAPTER X.

CENTRAL PRAIRIE COUNTRY CONTINUED—FERTILE REGION ON THE ASSINIBOINE.

CHAPTER XI.

CHAPTER XII.

CHAPTER XIII.

CHAPTER XIV.

CHAPTER XX.

SLAVE RIVER, HAY RIVER, AND RIVER OF THE MOUNTAINS.

CHAPTER XXI.

CLIMATE OF CENTRAL PRAIRIE COUNTRY—FITNESS FOR CULTIVATION—CROPS RAISED.

CHAPTER XXII.

COAL, PETROLEUM, AND BUILDING MATERIAL.

CHAPTER XXXIII.

INTERESTS OF CANADA, THE HUDSON'S BAY COMPANY AND THE INDIANS, COULD
BE COMBINED.

CHAPTER XXXIV.

COMPARATIVE VALUE OF THE SEVERAL SECTIONS OF TERRITORY TO CANADA;

INDEX OF SUBJECTS

IN REPORT ON THE LINE OF ROUTE BETWEEN LAKE SUPERIOR AND THE
RED RIVER SETTLEMENT.

THE RED RIVER COUNTRY,

HUDSON'S BAY & NORTH-WEST TERRITORIES,

CONSIDERED IN RELATION TO CANADA.

CHAPTER I.

INTRODUCTION.

ABOUT two years ago an eminent Canadian statesman told us that Her Majesty had been graciously pleased to express her willingness to consent to the acquisition, by Canada, of all the great northern and north-west territories of British North America. Since then the "British North America Act" has been passed, erecting the Provinces of Canada, Nova Scotia and New Brunswick into the "Dominion of Canada," and providing for the union of these territories with it, by Her Majesty, on an Address from the Parliament of Canada, expressing conditions she may approve of; and both Houses of Parliament of the Dominion have addressed Her Majesty praying her action accordingly.

As paying any just claim of the Hudson's Bay Company for any interest or right of property, that may be acquired from them, will be a condition in the transaction, it is desirable that we should endeavour to form a correct estimate of the value of these territories to us.

In doing so we have to consider their extent and character—and what use we can make of them;—to inquire if we need them or any part of them, and for what purposes; and of what importance ultimately they may be to us as respects the great objects aimed at by the Confederation we have entered into.

We have also to consider what is the best way of getting in to them; if we can have such a way on our own ground and at all seasons of the year, and if the ways of communication through our own ground will be the best for the freight and travel of these territories.

These heads cover a wide range of matter. Without professing to enter fully into them, we may take a brief glance at the subjects of them, and endeavor to put a few facts together as to what is known of this great northern part of the continent of America, of which it seems destined that we are to have the control.

1

If we include all the vast region heretofore held by the Hudson's Bay Company, alike under its charter and its lease of Indian territory, which has not been renewed since its expiration in 1859, the extent is very great indeed. It embraces all the northern part of this continent, from the boundary of Labrador to that of Russian America, lying north of Canada, the United States and British Columbia. It is three thousand miles in length from East to West, and fourteen hundred miles in breadth from North to South ; and has an area of about two millions two hundred and ten thousand superficial miles.

If its value could be measured by its magnitude it would be enormous ;—but such as it is, it is not much inferior in natural value to Russia in Europe, which it more than equals in extent and in many respects resembles in character.

Russia in Europe sustains a population of sixty-nine millions of souls. If this territory of ours be only half as good, it may sustain a population somewhat over the thirty millions Lord Selkirk estimated it as capable of supporting.

If this great territory be added to our Confederation, together with Vancouver's Island, British Columbia, Prince Edward's Island and Newfoundland, with Labrador, the Dominion of Canada will then include an area of upwards of three millions of superficial miles. That is more than three-quarters of the area of the European continent,—or one-half greater than Russia in Europe in extent.

Besides much exceeding Russia in Europe in extent of territory, Canada, when so augmented, will possess immensely greater maritime advantages. Instead of being almost excluded from the ocean, like that great country, she will have, on the Pacific, twelve hundred and fifty miles of the coast line of British Columbia and Vancouver's Island, open to navigation at all seasons ; besides three thousand seven hundred and fifty miles of coast, south of Latitude 60°, on the Atlantic and Gulf of St. Lawrence, (a great part of it open to navigation in winter,) exclusive of bays and inlets, and the estuary of the St. Lawrence ; possessing also that mighty river, and eighteen hundred miles of coast on its great lakes; far surpassing any river in European Russia in importance as a commercial outlet. Without the St. Lawrence the Saskatchewan is equivalent to the Volga, and the ports of York and Moose Factory, and others in Hudson's and James' Bay, are naturally about equal to Archangel in value as means of access to the ocean, though as yet used only for the traffic of the Hudson's Bay Company.

To avoid seeming to base our comparison merely on territorial extent we may carry it a little further :—

Of the four hundred and two millions of "decatines," (of about two and one-seventh English acres each,) forming the total area of Russia in Europe, M. Schnitzler, in his "Essai Statistique de la Russie," estimates that the whole of the cultivated lands and the meadows taken together, does not exceed sixty-seven and a half millions, or about one-sixth part of the surface; and by the Official Returns made about the time he wrote, the average yield was four and a half fold to one of rye sown, and nearly four to one of wheat.

No doubt an equal proportion, at least, of the total area of our Provinces and Territories taken together is fit for cultivation, if returns like these be taken as the lowest standard; but if even one-twelfth part, instead of one-sixth of it, be capable of yielding the general average returns of Lower and Upper Canada, which by the last census are from two and a half to three and a half times as great as these rates, the ultimate productive capacity of our Dominion and territories will probably be one-half greater than that of Russia in Europe, even if fifty per cent. were added to her rates of produce mentioned. We have good grounds, therefore, for assuming that the comparison as to extent of territory and its capacity to sustain population is rather in our favor.

As to the value of our maritime advantages, we have no need to rest on calculations of what may be, or estimates of future progress for the result. The Dominion has afloat to-day a commercial navy, that, in tonnage and number of men far surpasses that of the Russian Empire, exceeding that of any other continental power of the old world, excepting France, which it nearly equals.*

In respect to this it is proper to remember that the Maritime Provinces, in confederating with Canada, have augmented her importance and power in a degree immensely exceeding the mere proportion of their population or extent of their territory. They have given her an ample sea-board, thickly studded with excellent harbours,—coal fields nearly as extensive as those of Great Britain,—and many thousands of hardy, skilful sea-faring men, who, to use the language of Governor Andrews in his

* Note, since the above was written.—Merchant Navies of Europe from "The Statesman's Year Book for 1868."—Great Britain, 5,452,862 tons ; France, 1,008,084 tons ; Italy, 660,662 tons ; Russia, including Finland, 365,000 tons in 1866 ; Dominion of Canada, by Canadian Parliamentary return on 1st July, 1867,—

	776,343 tons.
Add for Guysboro, &c., not in return	36,000 "
	812,343 "
Newfoundland in 1866, by Canadian Year Book.................	83,204 "
Prince Edward's Island in 1865 do	30,549 "
	926,096 tons.

report to Congress on the British Provinces, from their superior intelligence and bodily vigour, and their experience in the navigation of cold and stormy coasts, are the best of seamen, and well qualified to maintain the honor of their flag on every sea.

The Dominion, though but in the beginning of her power, owns already about 800,000 of tons of shipping;—bearing a proportion of about twenty per cent. to her population, while that of Great Britain, the greatest maritime power in the world, without her colonies, is only about eighteen per cent. per head.

We see, therefore, that we have before us a greater and more advantageous field, as a basis of future national prosperity and power, than that on which has risen that empire whose greatness has not a little intimidated Europe, and has been supposed to threaten her independence. In view of this fact,—with superior civilization and institutions in our favor—we may surely hope to develop at least equally advantageous results from the territories at our command and their resources, though less arrogant in our pretensions.

This comparison is made for the purpose of showing that we have now no longer to look on outlying territories with that indifference with which they might have been regarded when our autonomy was limited to that of a single province, to which they might stand in little or no closer relation than a foreign land, but as integers, the utmost value of which will ultimately go to swell the balance in favor of our national strength and prosperity.

In that view, while drawing the distinction broadly between what is immediately of high value to us, for the extension of settlement, by our present standard of the value of lands for that purpose, we must also take into account not only the inferior portions capable of any degree of agricultural occupation, in future time, under the influence of increasing demand and improved means of communication, but also regions which have no other value than that which their fisheries, their metals and other mineral resources may be found to present.

We have already had a little experience of the error of undervaluing territory, under the idea that we had land enough without it. Many were indifferent to the loss, some years ago, of what was called the disputed territory, on the head waters of the River St. John of New Brunswick; but now we find that our railroad to Halifax, in order to avoid going straight through that territory, has to be made a hundred miles longer than it otherwise would have been; adding about six millions of dollars to the cost of making it, and about a dollar and a half for ever to the freight of every ton of goods passing over it. We are now making colonization roads to let settlers into the scraps left us of that territory, and the loss of it has seriously weakened our frontier. Our experience in this instance should be a warning to us against undervaluing our opportunity of acquiring useful territory now.

In briefly describing the great Northern Territory of British America, it may be divided into the following sections, partly on account of their distinct natural character or geographical position, and partly for convenience in speaking of them.

1st. East Main or the Peninsula of Labrador.

2nd. South Hudson's Bay Territory,—between that Bay and Lakes Winnipeg and Athabasca, from the northern water-shed of the St. Lawrence to lat. 60° N.

3rd. North Hudson's Bay Territory or Barren Ground, extending from the preceding to the Arctic Ocean.

4th. The McKenzie River country, from lat. 60° N., to the Arctic Ocean.

5th. The Pelly River or Mountain Territory, embracing all north of British Columbia from the crest of the Rocky Mountains to Russian America.

6th. The Red River, Saskatchewan and Peace River Country, or Central Prairie Land, extending from the Lake of the Woods and Lakes Winnipeg and Athabasca to the Rocky Mountains, and from the United States boundary, lat. 49° N up to lat. 60° N.

The last of these divisions only is of great and immediate importance to us, for the extension of settlement and commerce, and for the command of communication to the Pacific Ocean;—objects alike eminently important for the expansion and consolidation of national power.

Before proceeding to consider its value in relation to Canada, and the means of communicating with it, the other sections mentioned may be briefly noticed. Though now only of value for their fur trade, and of little or no interest beyond that, at present, excepting to naturalists and other men of science,—we are unable to say that they may not, in future, become of some importance for their mineral wealth or other natural resources, now unknown or unavailable.*

* Note.—Since the above was written, British Columbia and Newfoundland have decided in favor of union with Canada. And it has been agreed between the Imperial Government and the Hudson's Bay Company, that Canada is to have all the territories held or owned by the latter for £300,000, Stg., (which Great Britain guarantees), the Company retaining their trading posts, with an allowance of land around them, and one-twentieth of the land, as sales to settlers take place, for fifty years; which unites their powerful interest to ours in the tranquillity and speedy settlement of the country.

CHAPTER II.

EAST MAIN, OR THE PENINSULA OF LABRADOR.

This great peninsula, lying between Hudson's Bay and the Atlantic ocean, extends a thousand miles from east to west, between Cape St. Charles, at the entrance of the Straits of Belle-Isle, and James' Bay, and eight hundred miles from north to south, from Cape Wolstenholme, its northern extremity, to the height of land dividing the waters of Rupert's River from those of the Saguenay.

Geographically it might be described as bounded on the south-west between James' Bay and the mouth of the St. Lawrence, by Rupert's River, up to its source, and thence eastward by a line to the Bay of Seven Islands; which would give it an erea of about four hundred and eighty thousand superficial miles. But the southern part of the peninsula of Labrador, facing the Gulf, as far eastward as Ance Blanc Sablon, and back to the sources of the rivers falling into the Gulf, belongs to Canada. (Blanc Sablon is ninety miles within the eastern entrance of the straits of Belle-Isle.) Deducting this part, the remainder of the Peninsula has an area of about four hundred and twenty thousand superficial miles, or a little more than Denmark, Norway, Sweden and Lapland, taken together.

The eastern part of it, facing the straits of Belle-Isle, and the Atlantic, as far northward as the entrance of Ungava Bay, called Labrador in the strictest sense, is under the jurisdiction of Newfoundland. The remainder, which is much the larger part, is held by the Hudson's Bay Company, and is commonly known by the name of East Main.

Labrador was first discovered in A.D. 986, by the Northman Bearne, the son Heriulf, who called it "Helluland it Mikla" or "Great slate land," from the stratified rocks (secondary limestone) seen on its coast. It was re-discovered by Sebastin Cabot, and five years afterwards, in A.D. 1501, it was visited by Corte Real, who, with less accuracy, called it "Terra Labrador" "Cultivable or laborers' land," believing it to be so from the growth of trees he saw upon it.

It is remarkable of this great peninsula, that though it lies next to Europe, and is the first discovered part of the American continent, very little is known of its interior; and that but lately. What is known of it, is such as to impress the mind powerfully with a sense of its vast and stern desolation. From the coldness of its climate and its general sterility, it seems utterly unfit for occupation by civilized men; except where a scattered population might live by the fisheries of some parts of its coast; or where its mineral resources may give profitable employment to industry.

As might be expected in so great an extent, it presents considerable variety of character. The interior of the eastern part of it, where traversed, is found to be a high table land upwards of 2,000 feet above the level of the sea; with occasional mountains, rising to 3,000 feet, and some nearly to 4,000 feet. The valleys and lower slopes are covered with spruce, fir, and birch woods, of a moderate growth, in favorable positions; the spruce trees in some places averaging eighteen inches in diameter and fifty feet in height; in rare instances they have been found two feet in diameter, even as far north as the Moravian missionary station of Nain, on the Atlantic.

Much of the coast on the Atlantic and the Gulf is utterly barren of timber for many miles inland, and often destitute of soil; and much of the interior is burned bare to the rock by running fires more or less recent.

Advancing northward, the trees become more scattered, in groups, and stunted, till towards its northern extremity, and Hudson's Straits, it assumes the character of the Arctic "Barren Grounds" and the "Tundrens" of Siberia, and is like them the abode of the reindeer, that feed on the lichens and other Arctic vegetation its rocky surface affords.

As to surface, the western part of the peninsula seemingly contrasts with the eastern part. It is represented by physical geographers as being chiefly a plain country, for two hundred miles or more back from Hudson's Bay.

From what is known, its geological character seems considerably varied. The formation of the great Silurian basin of Hudson's Bay extends in a broad band far into the southern part of the Peninsula, and has even been represented, though doubtless on imperfect data, as connecting with the limestone formation of the east coast.

Though lying in the same latitude as the British Islands, the climate of this immense peninsula, taken as a whole, is no better than that of Lapland; in the northern parts it is even colder. But like that country, in the most southerly parts, it is such as to admit of the cultivation of vegetables, in favorable situations.

Mr. Gladman had a good opportunity of observing, during his thirty-one years' service in the Hudson's Bay Company. He states in his evidence given to a committee of the Canadian Legislature, that at East Main Old Factory he raised good potatoes, turnips and other vegetables. East Main Factory is sixty miles north of Rupert's River. He says further, that a large herd of cattle was kept there, at that time, as a resource in case of the company's ships wintering in the bay, an abundant supply of hay being made in the salt marshes on the shores of the bay: that vetches grow wild on the point of the river, and abundance of strawberries and currants.

He says that at Big River, a hundred and eighty miles north of Rupert's River, potatoes and other vegetables are grown. The cold in winter is evidently intense. He states the lowest degree of temperature registered by him was 50° below zero at East Main. He says that at Rupert House the soil is much better and the station more sheltered than East Main Factory, or Big River, and more favorable for garden cultivation. The Finish colonists who raised barley at Alten, (lat. 70°) in Lapland, would no doubt be quite successful in doing so on the warm rich soil of the Silurian basin at Rupert's River.

The climate of Hamilton River, in the south-eastern angle of the peninsula, is apparently similar. Notwithstanding the lofty, rugged and extremely barren character of the shores of Hamilton inlet, into which the river falls, Mr. Davis, in an article read before the Literary and Historical Society of Quebec, speaks of the pleasing aspect of the valley of Hamilton River, of its being well timbered and having a loamy soil in parts, with some advantage in climate, and mentions the Hudson's Bay Company's farm, where cows, pigs and sheep were kept.

In respect to the growing of garden vegetables, and having forests, such as they are, the southern parts of the peninsula of Labrador much resemble the more favorable part of Lapland.

These facts are not altogether unimportant in connection with the probable ultimate extension of fishing settlements, or the formation of mining establishments, should minerals of value be found in the confines of the Silurian and Laurentian formations.

That part of the peninsula under the jurisdiction of Newfoundland is evidently very valuable for its fisheries. As early as 1832, the value of its yearly exports are stated by Mr. McGregor to have amounted to upwards of three hundred thousand pounds sterling.

The west coast of the peninsula, within Hudson's Bay, forming part of the Hudson's Bay Company's territory, is much less valuable in that respect. The entrance to the Bay is much obstructed by ice late in spring, and early in the fall; the Company's ships, which make but a single voyage into the Bay each summer, being sometimes, though rarely, prevented from returning to Europe, till the following season.

To fishing for foreign markets this would be a very great disadvantage. The absence of salmon on that coast, and the streams falling into it, is another. A salmon, not of the ordinary kind,— probably the "Salmo Rossii" of the Arctic, is occasionally, though rarely seen, in some of the rivers falling into Hudson's Bay.

Though Codfish are well known to be exceedingly abundant at Davis' Straits, (see Report of Commissioners of British Fisheries for 1846,) they are not generally noticed in such a way as to indicate that they are so in Hudson's Bay ; nor are they mentioned as forming part of the food of the native or other residents.

Seals and porpoises, however, are abundant. Some are of opinion that the absence of salmon is due to the seals being so numerous. Umfraville, in 1790, says that whales, white and black, sea horses, bears and seals, are killed in great numbers by the Esquimaux ; and Lieut. Chappel, in 1817, proposes the opening of a free intercourse with Canada as likely to animate the exertions of the Esquimaux in their seal and whale fishing.

The natural facilities for opening a direct interior communication with Hudson's Bay will be briefly noticed in the following section.

As, apart from whaling, " Seal Fishing" would seem to be the only profitable industry that the west coast of the peninsula admits of, it becomes natural to inquire what the importance of Seal Fishing is, as a branch of trade, where it can be carried on successfully, and what employment it would afford.

The Seal Fishery of Newfoundland may serve to explain this. Mr. M. H. Perley, in his " Report on the sea and river fisheries of New Brunswick," says that the outfit for the seal fisheries of Newfoundland, for 1847, consisted of 321 vessels, making in all 29,800 tons, with 9,751 men. The average yield for ten years was about half a million of seal skins, and three millions of gallons of oil. It is roughly estimated that about a million of seals are killed annually on the coast of Labrador proper, by the Esquimax and other seal fishers.

What may be the comparative value of Hudson's Bay as a site of seal and other fisheries remains to be known. It would seem desirable that it should be ascertained by one or more practical men of business, engaged in the trade of Labrador, commissioned for that purpose.

CHAPTER III.

SOUTH HUDSON'S BAY TERRITORY.

We may next turn to the adjacent section of country, held by the Hudson's Bay Company, lying between Hudson's Bay and the Lakes Winnipeg and Athabasca ; extending from the northern water-shed of the St. Lawrence and its tributaries—the reputed boundary of Canada, to the parallel of lat. 60° N.,—including with it the Abittibbi District, between the water-shed and Rupert's River :—containing in all an area of about four hundred and thirty thousand superficial miles.

For the convenience of description it may be called the South Hudson's Bay Territory.

Though this territory has a very cold climate, exceedingly so in winter, (the greater part of it is too cold to admit of agricultural occupation of any kind,) it is nevertheless far more valuable than East Main, besides being especially so in relation to Canada.

It is the coldness of the climate alone that prevents this territory from being very valuable as an agricultural country. One-half of it lies in the great northern Silurian basin, in which Hudson's Bay is situated. That formation besides underlying the greater part of the district of Abbitibbi, (which is a little larger than New Brunswick,) is represented by Sir John Richardson as extending from two hundred miles in the north part to four hundred miles in the south, due westward from Hudson's and James' Bay. It is shown as extending also to the distance of two hundred miles southward from the south end of James' Bay, and comes to the boundary of Canada at the sources of the northern tributaries of Lake Temiscaming of the Ottawa*, where it is called the level clay country by the Hudson's Bay Company's people. It is so called in contradistinction to the rugged Laurentian Country forming the height of land, where the waters of the Ottawa and northern tributaries of the Great Lakes, and those of Hudson's Bay interlace, and which extends over the Ottawa Valley and the country north of the Lakes Huron and Superior, rendering so much of them unfit for settlement.

The boundary of this Silurian plain country is probably quite irregular, and may in many parts not be accurately known. Mr. Ballantyne, who resided there, places it about Martin's Falls, on the Albany River, two hundred and fifty miles due west of James' Bay ; and says the river flows through a limestone and clay country to the Bay. Lieut. Blackiston, in ascending Hayes' River from York Factory, describes the country on it as alluvial, without any rock being visible, for a hundred and twenty-four miles, to the first portage, where he says the primitive formation commences, and that is two hundred miles due west from the coast of the Bay.

It will be seen by the accompanying map, that this broad band of Silurian formation, which sweeps round Hudson's Bay, in a north-westerly direction, attains a width of five hundred miles about

*Note.—By an extensive survey, just completed by Provincial Surveyor L. Russell, it has been ascertained that though the clay land of Hudson's Bay extends south of Lake Abbitibbi to the northern waters of the Ottawa, the underlying rocks are there Laurentian.

Lat. 63° N.; then turning north-eastward continues to the Artic Sea, which its western outline intersects about Long. 97° W.

It will be seen also that it, again, is encircled by that broad band of primary formation, known in Canada as the Laurentian Range, which skirts the lower St. Lawrence, and forms the northern boundary of the great plain of Lower Canada. Gradually declining in height, and increasing in breadth, to two hundred miles, it crosses the Ottawa above the mouth of the Bonnechère, and sweeps round the north shore of Lakes Huron and Superior. Curving north-westward with a breadth of two hundred miles, this Laurentian Belt continues along the rear of the Silurian country of Hudson's Bay, with varying breadth, increasing to four hundred miles where it joins the Artic. Its western boundary, commencing at Rainy Lake, passes north-westward, through the Lake of the Woods, and along the east shore of Lake Winnipeg; then curving more westerly, through Cedar Lake, on the Saskatchewan, to Methy Portage, and thence on a more northerly course, through the west end of Lake Athabasca, and near the middle of Slave Lake, it passes to the east end of Bear Lake, and thence north-eastward to the Artic Sea, at the west end of Coronation Gulf.

This broad range of primary formation divides the great Silurian basin of Hudson's Bay from the still greater central basin, or sloping plateau, of Silurian and more recent formations, lying between it and the Rocky Mountains, and extending from the Artic Sea to the Gulf of Mexico; it also divides both of them from Canada.

Though east and north of Quebec the summits of this range rise from two to three thousand feet, fronting the River St. Lawrence,—and four and five thousand feet in the interior—it declines so in height as it goes westward, that where it traverses the Ottawa, its summits rise only from five to thirteen hundred feet,—and very rarely the latter, over that river. After ascending through the Laurentide Range, by the valley of the Ottawa, the water-shed between its waters and those of Hudson's Bay, has, in parts scarcely any perceptible elevation, and is passed unnoticed.

Though presenting a lofty and very rugged barrier along the north side of Lake Superior, especially where it goes westward towards the frontier of the United States,—and the same north of Lake Huron—it becomes lower further northward, rising but little over the adjoining country.

Where it divides the two great Silurian basins, and forms the west half of the territory we have now under consideration, Sir John Richardson says "its altitude nowhere entitles it to the apellation of mountain chain. Its hypogenous rocks, which are chiefly granite and gneiss, scarcely rise above the mean eastern slope, and in no case present continuous ridges or acute peaks. They exhibit generally rounded or dome-shaped summits, or form oblong eminences, separated by narrow inclined valleys, the larger ones occupied, without exception, by deep lakes; and the proportion of water is very great."

This declination in height and peculiar character of the range, are mentioned, not only as meriting notice as descriptive of a large part of this section of territory, but especially because they are of importance to us, as admitting of a most direct line of Railway from Montreal to the Red River settlement, (and the Pacific,) about four hundred miles shorter than the route through Minnesota, now used; as favorable as to the character of the ground as much of what is to be made of the Intercolonial Railway, in the country between the St. Lawrence and New Brunswick, and passing through much land as fit for settlement, and with as good a climate; but with less depth of snow in winter.

The probability of this fact as to a direct route to Red River, was stated in evidence given before the last Canadian Parliamentary Committee on the North-west Territory. It has since been to an important extent confirmed by the results of surveys of the Montreal River, a north-western tributary of the Ottawa, and of a line, from it, a hundred and five miles westward, performed last winter by Provincial Surveyors A. G. Forrest and D. Sinclair. The valley of the river for a hundred miles was found to present a good site for a railroad, while it was learned that the line of a hundred and five miles was, at its commencement, only about fourteen miles south of the continuous level clay country, and about twenty miles from it at its termination; the intervening distance, at the commencement, to the clay country, being traversed by an arm of the river. These surveys have on that account a peculiar value.

CLIMATE OF SOUTH HUDSON'S BAY TERRITORY.

In order to see what reason there is for speaking so favorably of the climate of this part of the south Hudson's Bay Territory, let us consider a little more closely what is known of it as a whole.

The north-east part of it is extremely cold. The Barren Ground of the north, where trees of every kind almost entirely cease to exist, sweeps down into the north-eastern part of it, as much as a hundred and fifty miles southward of the sixtieth parallel of latitude; closely approaching Churchill River, towards its mouth. Even at York Factory, nothing but the hardiest vegetables can be raised. In summer there is a thickness of seven feet of perpetually frozen ground, at ten feet below the surface, and spruce trees, the prevailing wood, are almost uselessly small.

But the climate improves equally southward and westward; the western side of it, even to its north-west angle, is wooded thickly, and flanks the great central region suitable for cultivation.

Umfraville, writing in 1790, says that the pine trees (spruce probably) on the coast of Hudson's Bay, near York Fort, are "too small and knotty to be used for good building; but on leaving the marshy country and going inland to the southward, trees are of a more stately growth ; and about Albany and Moose Forts they are found of all diameters ;" and adds further that "potatoes, turnips, and almost all kitchen garden stuff, are raised with facility, and no doubt corn could be raised," but the Company, he says, discourage anything like cultivation.

Mr. Gladman, whose evidence has been already quoted, resided fifteen years at Moose Factory ; he says its climate and soil are good, that he raised potatoes and other vegetables there in great abundance, that barley ripened well, and that horned cattle, horses, sheep and pigs were kept there. It is to be observed that Moose Factory is upwards of two hundred and thirty miles north of the boundary between this territory and Canada. He adds that the soil and climate of Albany, which is a hundred miles further north, does not differ much from Moose, that it is well sheltered, and that the extensive marshes on the coast furnish abundant fodder for domestic cattle. He also says that the soil around the posts of Henly, Martin's Falls, Osnaburg and Lac Seul, is of a quality that enables the servants of the company to raise fair crops of potatoes.

At New Brunswick House, which is a hundred miles further south, he says the soil is very good, that excellent potatoes are raised there, also every description of vegetables. Oats ripened well, and made good oatmeal, ground with a hand mill ; wheat was tried afterwards, he was informed, with good success. He says further, "*that he does not know anything to prevent a good settlement from being made there, but its being rather distant from market.*"

South of Lake Abbitibbi, near the southern boundary of this territory, the mean summer temperature probably exceeds that of Halifax, Nova Scotia, as it well may, seeing the mean temperature on Lake Temiscaming, about one degree further south, so nearly resembles that of Montreal ; the mean of the summer of the former being 65°20, and of the year 39°49, and the corresponding mean température of the latter 65°55 and 42°86, by the tables given by Sir John Richardson in his "Arctic Researches."* Lake Abbitibbi lies nearly in the same latitude as the west coast of

* His published tables differ slightly in fractions from the above, owing to typographical errors.

Lake St. John, on the Upper Saguenay, which has the climate of Three Rivers, and yields excellent wheat.

Speaking of Martin's Falls, a post on the Albany River, upwards of two hundred miles westward from James' Bay, and two hundred miles north from Lake Superior, Mr. Barnston, who resided there, says that " it has the winter of Russia and the July and August of Germany and France; that in the usual course of seasons the buds of the trees begin to swell about the 12th of May, and leaves expand about 28th May," (which is as early as they did at Ottawa this last Spring.) He says that "a night's frost will sometimes intervene as late as the 10th June," (which is the case in central Canada, occasionally about the 15th of June,) that " by the 1st October foilage is yellow and falling. Usually there is a little snow by 20th October, and it covers the ground by 1st November." In Johnson's Physical Atlas the line of wheat cultivation is represented as passing here. It is quite possible that it may.

At the north end of Lake Winnipeg, on the western side of this section, three hundred and fifty miles north of Rainy River, its southern boundary, Captain Blackiston, of the Imperial Exploring Expedition, states that barley, potatoes, onions, carrots, peas and pumpkins, flourish in the open air, and melons can be forced ; but he adds that at Holy Lake, a hundred and sixty miles north-east-ward, near the centre of this section, potatoes do not always attain full size.

Towards the south end of Lake Winnipeg, at Fort Alexander, on the mouth of the River Winnipeg, at a hundred and fifty miles north of Rainy River, spring wheat grows well. Mr. Dawson, in his report of his Red River exploration, states that the Indians have always raised Indian corn with success on the islands of the Lake of the Woods.

The south-western part of this territory is quite fit for cultiva-tion, as regards climate ; but unfortunately, instead of being a fertile Silurian plain, like the north-east side bordering on Hudson's Bay, it is chiefly of the Laurentian formation, and is generally very rocky ; more so, as far as known, than the Laurentian, or greater part of the Ottawa country, but presenting, like it, excep-tional tracts of good land.

BOUNDARY OF THE GREAT SILURIAN BASIN OF HUDSON'S BAY.

Excepting on the canoe route from Lake Superior to Red River very little information is before the public respecting this section of territory. Its character and value may be found to be in a con-siderable degree affected by the extent to which the Silurian basin of Hudson's Bay may reach into it. Authorities differ widely as to the position of the boundary of that formation. Mr. Ballantyne would seemingly place it a little above Martin's Falls, on the Albany River; Sir John Richardson carries it two hundred miles further west, on that river, to the Head of Lake Joseph, near longitude 91° W.; but not beyond the south side of that lake. In the geological chart of Johnson's Physical Atlas, it is shown as curving downwards there, fully a hundred miles south of Lake Joseph. We would naturally suppose there must have been some basis of fact for such a representation, perhaps the existence of a considerable outlier of Silurian formation, like the limestone at the head of Lake Temiscaming, which in that chart is erroneously represented as an arm of the Silurian basin of Hudson's Bay. Perhaps the diluvial clay of that basin which overlaps the Laurentian formation to and over the water-shed of the Ottawa, north of Lake Temiscaming, and appears to have led to mistake as to the boundary of the Silurian basin there, may have obscured its position elsewhere.

As outliers of Silurian limestone and tracts of level clay soil, within the limits of possible agricultural occupation, in the great region between us and the Red River country, may ultimately prove of some importance, from their soil being more suitable for cultivation than the rocky Laurentian ground prevailing nearer, further and more accurate information as to the geological and topographical character of the country upon and immediately beyond the northern water-shed of Lakes Huron and Superior, is most desirable. The highly interesting information respecting Lake Nipigon, furnished last summer to the Crown Lands Department by the private enterprise of Mr. W. Armstrong, C. E., is an instance of what may be obtained even by cursory exploration.

FERTILE TRACT ON RAINY RIVER.

As an exception to the generally rough, rocky, marshy and poor character of the country, between the water-shed of Lake Superior and Lake Winnipeg, forming the south-west angle of the section under consideration, the fertile tract along the north side of Rainy River is of much importance, from its lying on the line of communication with the Red River country.

This tract is described as extending from Fort Francis, on the outlet of Rainy Lake, to the Lake of the Woods, sixty miles in direct distance, or eighty by the course of the river, with a breadth back from it of from half a mile to twelve miles, and is estimated, by Professor Hind, as containing over two hundred and twenty thousand acres of rich alluvial land, highly suitable for cultivation. On the other hand it is stated that the front of it only is dry enough for cultivation, and that the ground behind would need draining, to render it available. In either case, however, it would admit of continuous settlement for eighty miles along a central part of the route to Red River, which is important.

Rainy River is here the boundary between the State of Minnesota and British territory. It is a noble stream, described by our Canadian explorers as from two to three hundred yards in width and six feet in depth, with a current of about two miles an hour. The great Falls at Fort Francis, of about twenty-three feet, and two small rapids, the Manitou at thirty-four miles lower, with a fall of three feet, and the Long Rapid below it, with a fall of two and a half feet, are the only obstructions to navigation, from the east end of Rainy Lake to the west end of the Lake of the Woods, a distance of about one hundred and seventy miles. This navigable reach forms an important part of the proposed line of communication between Lake Superior and the Red River Settlement.

The banks of Rainy River are from fifteen to fifty feet in height, wooded with a large growth of elm, balm of Gilead, ash, oak and basswood. The soil is a rich dark sandy loam, mixed with much vegetable matter, and resting on clay. From the masses of limestone occasionally seen, there is reason to think that it underlies the bed of the river, and extends westward to Red River.

Mr. Pether, who was in charge of Fort Francis, described the climate as much the same as that of Montreal, only colder in winter. Wheat, root crops and kitchen vegetables, are successfully cultivated at Fort Francis.

Behind the fertile plateau Mr. Pether states that there is a peaty marsh of immense extent, with a depth in parts of thirty feet. It is bare of timber; nothing but low bushes grow on it.

As we already begin to use peat fuel with advantage in Canada, we can see in this bog an unlimited supply of fuel for the fertile tract when cultivation has removed its woods.

On the shores and islands of the Lake of the Woods, there are patches of good land, where the Indians have gardens, and have raised Indian corn without failure for many years. At the Mission of Islington, about thirty-five miles down the River Winnipeg, from the Lake of the Woods, and a hundred and twenty miles further north than Fort Francis, Mr. Hind states in his report that wheat is sown about the 20th of May, and reaped about the 26th of August, that Indian corn ripens well, and potatoes had never, during five years' cultivation, been injured by frost.

A hundred miles east of Islington, and as much north of Rainy Lake, there is reported to be a good grain-growing tract on the north shore of Lac Seul. The existence of the Rainy River tract renders it likely that there are others. As elsewhere in Laurentian countries, many tracts of good arable land, of limited extent, no doubt exist on the banks of the lakes and rivers, as remarked alike by Mr. Dawson and Mr. Hind, and in the valleys between the low dome-shaped hills that prevail over this region; but from being scattered and isolated they will long remain valueless, unless near the line of communication, or where they can be occupied in connection with mining operations, lumbering or fisheries.

Among these we might include the small tracts of drift occurring on the portages and on the islands in Lac de Mille Lacs, near the height of land, on the canoe route to Rainy Lake, noticed by Mr. Hind, who elsewhere says that there is no scarcity of arable land between the low hill ranges of Lac de Mille Lacs and Baril Lake to support a mining population. But their being on the coldest part of the route and subject to frost in summer, owing apparently to their elevation, is not to be overlooked.

As there is evident scope for the branches of industry mentioned, even the isolated tracts will, after the opening of a line of communication, be profitably occupied, but slowly, in the face of the greater inducement westward; while the good lands on the route will be more speedily taken up where the climate is favorable, as on Rainy River.

It may seem difficult to reconcile what is stated with regard to the growth of wheat at the places mentioned, with the fact that it seldom ripens well at Fort William; but not so when we consider that, owing to its vast extent, the very low temperature of Lake Superior, (excepting near the shore,) scarcely 40° on the last day of July, necessarily reduces the summer heat on its northern coast, while the temperature of the heights of land which are comparatively near it is reduced by their elevation. Thus, decidedly greater warmth of climate, after crossing the height of land and approaching Rainy Lake, is noticed alike by Sir John Richardson and other explorers.

At Fort Francis on Rainy River, where this tract of rich alluvial land commences, Sir John Richardson and others say that wheat is sown from the 1st to the 23rd of May, and reaped in the latter end of August.

To army officers, gentlemen from England, who have explored this region, the climate at Fort Francis might seem by no means favorable; and men even from the western peninsula of Canada might look upon it as much inferior to that of their own country; but those accustomed to the north-eastern settlements of Lower Canada see it in a different light.

When I was a backwoodsman engaged in farming and assisting to locate settlers, from thirty-seven to forty-five years ago, in the county of Megantic, fifty miles south-westward of Quebec, we sowed our wheat rather later than it is done at Fort Francis, and instead of reaping it in August, we were glad to get it all secured in September—were lucky if early frosts did not damage it, and if we got our other crops secured in October.

Superior cultivation may have mended matters somewhat now, but many of the north and east parts of Lower Canada are inferior to Megantic in climate. I have seen rather green rye carted home in the beginning of November, with a snow storm coming on, in the parish of Les Eboulements, from rich clay soil, generally well worth cultivation, nevertheless. But as to the soil and climate, at least, practical men would prefer the rich alluvial lands of Rainy River and its August harvest, with its broad navigable stream, and exceedingly rich fisheries, to either Megantic or Les Eboulements.

We see, therefore, that the south side of this territory, for a breadth of upward of a hundred miles in some parts, (as at Fort Alexander and New Brunswick House,) is as suitable in climate for raising wheat as parts of Lower Canada, where settlements have long existed, or are now being formed ; and no doubt much of the remainder which we class as suitable, for the growth of barley only, may, on account of the soil, which its level Silurian character indicates, be quite as profitably cultivated as the tracts on the north-east parts of the Taché Road in Rimouski, now being opened for settlement. The Intercolonial Railroad has to pass through such a region as the latter, in soil and climate, on leaving the St. Lawrence.

From the preceding facts, it will be seen, that if a line be drawn north-westward, from Rupert's River to Oxford House, and continued a little beyond the head of Lake Winnipeg, it roughly divides this territory into halves, and, with slight curves, may be taken as representing the limit of the cultivation of barley ; while a similar line from the north side of Lake Abittibbi, passing more westerly, a little north of New Brunswick House, and a hundred and twenty miles north of Rainy Lake, striking Lake Winnipeg north of Fort Alexander, may be taken as the northern line of the cultivation of wheat.

The southern half, or about 230,000 square miles of this territory, therefore presents an area nearly twice as large, and quite as favorable for cultivation, as Finland, which was formerly called the Granary of Sweden. European works on Physical Geography, scarcely include any of Finland within the limits of wheat cultivation ; but all of it within the line of barley. But Finland is all of primitive rock formation, and is therefore inferior in soil to this territory, which has 50,000 square miles of Silurian formation within the limits of cultivation ; yet Finland maintains upwards of a million and a half of people.

It is worth mention further that this territory offers a great extent of timber lands on the eastern tributaries of Lake Winnipeg, especially the upper part of the water system, which forms part of the proposed communication with Red River. This fact is given by S. J. Dawson, Esquire, in his Report of Exploration, who, from great experience in the lumber trade, is an excellent judge. The pine, though much smaller than Ottawa timber, is with other woods, on these streams, the best that can be had for the adjoining parts of the great prairie land westward to which the streams will carry it.

The south-western part of this territory will therefore become the site of an important lumber trade, while its rivers and numerous lakes offer more abundant fisheries than those of the great lakes of the St. Lawrence, where so many thousand barrels of white-fish are taken annually for use and sale. The white-fish is really much superior, as an article of food, to that much boasted fish the salmon.

Before leaving this territory we may observe, that the country between Hudson's Bay and Canada is intersected by various large rivers, falling into Hudson's Bay, that interlace the tributary waters of the Ottawa and the Lakes Huron and Superior, on the summit plateau, in long, deep lake-like channels. They present natural highways that with tow-paths and waggon portage roads, and occasional slight dams in their further courses, would form excellent inland routes of transport to Hudson's Bay, should fishing settlements be established there, or for communication in the future with the cultivable part of the Silurian basin.

To carry provisions by sea from the Great Lakes, where they are so cheap, to fisheries on Hudson's Bay, would take a voyage of four thousand miles, which from the difficulty of its entrance and navigation, could be performed but once in a season. From Lake Superior the direct distance to Hudson's Bay is only three hundred miles, and from Lake Temiscaming, on the Ottawa, only two hundred and forty-nine.

By the rivers this distance would be of course increased considerably. There is a route heretofore used by the Hudson's Bay boats through from Michipicoten, and there are good canoe routes through from Lake Temiscaming.

These routes would well merit the cost of a cursory exploration of them by a competent practical man, accustomed to road and river works in new countries, with a view to ascertain their capacity and the facilities they offer of improvement on an economical scale.

In exhibiting these facts I by no means pretend to say that this section of territory is of importance to Canada for immediate settlement. It may be long before any but a few enterprising adventurers, on routes of communication, will occupy it, from the simple reason that the prairie land beyond it is so much preferable. But it seems quite within the bounds of cautious moderation to say, that a country quite equal to Finland, and about double its extent, with forests of considerable importance, and rich fisheries, and that commands a line of communication of great importance to us, may at least ultimately be of much value to Canada.

As the opinions here given may differ widely from the views of gentlemen in the service of the Hudson's Bay Company, it is necessary to explain that there is such a thing as prejudice of occupation and upbringing, of which we have powerful instances. When the question of the division of Canada into two provinces was discussed, in the end of last century, Mr. Lymburner, a most experienced and intelligent Member of Assembly, argued against the measure, on the ground that it was an indisputable fact that the country above the Falls of Niagara would never be inhabited by civilized men.

When the first township of what is now the South Riding of Renfrew was surveyed, the earliest lumberers laughed at the idea that settlement would extend there; not from opposition to it, for they desired settlement to aid them, but from the stereotyped idea then in force, that the country was too remote and rough to be inhabited.

Even in the year 1839, a gentleman of unquestionable honour and experience, who had been engaged in the fur trade in the Upper Saguenay country, informed an officer of long and high standing in the Crown Land Department, that the Saugenay country was so utterly valueless for occupation that no man need ever take a mill stone or a mill saw into it. Twelve years afterwards, when sent by Government to project colonization roads there, I traversed, in a short time, unoccupied good land enough to make seven parishes, besides thriving settlements well advanced, where excellent wheat was raised; and many ships were even then employed in exporting its sawn lumber. Now there are twenty thousand people living there on the local produce of the mill-stone and the employment the saw mills afford them. I must apologize for stating these facts so fully; but they are important as regards the question of settlement.

CHAPTER IV.

NORTH HUDSON'S BAY TERRITORY, OR BARREN GROUND.

Little need be said of this section of territory; it is here noticed separately to distinguish its valueless character as a whole.

It may be described as the country lying north and west of Hudson's Bay, from latitude 60° to the Artic sea, back to Great Bear Lake and Slave Lake, assuming for its western boundary the dividing line between the primary formation and the Silurian basin of the River McKenzie, from the middle of Slave Lake to the east end of Bear Lake and to Coronation Gulf; corresponding roughly with the line of longitude 117° West,

Its extreme length from east to west is nine hundred and fifty miles, and its breadth from north to south six hundred. It includes an area of about four hundred and twelve thousand five hundred square miles.

Only one-sixth part of this section of territory, forming its south-west angle, from Bear Lake to a little east of the east end of Slave Lake, and nearly on that course to latitude 60°, is wooded.

The remainder, forming five sixths of its area, is the treeless Artic desert of the Barren Ground.

Its surface is varied with rocky hills of moderate altitude; some, however, as at Cape Barrow, rising to an elevation of fifteen hundred feet. It is watered by one large river, the Great Fish or Back river, and many smaller streams, and lakes.

Its vegetation consists of a close covering of lichens where it is dry, mixed with reindeer moss in moister spots. Other plants flourish where the soil is suitable, with depressed willows, blue berries, bear berries, &c. In favorable sheltered meadows grass and bents flourish, and many flowering plants. Notwithstanding the generally desolate character of the country, it, in parts, affords sustenance for herds of hundreds of reindeer and of the musk-ox, as described by Capt. Back, on the river to which his name has been given.

The Indian cannot live in it in winter on account of the want of fuel. What little is used by the Esquimax, who inhabit the coast, is the oil and blubber their fisheries afford; their fuel is got in the deep.

Even the reindeer retire from it to the bordering woods in winter, to shelter them from the season's storms. They go in numerous bands by certain passes among the lakes and hills, where the Esquimax and Northern Indians waylay and slaughter them for winter use, sometimes with the most wasteful reckless-ness.

If the natives could be taught to tame the reindeer, which is said to be easily done, and use them as domestic herds, as the Laplanders do, they might live in greater comfort and security.

The chief permanent inhabitant of this vast desolate region is the Musk Ox, the cotemporary of the mammoth and other extinct animals. He feeds in winter on the high spots where the vegetation, preserved with all its juice by the sudden severity of the winter's frost, is bared of snow by the winds.

His extinct cotemporaries are gone, and the buffalo and the moose deer are rapidly following; even the lion of Africa is hunted in his home; but the inhospitable desolation of this, the only abode of the musk ox, will be his security.

In connection with this section, its probable mineral wealth may be noticed. Speaking of the country north of Lake Winnipeg, Sir John Richardson says that Government, or the Hudson's Bay Company, should ascertain, without delay, the " mineral treasures it contains," and adds, " I have little doubt of many of the accessible districts abounding in metallic wealth *of far greater value than all the returns of the Fur trade can ever yield.*" This observation would seem to apply not only to the western skirts of the band of primary formation immediately north of Lake Winnipeg, but also to this section as far north as Copper Mine River.

CHAPTER V.

THE NORTH McKENZIE RIVER COUNTRY.

That part of the great central Silurian plain, west of the foregoing section, extending from latitude 60° N. to the Artic Sea, and from the west edge of the primary belt to the Rocky Mountains, may be designated as the North McKenzie River Country.

It is about seven hundred and forty miles in length from north to south, with a breadth of four hundred miles at latitude 60°, varying to over six hundred miles, where it meets the Artic Sea; and contains an area of two hundred and seventy-four thousand square miles.

Though lying in precisely the same latitude, its climate is not so intensely severe as that of the foregoing section; from which it differs much in other respects, that render it of more value comparatively.

Instead of being a rocky, barren, treeless waste, chiefly of infertile primary formation, like the preceding, it is, as mentioned, a Silurian plain, more or less wooded throughout, almost to the shore of the Artic. In the southern half of it barley and garden vegetables can be raised. It is traversed by the McKenzie, a first class navigable river, and it abounds in rich beds of lignite coal, with, in parts, liquid bitumen, which may ultimately prove of some value commercially.

The effect of its rich alluvial soil, and some superiority in climate, due perhaps in part to the prevalence of limestone, is such as to admit of the growth of trees, as far as the mouth of the McKenzie. Stunted generally in the most northerly parts, and of the hardiest kind—white spruce—but in sheltered positions, sometimes attaining a useful size. Even at the north-eastern extremity of this section, at the mouth of the Copper Mine River, in a sheltered grove, one is noticed as being thirty-seven inches in girth, and on Kendal River, near the same locality, in a fine grove of white spruce, one was found sixty-three inches in girth, twenty feet without taper, and fifty feet in height; but such trees are exceedingly rare in the north end of this section.

Being of Silurian and more recent formation, and generally a plain, it would have been a good agricultural country had its climate admitted. Such as it is, though its southern boundary is the limit of profitable wheat cultivation, Col. Lefroy and Sir John Richardson say, that at Fort Simpson, a hundred and fifty miles further north, with a mean summer temperature of $59\frac{1}{2}°$ Fah., barley grows well, and the latter says that at Fort Norman, three hundred and forty miles north of lat. 60°, (the assumed southern boundary of this section,) potatoes are raised, and in good seasons barley ripens well, and that lat. 65° may be considered as the northern limit of the growth of barley. He adds, that at Fort Good Hope, a hundred and eighty miles north of Fort Norman, that is fifty north of the Arctic Circle, turnips attain the weight of two or three pounds in favourable seasons, but barley has failed there when tried. Fort Simpson is evidently far within the limit of barley cultivation, for which, on the authority of Ernan, quoted by Sir John Richardson, it is necessary only that the mean temperature of any one of the three summer months shall not fall below 47°75 Fahr. At Fort Simpson, the mean of each of five months is above that, being for May, 48°16 ; June, 63°64; July, 60°97; August, 53°84; September, 49°10. The three winter months, however, are there extremely cold, the mean being 10° below zero; that of the spring months, 26°66 above zero, and of autumn, 27°34.

If, therefore, we draw a line across this territory at lat. 65° N., we find that we have in the south part of it, an area of a hundred and twenty thousand square miles, which, with the necessary allowance for waste lands and positions unfavourable in elevation or aspect, nearly all admits of the growth of barley as well as vegetables, and that must admit of the growth of rye in the part of it adjoining the limit of profitable wheat cultivation.

That is to say, we have there a country resembling in extent, and in partial fitness for cultivation, the Russian Province of Vologda, which lies in a similar Silurian formation, and is embraced in the same manner between the northern limits of wheat and barley cultivation.

Of Vologda a great part is unoccupied, but for the chase or fur trade; yet such as it is, with much marshy and sandy land, it sustains about eight hundred thousand inhabitants. But it is to be observed, that Vologda lies on the northern Dwina, which, though insignificant compared with the McKenzie, leads to a seaport open during a short season, an advantage greatly in its favour, in giving value to its products.

The River McKenzie, though not giving that advantage, presents some others that may in some degree make up for the want of it. It traverses this section of territory diagonally, presenting a course of a thousand miles of deep, uninterrupted, navigation, (besides Slave Lake, three hundred miles in length, which connects with the Arctic Sea.) Sir Alexander McKenzie states its depth to be from four to fifty fathoms, and its breadth from two miles to a half mile, running six miles an hour at the latter breadth, and twelve fathoms deep. This, with the usual large deductions necessary in such calculations, gives a passing volume of upwards of a million of cubic yards of water per minute, double Niagara or the River Missouri, which it well might be, as it drains both sides of the Rocky Mountains. The Missouri drains but one.

The McKenzie offers a great navigable communication for large vessels, with coal on its banks, connecting the vast interior region south of it, suitable for cultivation, with the rich fisheries of the Arctic sea.

The whale fisheries it leads to, inside of Behring's Straits, are the richest known, and are fished extensively by American whale fishers, who have to sail sixteen thousand miles to get there. When our great central prairie country is occupied by millions of people, they will have but one-tenth of the distance to reach these fisheries by the McKenzie, to obtain the products of the sea; it will no doubt then be a highway of some importance.

Sir Alexander McKenzie's journal of his exploration of this river is simple but very interesting. The heroic age of discovery lasts long—we are scarcely through it yet. It has its heroes, and he was one of them.

His voyages through this continent to the Arctic and Pacific Oceans may be said to have first lifted the veil that till then shrouded the vast intervening regions in obscurity.

On the 3rd of June, 1789, he left Fort Chipeweyan on the Lake of the Hills, on his voyage to the Arctic, with all the difficulties and hardships before him of first exploration in unknown, inhospitable regions, inhabited by savage tribes. Even his Indian guides had no experience of the way before them, deserting him through fear of the unknown, like that felt by the sailors of Columbus.

He had but limited supplies, for his small force depended chiefly on what they killed.

His narrative is simple, but the incidents are grand. They passed great plains of unknown extent, great tributaries like the River of the Mountains, half a mile in width,—lofty mountains with their summits clad in snow or veiled in clouds and mist. They looked upon the vast panorama that took day after day and week after week to unfold, for the first time since creation, to civilized man.

Then comes the region of eternal frost under the surface, and stunted trees ;—the increasing terror of his men,—the alarming stories of the Indians, that they would be old men and grey before they returned, if they ever did, from the regions where there was no game to kill, inhabited by terrible and cruel nations—the Island of the Evil Manitou, who swallowed every man that came his way—and beyond that the land of gigantic men who could kill other men with their eyes.

Then the arrival at the Esquimaux country, and the astonishment of his men at the sun that did not set, and the tide. Still singularly vigorous vegetation for the high latitude, 63° to 68° N.—and abundance of berries—innumerable islands in the river approaching its mouth, covered with trees of a small growth, and in places spruce and fir of a larger size. The banks, where high, wooded partly with birch and fir ; and the ground in places covered with short grass and flowers, though the frost was only four inches out of the earth on the 12th of July.

McKenzie was then two thousand miles beyond the Lake of the Woods, in direct distance north-westward, and three thousand miles in direct distance from Montreal—or as far from that city as it is from the mouth of the River Orinoco in South America.

This comparison is given to assist in realizing the extent of country that we may now acquire,—and of that extent three-quarters of the distance is through territory which, by way of Red River, is fit for agricultural occupation.

McKenzie returned to Fort Chipeweyan on the 12th September, having performed his voyage of three thousand miles in a hundred days, showing that so long, at least, annually this great Arctic River is open for navigation. In returning, the air for some part of the way was laden with a heavy smell of sulphur, which is found to be caused by the burning of coal in the banks of the river,—it was the lignite coal that is so abundant in this territory.

Lignite varies much in quality. Its average heating power may be taken as equal to that of five-sevenths of an equal weight of good Newcastle coal, though it often exceeds that proportion. The lignite coal of Nanaimo in Vancouver's Island is only ten per cent. less valuable than the true coal of the Carboniferous epoch, according to Dr. Hector.

Its prevalence in immense quantities and in positions where it can be most easily made available, in a climate where fuel will be so much needed, the comparative fertility of the soil of this section, and its great navigable river and the fisheries connected with it, will no doubt ultimately lead to the partial occupation of the southern half of it, where hardy grains and vegetables can be cultivated. Therefore, though owing to its remoteness and the exceeding coldness of its climate, it is utterly useless now, excepting for its fur trade, we should not consider it altogether valueless with reference to the future.

Speaking of the possible future occupation of the south half of this section of territory, notwithstanding the severity of its climate, it is worthy of remark, that in the province of Vologda, to which we have compared it, hemp and flax are cultivated with success. Even in the province of Archangel, north of it, with a climate much more unfavorable, considerable quantities of hemp and flax are raised, and coarse linen cordage and mats are manufactured. .Hemp and flax, with cordage and linseed from these provinces, are the principle articles of export at Archangel. It is reasonable to think that in the future they may be cultivated and manufactured in this territory.

This observation, however, applies with much more force and more immediately to the country south of Hudson's Bay, already noticed, as well as to the great Central Prairie Country, the chief subject of this pamphlet. As they are remote from markets, the cost for transport of flax exported, especially if manufactured, will be insignificant compared with that of ordinary agricultural exports ; an important advantage, even with improved means of communication.

CHAPTER VI.

THE PELLY RIVER AND MOUNTAIN COUNTRY.

Continuing to notice the less important or comparatively valueless sections of territory before directing attention to the great central prairie land, the last of these inferior territories may be designated the Pelly River and Mountain Country.

It is a little more than a thousand miles in length, northward from Simpson's River, the northern boundary of British Columbia, to the Arctic sea at Point Demarcation, where it terminates in an acute angle ; and five hundred in breadth, from the eastern crest of the Rocky Mountains to Mount Saint Elias, on the coast of the Pacific Ocean. It contains an area of about two hundred and eighty-five thousand superficial miles.

This section of territory merits separate description, inasmuch as it differs as widely in its general character from those previously noticed as they do from each other. It differs especially from the last described, which is generally a plain country, while this, with little exception, is a vast mountain region, equal in extent to the Kingdoms of Norway and Sweden taken together.

In its mountainous character it chiefly resembles Norway. Had it embraced the coast of the Pacific and the islands along it, the resemblance would have beeen greater, for it then would have possessed a seaboard rendered temperate by the warm winds of the Pacific ; but from Mount St. Elias down to the boundary of British Columbia, a narrow stripe of American, formerly Russian territory, intervenes, along the Pacific coast, reaching back to the summit of the nearest mountain range, but nowhere exceeding thirty-five miles from the shore.

Though possessing a less genial climate than Norway and Sweden, the resemblance to them may be traced a little further. As little more than one-sixteenth part of the surface of Sweden is classed as arable land in cultivation, including meadows, and only about one-hundredth part of Norway, this territory is probably not much inferior to them in extent of land fit for such cultivation as the climate may admit of.

The Rocky Mountains on the east side, the Blue Range or Peak Mountains and the Cascade Mountains and Coast Range run nearly parallel to each other, north-westwardly through this territory, with many intermediate ranges and groups.

The Rocky Mountains, whose highest peak rises to sixteen thousand feet, at the sources of the Athabasca, gradually decline in height northward, to four and five thousand feet above the sea. The Coast Range, on the contrary, attains its greatest height at Mount St. Elias, which is stated to be 17,970 feet in altitude.

These ranges cover much of this territory ; but there are valleys between and among them, of considerable extent : not much known as yet, as might be expected of a country so remote ;—as Alpine in character as Switzerland and Tyrol and eleven times as large as both together ; presenting incomparably greater obstacles to exploration, in the coldness of its climate, and from its being uninhabited except by savages.

It offers a far more interesting field of study for the geologist and the naturalist than the regions east of it already noticed.

It is a country that presents the greatest possible obstacles of climate and surface to military operations; a country utterly impregnable from its character and extent, should it ever become inhabited, as it no doubt ultimately will, where it admits of being so, as similar countries in the old world have. It is therefore a great natural bulwark to the plain country east of it.

The cold climate of much of the southern part of this section of territory is due in a great degree to its elevation. Col. Lefroy argues that the part of it in which the sources of the Peace River lie, must be nearly six thousand feet above the sea. At Pelly's Banks, lat. 61°30', the valley of Pelly River is fourteen hundred feet above the sea; and there the mean temperature of the month of January is nearly 22° below zero, or nine and a half degrees colder than at Fort Simpson, on the McKenzie, nearly in the same latitude (61°51' N.,) three hundred miles eastward, but which is only four hundred feet above the sea. In April the difference is only five and a quarter degrees, and their summers are probably equal; a temperature which will admit of the cultivation of barley and vegetables at Pelly's Banks.

Pelly River is a branch of the great River Youcan, that discharges at the entrance of Behring's Straits, after a course of eighteen hundred miles, from the source of the Lewis Branch of the river Pelly, which flows for seven hundred miles through this territory.

The temperature of Fort Youcan, Lat. 66° N., at the junction of the Pelly and Youcan, in late Russian America, may be taken as that of the north end of this territory near it in the same latitude. The mean temperatures of its seasons are, spring 14°04, summer 59°71—autumn 17°33 above, and winter 23°80 below zero;—showing its summer to be warmer than that of Fort Simpson, which is only 59°48. From which it would certainly appear that barley and vegetables might be cultivated there and all along the valley of the Pelly River, within this territory, as well as at Fort Simpson. The temperature of Youcan is more than sufficient for the growing of barley, by Ernan's rule before quoted, that the mean of none of the three summer months shall fall below 47°75, —for the mean temperature at Youcan for June is 53°49, July 65°75, and August 59°90, though the mean for the whole year is only 16°85.

"Pelly's Banks" is in the middle of this territory, with the disadvantage of great elevation; and Youcan is nearly at the Artic

Circle,—towards the south-west, near the coast of the Pacific, and at lower levels, the climate must necessarily be widely different. To judge of the climate of these more favorable parts we may take, for data, the temperature of the seasons at Sitka, on the Pacific, about a degree further north than the south end of this territory, and about a hundred miles westward of it. Here we have a striking contrast to the preceding; Sitka has a warm winter and a cool summer; the mean of the former being 34°70 and the latter only 56°24; that of spring 42°28, and autumn 48°49—with a mean annual temperature of 45°44—much the same as that of Buffalo or Toronto; or 2½° warmer than that of Montreal, and sixteen degrees warmer than that city in winter; but yet with a summer inferior to that of Youcan or Fort Simpson for ripening grain.

We have here, therefore, between these points an extreme contrast of climates, extreme difference between the heat of summer and the cold of winter on the one hand, and extreme want of difference between the temperature of the seasons on the other, to such a degree as to prevent the ripening of the grain at Sitka, notwithstanding the high mean temperature of the year.

Consequently, somewhere between these points, a little removed from the too equalizing influence of the Pacific, and its humidity, in the valleys on the south-west side of this territory, we should find with a gradually diminishing annual temperature, and an increasing difference between summer and winter, and less humidity, localities with climates resembling those of Montreal and Quebec.

Consistently with the facts mentioned, physical geographers have drawn the line of New York mean winter temperature from twenty to one hundred and twenty miles within this territory, running north-westwardly through it, for six hundred and fifty miles. But this line must only be taken as applicable to low lands and valleys :—it will generally be exceedingly deflected and often largely interrupted by ridges and highlands.

When this peculiarity of temperature of the south-west side of this territory is taken into consideration, together with what is known of it from exploration, it would appear that there are some favorable parts of it, of considerable value from their position and mineral resources, and their fitness for cultivation, owing to the quality of the land.

By Mr. Downie's report of exploration of Skeena or Simpson river, which forms the boundary between this territory and the Province of British Columbia, it appears that after passing the coast range the valleys present extensive tracts of good land well suited for settlement. He took two days to traverse one of them, which he says is as fine a farming country as one could wish to see. On a large tributary on the north side, within this territory, the land is described as good and well adapted for farming; and there the Indians grow plenty of potatoes. He describes fine flats running back to the mountains, which recede four or five miles from the river; speaks of the Skeena country being in parts the best looking mineral country he had seen in British Columbia; alludes to gold which he finds there; mentions that the river Skeena passes through an extensive coal country, the seams cut through by the river varying from three to thirty-five feet in thickness; superior to any that he had seen in Vancouver's Island, (where the mines of Nanaimo are already of value commercially,) or in British Columbia; and in other reports he says, salmon and other fish are in inconceivable abundance.

Such advantages may not be common, and may be limited to a small part of this territory; but good lands with a moderate climate, on fine salmon rivers, with valuable timber forests and beds of coal, situated within a hundred miles of the continually open navigation of the Pacific and its commerce, taken together with the gold-bearing character of the country, (for which the river Stikene to the northward of the Simpson is already famous,) render the southern part of this territory of considerable immediate, and still greater future value.

CHAPTER VII.

THE RED RIVER, SASKATCHEWAN AND PEACE RIVER COUNTRY, OR CENTRAL PRAIRIE LAND—POSITION AND EXTENT.

The remaining section of the great north-west territory—that which is of by far the greatest intrinsic value, and of the greatest relative importance to the Dominion of Canada—may, in the absence of any general name, be designated as the Red River, Saskatchewan and Peace River country, or Central Prairie Land; using the latter term merely to signify that prairie land is more or less prevalent throughout the greater part of it.

It may be described as bounded on the south by the line of latitude 49° N., the Northern boundary of the United States, on the west by the crests of the Rocky Mountains, which divide it from the Province of British Columbia, as far northward as Peace River; on the north by the parallel of latitude 60° N., and on the east by Lake Winnipeg with its tributary waters, the River Winnipeg and the Lake of the Woods; and from the north end of Lake Winnipeg by a line drawn north-westward through the west end of Lake Athabasca to the line of lat. 60° N.

Its length, from the outlet of the Lake of the Woods westward to the sources of the Saskatchewan, is eight hundred and eighty miles. Its breadth northward from lat. 49° to 60° N., is seven hundred and sixty miles. It contains an area of about four hundred and eighty thousand square miles ; that is to say, an area equal to that of France and Germany with Belgium and Switzerland added together,—or about ten times that of the State of New York.

SUITABLENESS FOR SETTLEMENT, AND ITS IMPORTANCE.

It is highly important to observe that nearly the whole of this section of territory, within the boundaries stated, excepting where cold, arising from great elevation, renders it otherwise, is as suitable in climate for agricultural occupation as the parts of Canada and the Maritime Provinces already settled or now being settled, taken together. That is to say that the best parts of this section of territory are fully as rich in soil, and, where cultivated, yield fully as heavy returns of wheat as the best parts of Upper Canada ; and that with little exception the most northerly parts of it admit of as good crops of wheat or other grain being raised as the least fovourable parts of Lower Canada already settled or being now opened for settlement. Besides which, a great portion of it presents the very great advantage of being ready for the plough, without the trouble of clearing and taking out stumps and stones.

The acquisition of this territory, or the effective opening of it as a Crown colony with a view to federation with us, which is much the same, is therefore of the utmost importance to Canada, alike for immediate use for the extension of native settlement and as a receptacle for many immigrants who go to a foreign country to obtain such prairie land ; and also, and chiefly, as a necessary basis for that degree of strength of population essential for the maintenance of our national security in the future.

TOPOGRAPHICAL CHARACTER.

This section of territory forms part of the great plain that lies along the eastern base of the Rocky Mountains, already spoken of in describing the McKenzie River country.

This great interior plain extends from the Gulf of Mexico to the Artic Ocean, with but little interruption from lesser ranges and occasional groups of hills of insignificant elevation compared with the great range that bounds it to the westward. The water-sheds of its greatest river basins are but elevations of the same great sloping plain. Even the great parallel Azoic belt, the continuation of the Laurentides, that divides it from that other great Silu-

rian plain which encircles Hudson's Bay, presents but little interruption to the gradually descending slope of the continent from the
Rocky Mountains eastward.

It is described as presenting a general similarity of geological
character, varying as the different formations, from the Silurian
upwards, exhibit themselves in greater or lesser breadth.

Within the section of territory under our consideration, the
Silurian formation, that prevails along the eastern side of the
plain, dips westward under the Devonian, Cretaceous and Tertiar-
ies, to rise again in the ridges of the Rocky Mountains.

The absence of granite or other primitive rock, in the Rocky
Mountains, from lat. 49° as far as 52° N., is noted as remarkable
by Sir John Richardson. By the exploration of Capt. Palliser and
Dr. Hector, they are shown to consist of Silurian and carboniferous
rocks. Far beyond the scope of their examination, these mountains appear to be the same in geological character. Where
traversed by the Peace River about lat. 56° N., Sir Alexander
McKenzie describes the bed of that river to be of limestone, and
the mountains as solid masses of the same.

This formation of the Rocky Mountains is important. The
prevalence of limestone has no doubt contributed fertility to the
alluvial lands and low prairies of the plain country below; and
the presence of the carboniferous rocks is a favorable feature.
Sir Roderick Murchison, in passing a well-merited encomium on
the valuable exploratory operations of Dr. Hector, observes
that he shows the "structure of the chain, with its axis of slaty
subscrystalline rocks overlaid by limestone of Devonian and carboniferous age, and flanked on the eastern side by carboniferous
sandstone, representing probably our own coal fields, the whole
followed by those Cretaceous and Tertiary deposits which con-
stitute the subsoil of the vast and rich prairies watered by the north
and south Saskatchewan and their affluents."

This encomium was justly due to the Doctor, but hardly so to
the South Branch of the Saskatchewan; the dry prairies that
prevail on much of it resemble the steppes of Russsia in Europe,
of which, as Mr. Hauxhausen says, "some consider the larger
portion as unfertilizible deserts," while others think they require
'nothing but hands and judicious culture to convert them into rich
and fertile places," but adds that he thinks the truth lies between
these extremes.

However gratifying the prospect may be of discovering true
coal in the carboniferous formation of the Rocky Mountains, it has
not yet been realized, either from the explorations yet made being
very limited and imperfect, or from there being no true coal
measures there : for it is to be borne in mind that the presence of

the carboniferous formation merely indicates that it is there, and there only, that true coal will be found if it exists at all, or in useful quantities. Thus we have the carboniferous formation on the south coast of the district of Gaspé ; its presence led to extensive speculation and the formation of a mining company; but though it, the carboniferous formation, exists to a total thickness of three hundred feet, no coal to warrant mining was ever discovered.

Along the eastern base of the Rocky Mountains there extends a broad belt of geological formation, throughout the entire length, northward of this section of territory, (nearly a thousand miles,) and beyond it to the Arctic Ocean, as already mentioned, containing an inexhaustible amount of lignite coal; it has been seen in many places in beds from two to eight feet thick, and in some parts over a breadth of nearly two hundred miles.

As this immense region of lignite coal lies on the upper courses of great navigable rivers, which flow through vast fertile prairie countries on their lower courses, containing much of the richest wheat-growing ground in this continent, the value of it as a perpetual supply of fuel for them is incalculable ; it evidently much more than compensates for the infertile character of a large part of the dry prairie lands adjoining the boundary of the United States.

FORM AND NATURAL SUBDIVISIONS.

On the map of the section of territory now before us, this Central Prairie Land, bounded as mentioned, is an irregular diamond-shaped figure inclining westward. It is eight hundred and eighty miles broad at its base, on lat. 49° N., diminishing northward to three hundred miles in width on lat. 60° N. The length of its eastern boundary is a thousand and fifty miles, and its western one, by the curve of the Rocky Mountains, is nine hundred and fifty miles.

Its south-east angle, in the Lake of the Woods, is two hundred and fifty miles west with a little northing, from Fort William, on Lake Superior. Its north-east angle is six hundred miles due west from Hudson's Bay, and its north-west angle is at the same distance due east from the Pacific. Its east and west outlines are, at their middle parts, about four hundred miles in direct distance from Hudson's Bay and the Pacific, respectively. It therefore occupies a central position in the continent.

The south part of it, two hundred and eighty thousand square miles in area, or considerably more than the half of it, lies upon the waters of the River Saskatchewan, and the Red River and Assiniboine, and other tributaries of Lake Winnipeg. Next north-

3

ward, the head waters of the Churchill or Beaver River, occupy a triangular area of fifty thousand miles on the east side. Of the remaining part, north-westward, a hundred and twenty thousand miles lie on the Athabasca, and on the Peace River north of it; and about thirty thousand square miles of the north-west corner lie on the waters of the River of the Mountains, and Hay River; the last four rivers are branches of the River McKenzie.

GENERAL CHARACTERISTICS.

Before going into details as to the character of these subdivisions, it may be well to make a few observations of a general nature, on this section of territory.

Its elevation, though considerable, is not so great as might be supposed from its central position in the continent.

Its lowest levels are the two great lakes, Winnipeg and Athabasca, nearly at its south-east and north-east ends, which receive the waters of five-sixths of its area, and the River of the Mountains at Fort Liard, which is estimated to be only four or five hundred feet in height. Lake Winnipeg, which receives the waters of the River Winnipeg and others on the east side, besides the Red River and Assiniboine, and the River Saskatchewan, on the west, is six hundred and twenty feet above the level of the sea. Lake Athabasca, which receives the River Athabasca from the south, and others rivers from the east, and connects at its discharge with Peace River, from the west, is six hundred feet above the sea.

Having these for the lowest levels, the general fall of the surface towards them will be better understood by tracing the elevation of the circuit of this section of territory. The Lake of the Woods is three hundred and sixty-one feet above Lake Winnipeg, or nine hundred and eighty-nine feet above the sea. It is in a country of lake-like marshes of great extent, on the same level as itself, or nearly so. The elevation of Pembina near long. 97° W., where the Red River intersects the boundary of U. S., lat. 49° N., is estimated at nine hundred feet. Half way between Pembina and the Rocky Mountains, the boundary line rises on the "Grand Coteau du Missouri," the high arid plateau dividing the valley of the latter from that of the Saskatchewan, upwards of fifteen hundred feet in height, and gradually ascending till, at the entrance of the Kootanee pass, the plain terminates with an elevation of four thousand feet, and the further ascent to the summit of the pass is two thousand feet. This elevation of the plain at the foot of the mountains continues northward; the summits of the passes varying between five and six thousand feet, and the peaks of the mountains rising from seven or eight thousand to fifteen, and the highest to sixteen thousand feet above the sea. Speaking of this elevated country at the foot of the Rocky Mountains, between Saskatchewan and Peace River, Col. Lefroy observes that "it is a district remarkable for its gradual and regular ascent, preserving much of the character of a plain country."

Near the boundary of the United States and south of lat. 51° N., the base of the Rocky Mountains is not more than forty miles in width. They attain their greatest height about lat. 52° N., and also their greatest width, which is about a hundred miles.

Only between lat. 51° and 52° N., and a little above the latter parallel, are glaciers to be found. There close together, by Dr. Hector's valuable map, about lat. 51° 40 N., long. 117° W., in a grand nucleus of lofty summit glaciers, where the range is a hundred miles in breadth, the North and South Branches of the Saskatchewan have their sources, but a few miles apart; diverging to meet again, on their way to the Atlantic, after following their separate courses of eight hundred miles. Close between them rises one of the sources of the Columbia, flowing to the Pacific; and in glaciers near them, about lat. 52° 17 N., is the source of the Athabasca—the remotest source of the River Mc-Kenzie, which takes its course of two thousand miles to the Arctic sea.

Elsewhere, Captain Blackiston and others describe the Rocky Mountains as being well-wooded, excepting their summits; the timber on the eastern side inferior to that of the western; and add, that perpetual snow is only seen on some of the higher peaks. This peculiarity, we may observe, is the natural result of the high level of the plain; the line of perpetual snow depending more on the height above the mean elevation of the earth's surface, in the region adjoining, than its height over the level of the sea.

Returning to the elevation of the circuit of outline, on attaining latitude 60° N., the elevation of the mountains and the plain diminishes rapidly. Fort Liard, on the River of the Mountains, near that parallel, though only fifty miles east from the mountains, is only four or five hundred feet above the sea.

This depression of level in northing is favorable to cultivation. Had the elevation risen with the latitude, or even continued unabated, the climate would have been less suitable for the growth of grain. Fort Liard is the lowest point in this section of territory; and the altitude can be but little greater where the parallel of latitude 60° N. crosses Hay River, and meets the assumed east outline of this section.

The country traversed by this east outline, rises but little above the height of Lake Winnipeg, excepting the northerly part between Beaver River and Lake Athabasca. There this assumed boundary

passes over a great bend of the Laurentian formation. Even
hundred miles westward, where that formation joins the Silurian
Methy Lake is fourteen hundred and ninety feet* above the sea.

This tract of Laurentian country will be valueless unless it b
for such minerals as it may be found to offer, near the junction c
these formations.

Turning to the interior, we find at Fort Dunvegan, on Peac
River, a hundred and fifty miles east from the Rocky Mountain:
the plateau sloping from their base has declined to sixteen hundre
feet, while the river is only nine hundred and ten feet above th
sea, or three hundred and ten above its mouth at Lake Athabasc;
from which it is three hundred miles distant in a direct lin
though double that by the winding course of the river. The ele
vation of Fort Edmonton, on the North Saskatchewan, two hun
dred miles east from the mountains, is eighteen hundred feet; tha
of Carleton House, near the Forks, at three hundred miles in direc
distance eastward, is eleven hundred feet; and Cumberland Hous
two hundred miles further east, and a hundred miles in direct dis
tance from Lake Winnipeg, is nine hundred feet above the sea, c
two hundred and seventy above the mouth of the Saskatchewan 8
the Lake.

These points being on the banks of rivers, are the lower level:
and indicate the general inclination of the plain. It is only a com
parative plain, however, varied in surface by scattering groups c
hills, rising to six hundred, and occasionally a thousand feet an
upwards over the plains below them; or the equally lofty edges c
high plateaus, forming long ranges of highlands towards the lowe
levels.

Of the former, the Riding Mountains, west of Lake Manitoba]
have an altitude of a thousand and thirty feet above that Lake, c
seventeen hundred feet over the sea. The north-east face of th
Missouri Plateau advances towards the South Branch of the Sa:
katchewan and River Qu'Appelle, with an elevation of six hundre
feet above the plains; showing a tertiary formation, with brow
coal and silicified wood. Its north-west face, under the name c
the Cypress Hills, rises to the height of four thousand two hur
dred feet above the sea. Its southern slope is watered by tribu
taries of the Missouri, that here extend into this territory. Th
Hand Hills, north of Red Deer River, long. $111\frac{1}{2}°$ W., rise to th
height of three thousand eight hundred feet above the sea; presen
ing the same formation, capped with tertiary shingle beds of th
highest plains.

* 1,540 feet by Col. Lefroy.

It is interesting to observe that while the Rocky Mountains present everywhere evidence of disruption and upheaval in their origin, these hills and high ranges of the plain exhibit with equal uniformity, in their abraded strata, that they were formed by denudation by water; by the scoping out of the plains around them.

By the elevations given it will be seen that the height of the sloping plateau, forming the chief part of this section of territory is considerable; but it is worthy of remark that it nevertheless has in some degree the character of a basin. We have noticed the great elevation of its western edge. That of its eastern Laurentian boundary is in parts considerable. The Branch of that range which bounds it at its south-east angle, dividing it from the basin of Lake Superior, is from fifteen to eighteen hundred feet in height over the sea, at the lowest parts. The Lake of the Woods is five hundred feet lower than Lake Itasca, the source of the Mississippi, immediately south of it. Fort Garry, on Red River is twelve hundred feet lower than Fort Clarke, on the Missouri which lies south-west of it, Carleton House on the Saskatchewan is about a thousand feet lower than Fort Union on the Missouri which lies south by east from it; and we have already seen that the ridge of the Coteau de Missouri, dividing its waters from the basin of the Saskatchewan, rises to the height of four thousand two hundred feet above the sea.

The basin forming the chief part of this section of territory is therefore about a thousand feet lower, generally, than the northern parts of Minnesota and Dakota adjoining it.

The term Central Prairie Land as applied to it, is, as before mentioned, merely intended to indicate that in it prairie land is to be found more or less prevalent; with this distinction, that in the southern half of it, the extent of prairie land very much exceeds that of wood land; while in the northern part of it, say from about lat. 54° to lat. 60° N., the country is generally wooded, though prairies are interspersed through it, some of great extent. Prairies extend as far north as the east branch of Hay River, on which they terminate near lat. 60°, and as far east as Methy Portage between the waters of the Churchill and Athabasca Rivers, near the eastern boundary assumed for this section. Prairie land between these points, occurs so continuously as to admit of herds of horses being sent through, as mentioned by Sir John Richardson and feeding by the way: a condition evidently favorable to the extension of settlement, as well as indicative of land suitable for agricultural occupation.

In so great an extent of country there is naturally much variety in character and quality of soil. To assist in describing it, i may be suitable to do so by its rivers, commencing with the southern part of it watered by the Saskatchewan and other tribu-taries of Lake Winnipeg.

CHAPTER VIII.

LAKE WINNIPEG AND ITS TRIBUTARIES.

Looking at the map, we have lake Winnipeg in the south-east part of this section, forming there part of its boundary. Lake Winnipeg is two hundred and eighty miles in length, and fifty-seven in greatest breadth. Its southern extremity is three hundred and fifty miles west-north-west from Fort William on Lake Superior Its elevation above the sea is about six hundred and twenty-eight feet. From the mouth of the River Winnipeg, near its south end to its northern extremity, it is the boundary between the generally rocky Laurentian Country and the Silurian lime-stone formation o the east side of the great central plain.

It is very shallow at its southern extremity. Its shores are low and marshy at the entrance of Red River, and subject to inun dations. By the report of Captain Munn, at low water, the depth on the bar at the entrance of that river, in the shallowest part o the channel is only four feet. The narrows and islands in the south half of the lake afford good protection in the navigation o it from Big Island, as far as the mouth of the Little Saskatchewan in the expansion below Big Island the soundings are from three to five fathoms with good anchorage. From opposite the mouth o the Little Saskatchewan, he says, a vessel would have to depend on steam and an anchor, in the event of a storm, as far as the mouth of the Great Saskatchewan, where there is an excellen harbour and good anchorage.

The navigation of Lake Winnipeg derives an additional impor tance from that of its tributaries, the Great and the Little Saskat chewan; the former being navigable for steamers, with but three interruptions to Edmonton, on the North Branch, seven hundred and seventy-two miles, and probably farther, to the base of th Rocky Mountains; while the little Saskatchewan and its lake present a navigation of upwards of three hundred miles from it mouth, or five hundred from Fort Garry, without interruption.

THE RIVER WINNIPEG.

The River Winnipeg enters Lake Winnipeg, in a bay on the eas side, at forty-one miles by the shore, from the mouth of Red Rive the southern extremity of the lake; it has a course of about fiv undred miles, measuring from the head of the Savanne River, at he height of land, on the canoe route from Fort William to Red River.

Having large tributaries, and its sources being in a rainy region, it is a very large river;—it is considered by Mr. Dawson and Mr. Hind, of the Canadian Exploring Expedition, as resembling the Upper Ottawa in volume, say equal to the Rhine.

On its lower course the Ottawa, by the report of the Canal Survey, was found to have a mean discharge of 85,000 cubic feet per second, while the Rhine, as quoted, in the same report, from D'Aubuisson, has a mean discharge of 33,700 cubic feet per second.

The upper waters of the Winnipeg, Lac des Mille Lacs, the River Seine, Rainy Lake and Rainy River, with the Lake of the Woods, into which they flow, form the chief part of the proposed line of communication from Lake Superior to Red River.

The Lake of the Woods, seventy miles in length, and the River Winnipeg below it, a hundred and sixty-three miles long, by its crooked, turbulent and obstructed course, to Lake Winnipeg, form together part of the assumed easterly boundary of the great central section of territory under consideration.

The strip of rich alluvial land, eighty miles in length, on Rainy River, and its favorable climate, and the importance of the Pine forest on the upper waters of the Winnipeg, for the supply of the prairie lands adjoining, have already been mentioned.

From the Lake of the Woods to its mouth, the River Winnipeg, is described by our Canadian explorers, flows through the disk of the Laurentian formation : both banks are generally rocky and sterile. Between Islington Mission (thirty-five miles below the Lake of the Woods, where it begins) and Silver Falls, good soil occurs in the form of drift clay, in small patches of from fifty to three hundred acres. From Silver Falls, eighteen miles from Lake Winnipeg, well-wooded, fertile alluvial land prevails, on both banks, down to Lake Winnipeg ; forming on the south side the large fertile tract in which Fort Alexander is situated.

The Laurentian country, on the River Winnipeg, rises in dome-shaped hills, from a hundred to two hundred feet in height, that sink, irregularly, to the southward, into the plain country, which extends from the Lake of the Woods to Red River, a distance of about ninety miles.

COUNTRY BETWEEN THE LAKE OF THE WOODS AND RED RIVER.

This plain country is at first very level, and then falls gradually to the Red River. It is, more or less, thinly wooded, where not covered with water, for sixty miles westward from the Lake of the Woods. In this distance swamps and "muskeags," vast lake-like marshes, prevail. Some of the latter are many miles in extent; they cover the greater part of the country. They are undrained prairies, covered with two or three feet of water, thickly charged with vegetable matter, over a firm marly or clay bottom.

(This shallowness with firmness of bottom is singularly uniform; it was found so by Mr. Dawson's assistants in dragging their canoe through the muskeag, between the Lake of the Woods and White Mouth River; and it is the same forty miles further south in the muskeag between the Lake of the Woods and the River Roseau.)

As they are so shallow, and the fall from the Lake of the Woods to Red River is three hundred and sixty feet, they could, no doubt, to a great extent be drained, and would form vast fertile fields or valuable meadows; like the salt marshes on the Bay of Fundy, which have been reclaimed with great labor, in the construction of extensive dikes to exclude the tide. As the summer is equal to that of the district of Montreal, the marshes of the Lake of the Woods may yet be found as well worth reclaiming as the Westmoreland marshes referred to. Where there is much superfluous vegetable matter—or even three feet in depth of it, as it is stated there is in the swamps—it might be compressed for fuel.

The manufacture of Canadian peat is already yielding cheap fuel in Montreal, where it can be delivered at $3.20 per ton. It would be satisfactory if the bogs and swamps near the Red River settlements were found to contain sufficient material to supply the future demand for fuel there when the woods, which have hitherto met their requirements, fail. With a canal or a railroad passing through this tract, as part of the proposed route to Red River, such a supply would be made easily available, even from the great peaty morass behind the fertile strip on Rainy River.

A range, of slightly elevated ridges, which traverses this marshy country, commencing near the north-west end of the Lake of the Woods, was found to afford a good site for a road through to Fort Garry. From its being extremely even and free from obstacles, it is a most favorable site for a railroad. Immediately north of it there seems to be a favorable site for a canal; to both of which we shall have occasion to refer.

RED RIVER.

At its south end Lake Winnipeg receives the Red River—exceeding the Winnipeg in length of course, but far inferior to it n magnitude; yet a fine river, resembling the Richelieu in volume. By its windings it is nearly six hundred miles in length.

For the last three hundred miles of its course its general direction is due north. It crosses the United States boundary about ninety miles west of the Lake of the Woods, a little over a hundred miles from its mouth; and for that distance flows through his territory in a nearly level prairie plain of the richest alluvial soil.

Captain Palliser describes the soil as being that of an ancient lake bottom, consisting of variously proportioned mixtures of clay, loam and marl, with a remarkable deficiency of sand, overlaid with a great depth of vegetable mould, varying from two to five feet in thickness. Mr. Dawson and Mr. Hind speak of it as being generally from ten to twenty inches of black mould on a thick bed of alluvial clay.

This description of prairie country is described as extending back, on the east side of Red River, from four to about thirty miles; and on the west side about forty, to the ridge or hilly ground called the Pembina Mountains, the high disk of the unfertile dry prairie lands south of the Assiniboine. Parts of it are marshy, as might be expected of an alluvial nearly level plain, in a state of nature; but they are described as admitting of being drained with little trouble. The big swamp in rear of the Red River settlement is twenty-seven feet above the surface of the river; and the nine mile swamp on Rat River, a small tributary on the east side above the settlement, is described as capable of being drained with comparatively trifling labour, and would form the richest of prairie land. Marshes, great and small, and swampy spots requiring improvement—and capable of it, though of the richest soil—encroach largely on the area immediately available for cultivation; which is naturally less in proportion than in some of the higher prairie grounds of rich sandy loam.

From its lowness—(to which it owes its extraordinary fertility,) like many other alluvial valleys—parts of it are sometimes subject to inundations, but very rarely. About forty miles from its mouth the Red River receives its chief tributary, the Assiniboine. At their confluence is situated Upper Fort Garry, the chief commercial emporium and seat of government of the Red River settlement, (which extends from twenty miles above to thirty miles below it on the Red River, and about seventy miles up the Assiniboine.)

Red River is 480 feet wide and twelve feet deep at the middle settlement. It is navigable to the United States boundary and far to the south of it by boats of light draft; but the navigation of it is subject to interruption by drought in the dry season of the year.

From the settlement up to the United States boundary, about fifty-seven miles, its banks are fringed with wood, from a few yards to half a mile in breadth, and the peninsulas it forms are well wooded. The woods of elm, poplar, oak and ash towards its mouth, have supplied the wants of the settlement for upwards of twenty years.

The alluvial clay of the Red River and the Assiniboine is reported to be well fitted for the manufacture of bricks and common pottery in patches; which may be of importance for building in parts where stone cannot be had near. The prevalence of limestone however, will leave little occasion for the use of brick.

CHAPTER IX.

THE RIVER ASSINIBOINE.

By its very winding course the river Assiniboine is over six hundred miles in length. For two hundred and twenty miles in direct distance upwards from its mouth, its course is nearly west; above that, its course, for upwards of two hundred miles in direct distance, is north-westerly, lying nearly parallel to Lake Winnipeg, at a mean distance of two hundred and forty miles west of it.

At two hundred and twenty miles west from its mouth, where it turns northward, it receives its tributary, the river Qu'Appelle which continues directly westward two hundred and fifty miles further, having its source near the elbow of the South Branch of the Saskatchewan, four hundred and seventy miles directly westward from the mouth of the Assiniboine.

Though it and its tributaries drain a larger area than Red River, the Assiniboine, owing to the dryness of the country south west of it, drained by its principal feeders, and the loss of water in its lower course, is scarcely equal to the one-third of Red River at their junction. By Professor Hind's measurements the volume of the Assiniboine, at a hundred and forty miles from its mouth where it is two hundred and thirty feet wide and eight feet in mean depth, diminishes to half before its junction with the Red River The difference is seemingly lost in the sandy tract, of about fifty miles in breadth, which it enters about a hundred and twenty miles west of Fort Garry, a little above the mouth of its tributary the Souris or Mouse River.

The Souris is apparently upwards of three hundred miles in length. Its source is a little north of the U. S. boundary, and three hundred and fifty miles west of Red River.   A great bend of it at its middle course crosses that boundary.

By Mr. Hind's measurement the volume of water discharged by the Souris, though much broader at its mouth, seems to be about half of that of the Qu'Appelle.   The latter near its mouth is sixty-six feet wide, flowing a mile and a half an hour, with a mean depth of six and a half feet.

The small discharge of water by these rivers, compared with their length of course and the extent of their tributaries, indicates the generally arid nature of the light prairie country drained by them ; the greater volume of the Qu'Appelle being apparently due to the generally better description of country on its north bank. The main Assiniboine, above the Qu'Appelle, discharges twice as much water as the latter river, the area drained by it, though only half as extensive as that of the Qu'Appelle, being a very fertile country.

THE INFERTILE LANDS ON THE SOURIS AND QU'APPELLE.

Much the greater part of the country drained by the River Qu'Appelle, and very nearly all that drained by the River Souris, is classed as light prairie land on Professor Hind's shaded maps, distinguishing the quality of the land, published with his report in Parliamentary Papers on the Colonies of 1860.   In the body of his report, however, he estimates nearly a million of acres as fertile arable land; that is, only one-fortieth part of its area.

This region lies south of the great belt of fertile country described by Capt. Palliser as suitable for cultivation.

Much of its surface, especially south of an imaginary line from the great bend of the Souris across the middle course of the Qu'-Appelle, is described as bare and treeless prairie, covered only with short grass, and very deficient of water ; and in parts the soil is so light and sandy that it drifts with the wind, and in others the ground is strewed with fragments of shale and granite boulders.

A great obstacle to settlement in these treeless plains is the want of wood for fuel.   Were they otherwise suitable, that might probably be, in parts, overcome.   Dr. Hector's admirable geological section from Lake Winnipeg to Vancouver's Island shows brown coal in the Coteau du Prairie which extends from above the Elbow of the South Branch of the Saskatchewan, along the sources of the Qu'Appelle and the Souris, to the boundary line, with a height of six hundred feet above the plain.   Above the Blue Hills up the Souris, a little more than twenty miles from its mouth, Mr. Hind found beds of lignite boulders in its banks ; the water-borne debris of beds of lignite coal.

As so much has been seen in the course of the limited explora tions yet made, more may probably be discovered on further exam ination of the country.

This region, described as generally infertile, lying on the water of the Souris and the Qu'Appelle, and southward to the U. S boundary, is equal to England in area ; and continues westward, t a still greater extent.

But it is proper to notice that there are apparently considerabl exceptions to this generally valueless character. Mr. Hind speak of the bend of the Souris, near the Blue Hills, being " in the mid of a very lovely undulating country." A little further on he speak of a vast prairie of a rich dark green, " a beautiful level waste afterwards of " an extensive deposit of bog iron ore capped wit shell marl." Speaking of the Souris, further up, he says that i valley, " along which we travelled to-day, varies from a quarter t a mile broad. It flows through a rich open meadow 20 to 25 fe below the general level of the prairie, which on either hand is u dulating, light, and covered with short stunted grass." He speak of the valley of the Pipestone creek as being " narrow, but ric and beautiful."

In the same manner, beyond the region designated as the gre fertile belt, ascending the south bank of the Qu'Appelle from i mouth, he says " we left Fort Ellice and travelled due we through a pretty country, and the following day arrived at the cro woods. They consist of aspen with a splendid undergrowth. Th pasturage is excellent and the road good, passing through a fa rolling country, the soil consisting of a sandy loam with muc vegetable matter in the valleys. Aspen groves are numerous, an many little lakes." Again, " The trail continued through goc land for nine miles, with aspen groves on the crown of each und lation." " Then came a prairie, three miles across." " Ponds we numerous, abounding with ducks and ducklings." Speaking of th Indian Head Hills, near the middle course of the Qu'Appelle, l calls them " a hilly country for some miles : it contains many bea tiful lakes and is well wooded." Further on he speaks of a " exceedingly beautiful view, embracing an extensive area of lev prairie to the north, bounded by the Aspen Woods on the borde of the Qu'Appelle Valley. A portion of the old forest still exist of a large growth and very thickly set." Continuing, he say " on the 17th we entered a very beautiful fertile prairie at the fo of the Indian Head range ;" and further, " we reached the Qu'A pelle Lakes after passing through a magnificent prairie the who day. In fact, the country north of the Indian Head and Cha Hill ranges is truly beautiful, and will one day become a ver important tract."

Speaking of the Qu'Appelle Mission, he says : "the situation is beautiful. Here the Qu'Appelle Valley is one mile and a quarter broad and 250 feet deep. Both north and south a vast prairie extends, fertile, inviting, but treeless on the south, and dotted with groves of aspen over a light and somewhat gravelly soil on the north. Most beautiful and attractive, however, are the lakes, four in number, and from the rich store of fish they contain, are well-named Fishing Lakes. A belt of timber fringes their sides at the foot of the steep hills they wash, for they fill the entire breadth of the valley. Ancient elm trees, with long and drooping branches, bend over the water, the ash-leaved maple acquires dimensions not seen since leaving Red River, and the Mi-sas-ka-to-mi-na is no longer a bush, but a tree eighteen to twenty feet high, and loaded with most luscious fruit."

All this, and no doubt much more like it, is excluded from the belt generally spoken of as suitable for settlement; but though certainly inferior to the rich alluvial plains on the Red River, such lands are evidently better suited for cultivation than much of the poor and scarcely arable lands we have been eadeavoring to bring under settlement in the Ottawa and Huron territory. Infertile prairie lands, even of the worst description, are easily travelled over. They present no obstruction to communication, such as our rugged woodlands do. The hunting bands drive their carts all over them on natural roads, as good as our colonization roads, which, imperfect as they are, cost a hundred pounds a mile, and upwards.

Even the poor prairies, if they be little worth, at least cost nothing for clearing; and as their surface shows that they afford pasturage for numerous herds of buffaloes, it is evident they may do the same for domestic cattle and sheep.

When we read such descriptions, and turn to Mr. Hind's large map of exploration that accompanies his report, as published by the Canadian Government, and see large tracts, watered by fine streams, designated as "rolling prairie, good clay soil;" "level plain, dark rich loam;" "open level prairie of light sandy loam, with clumps of willows;" "rolling prairie of light clay loam, marshy in many places," (thirty miles of this in one tract apparently); "rich black soil;" "rolling prairie of sandy clay;" "level open prairie, full of marshy ponds;" and in the first great bend of the Souris, a tract of twenty miles, by ten apparently, with several streams issuing from it of "slightly undulating prairie of rich sandy loam, with clumps of young poplar;" and when we consider that these tracts, with the exception of marshy spots in them, are generally ready to receive the plough, without the trouble and cost we have in Canada in clearing and in taking out stumps

and stones, we are led to believe, that if these expressions hav
been used with accuracy, which there is no room to doubt; consi
derable tracts of this region, not included in the fertile belt, com
monly spoken of, are really far from being quite unfit for settle
ment.

These particulars are noticed here because, from the circum
stances of the large region in which they occur, being naturally i
generalizing excluded from the fertile country, the value of mucl
of it might be underrated.

They tend to show that the estimates referred to do not exag
gerate the extent of fertile lands, and are not the less valuable o
that account.

These remarks will be applicable to the large proportion of th
prairie lands on the south branch of the Saskatchewan, adjoinin
to the westward, which has also been classed as valueless and unfi
for settlement.

With the vast extent of far superior land which this territor
offers, even the exceptional good tracts, such as those describec
which are to be found in the infertile regions, may well be disre
garded for the present.

CHAPTER X.

FERTILE LAND ON THE ASSINIBOINE.

Ascending the Assiniboine from its mouth for upwards c
seventy miles to the Sand Hills, the country through which i
flows is described as being of the same rich alluvial character a
on the Red River; with the advantage of never being subject t
inundation.   Beyond that is the sandy tract, fifty miles in lengtl
westward; south of the river it connects with the dry prairie land
already mentioned; on the north side it extends twenty miles bac
from the river, to the great fertile region north of it.   Then, fo
about a hundred miles further west, to where it turns northward a
the mouth of the Qu'Appelle, and for nearly fifty miles north c
that, the Assiniboine may be considered as the boundary betwee
the great fertile prairie region and the equally great region of ligh
prairie land south and west of it.

Between the Sand Hills and the Qu'Appelle the Assiniboin
receives, on the north side, five considerable tributaries, from fift
to a hundred and fifty miles in length.   Their courses are in th
fertile region.   The land on their head waters is described as goo
sandy loam.   The description of one of them, the Rapid River, in

licates their general character. Of it Mr. Dickinson of the Canadian exploring party says: "The valley is about eighty feet below the general level of the country; the bottom of it is from half a mile to a mile in width, through which the river winds its way, flowing rapidly and uniformly; it is about fifty feet wide, and at this time (August) five feet deep. There is no appearance of the valley being flooded. There are large open flats occurring frequently, on both sides of the river, where the richness of the grass and the beauty of the various flowers prove the great fertility of the soil, places marked out by nature to be cultivated and inhabited by man. There is abundance of good sized poplar and balsam, spruce sufficiently large for building and farming purposes. I followed the course of the valley down to its junction with the valley of the Assiniboine, (a hundred miles,) and for the greater part of the way it is rich and fertile, as is also the land adjoining. Within a few miles of the Assiniboine the country changes considerably, the soil is much lighter, and the trees fewer and smaller." A strip of sandy ground extends for eighty miles above the Rapid River along the north bank of the Assiniboine.

Rapid River is navigable for a hundred miles for canoes and bateaux.

Speaking of the northerly part of the Assiniboine above the Qu'Appelle, S. J. Dawson, Esquire, who was in charge of the Exploratory Expedition of 1858, after describing the river as crooked and rapid for eighteen miles below Fort Pelly, says: "it is then joined by the White Mud River from the west, which drains a considerable portion of the great alluvial prairies which travellers pass on their way to Carleton House, and which have excited such general admiration on account of their great fertility." He describes the river as winding in a deep valley, from a mile to two miles in width, for a hundred miles, from White Mud River to Fort Ellice; the banks increasing in height from a moderate elevation at the former to two hundred and fifty feet at the latter place. He says: "With regard to the quality of the soil; on going inland a little we found it to be of an alluvial character, differing in no respect from the soil in the prairie lands at Red River." He speaks of its tributary brooks as flowing in "glens stretching far inland; with winding banks, covered in some cases with green herbage and in others with forests that ascend to the level of the plain above." He describes the course of the Assiniboine as being remarkably crooked, occasionally crossing its valley as much as three times in the direct distance of a mile,—(very unfavorable for navigation were it otherwise suitable.) He says: "The margin of the stream is in general wooded; sometimes the woods extend across the whole valley; in other cases the green banks slope down from the prairie level to the water's edge."

Such is the character of the northerly part or upper half of the Assiniboine and its valley. North-eastward of it the prairie plateau extends to the base of the Riding, Duck and Porcupine Mountains, a distance varying from sixty to thirty miles. It is described as a fertile country, often exceedingly beautiful, interspersed with forests and clumps of wood, generally of young trees and of a small growth; marshy in spots and abounding in lakelets or ponds, with wild fowl exceedingly abundant. Its soil is a rich sandy loam; limestone boulders and gravelly spots occurring but rarely.

Westward of the Assiniboine, above the light prairie tract already mentioned, this same description of fertile country, interspersed with woods, and abundantly watered by ponds and streams, extends a hundred and thirty miles to and beyond the base of the great and the little Touchwood Hills.

These ranges of hills extend in a south-west direction, about twenty miles from each other. The greater is about eighty miles, and the lesser about sixty miles in length. They lie between the upper courses of the Assiniboine and the Qu'Appelle. The transverse breadth of country occupied by them, and their gently ascending bases, measuring north-westward, is about fifty miles.

'Speaking of them, Professor Hind says: "We reached the summit plateau, and then passed through a very beautiful undulating country, diversified by many picturesque lakes and aspen groves, possessing land of the best quality, and covered with most luxuriant herbage;" further he says: "The country between the two ranges is dotted with lakes and groves of aspen. From a small hill near the Fort, I counted forty-seven lakes;" and further "So rich and abundant is the vegetation here, that the horses remain in the open glades all the winter, and always find plenty of forage to keep them in good condition. Buffaloes congregate in the beautiful prairie south of the Fort every winter, sometimes in vast numbers." A little further he says: "Not only are lakes very abundant and well supplied with water, but there are several living streams flowing from the range. Indeed, the whole country from Touchwood Hills to Riding Mountain," (upwards of two hundred miles,) "including the country about the head waters of the Assiniboine, is dotted with innumerable lakes annually replenished by summer rains."

North of the Touchwood Hills, the fertile prairie plateau, with an increasing proportion of woods in its northern and eastern parts extends from the Duck Mountains, westward to the South Branch of the Saskatchewan, two hundred and twenty miles, and beyond it, up the valley of the North Branch, four hundred miles further In a northerly direction it extends to the main Saskatchewan below the junction of the two branches, upwards of a hundred miles north of Fort Pelly, on the Assiniboine, and to the wooded country on Root River, which projects from the north-east into the prairie country.

Fertile ground continues through the wooded country for some distance north of Root River, till it merges in the poor marshy grounds towards the main Saskatchewan.

CHAPTER XI.

LAKES MANITOBAH AND WINNIPEGOOS.

A little east of the middle of the tract of two hundred and forty miles in width, between Lake Winnipeg and the Assiniboine, and roughly parallel to them, extend Lake Winnipegoos in the north and Lake Manitobah in the south; the latter receives the waters of the former by an elbow-shaped stream, and discharges its own into Lake Winnipeg, from a bay on its east side, by a river called the Little Saskatchewan, which is fifty miles in direct length to its mouth.

These lakes are each a hundred and twenty miles in length. The greatest breadth of Manitobah is twenty-four miles, and of Winnipegoos twenty-seven. Taken together, they extend two hundred and twenty miles from north to south.

They enclose between them and Lake Winnipeg a peninsula of two hundred and fifty miles in length by a hundred miles in greatest breadth, which is cut across at the middle by the Little Saskatchewan.

This peninsula, though as large as the Kingdom of Denmark, counts for little in the Nor'-West. Its interior has not been examined by our explorers. It is reported to be a low flat country, abounding in lakes and marshes. On its coast, on the north-east shore of Lake Manitobah, Mr. Dawson states that from the marsh which lies behind its high shingle beach, a rich alluvial soil rises gradually to a moderate height, not subject to be flooded. The section it shows, where traversed by the Little Saskatchewan, is less favorable, having much very low ground; which is natural, as the river would seek its way over the lowest part. As it is a limestone country and thickly wooded, the soil must necessarily be very fertile, where there is depth enough of it; which should at least frequently be the case in a low level country.

We may expect that it will be found so when explored; but it is of little present importance.

4

Round the south end of Lake Manitobah, for a circuit of about fifty miles, the soil is that of the richest description of prairie land. The few settlers consider it even superior to that of Red River. It is an undulating country of mingled woods and open prairie.

The White Mud River, a stream of about eighty miles in length by its course, which has its sources in the southern skirts of the Riding Mountains, and flows eastward to the south end of Lake Manitobah, is described as passing through an exceedingly beautiful and fertile country of prairies, thickly interspersed with woods, the soil of which is a rich sandy loam. This very rich prairie land extends southward to the Sand Hills on the Assiniboine, and eastward to Red River.

Between the upper end of Lake Manitobah and the Riding Mountains, and around Lake Dauphin, there is much rich ground, and much of it very marshy. Mr. Dawson and Mr. Hind agree in thinking that these marshes could generally be drained, and would form rich meadows. But Mr. Hind does not consider the country on the shores of these lakes, and between them and the Riding and Duck Mountains, as generally suitable for settlement, excepting the south end of Lake Manitobah. Mr. Dawson's opinion is more favorable, owing probably to his greater experience of rugged countries like the Ottawa and eastern districts, where the standard by which land is estimated is not so high as in the western parts of Canada.

Mr. Dawson states that "the country bordering on the western extremity of Lake Winnipegoos is, in general, of a fair elevation, and the land appears to be remarkably fertile; between the Red Deer River and Swan River," (a distance of seventy-five miles), "a level country extends to the base of the Porcupine Hills. It is well wooded, and upon the whole, I consider this tract well adapted for settlement."

THE DAUPHIN RIVER.

Reporting on the River Dauphin, Mr. A. Wells says, "that is a fine stream, forty yards broad, having five feet of water in the shallowest parts. Its banks are of a strong gray clay, covered with black mould and timbered with oak, elm and poplar, and adds, "there are several places on the Dauphin River where the Indians grow potatoes, indian corn and melons."

THE RED DEER RIVER.

The Red Deer River, which falls into the north-west end of Lake Winnipegoos, is said to flow through a country that is very ertile.   The fact that maple is to be found there in considerable quantities (as noticed by Sir Alexander McKenzie) is a favorable indication alike as to soil and climate.   It is a stream of about two hundred miles in length by its course.

THE SWAN RIVER.

The Swan River, which enters a bay of the north end of Lake Winnipegoos, after passing northward through Swan Lake, is about two hundred miles in length by its course.   Speaking of it Mr. Dawson says : " Ascending from Swan Lake for two miles or so, the banks are rather low, in the succeeding ten miles they gradually attain a height of nearly a hundred feet, landslips occur in many places, where the banks are high, exposing an alluvial soil of great depth resting on drift clay, or shale of a slightly bituminous appearance."

"About thirty miles above Swan Lake, the prairie region fairly commences.   There the river winds about in a fine valley, the banks of which rise to the height of eighty or a hundred feet.   Beyond these an apparently unbroken level extends, on one side, for a distance of fifteen or twenty miles to the Porcupine Hills, and for an equal distance on the other, to the high table-land called the Duck Mountain. From this south-westward to Thunder Mountain, the country is the finest I have ever seen in a state of nature. The prospect is bounded by the blue outline of the hills named, while, in the plain, alternate wood and prairie present an appearance more pleasing than if either entirely prevailed."   Leaving Swan River to cross Fort Pelly, he says, " the road then follows for some distance a tributary of Swan River, which runs in a beautiful valley with alternate slopes of woodland and prairie.   Numbers of horses were quietly feeding on the rich pasture of the valley as we passed, and what with the clumps of trees on the rising grounds and the stream winding among green meadows, it seemed as if it wanted but the presence of human habitations to give it the appearance of a highly cultivated country."

This description carries us round again into the rich prairie country, already described, on the upper course of the Assiniboine, which as before observed is bounded on the east by the Porcupine, the Duck and the Riding Mountains.   It is in a broad valley between the two latter that the Swan River finds its way eastward.

THE PORCUPINE, DUCK AND RIDING MOUNTAINS.

These mountains are thickly covered with wood of a large growth ; they rise gently, in successive plateaus, from the prairie plain, which is much higher than the low country on the shores of the lakes east of them.

Taken together, they extend in a curved line of two hundred miles in length, nearly parallel to the Assiniboine, about half way between it and the Lakes Manitobah and Winnipegoos.

Mr. Hind gives the Riding Mountains an elevation of a thousand feet above the land on the shore of Lake Manitobah ; and Mr. Dawson estimates the Porcupine Mountains as rising to about fifteen hundred feet over the plain at their eastern base.

The Riding and Duck Mountains are more properly described as portions of the elevated disk of the high plain country on the Upper Assiniboine, which rises gently from the prairie in successive plateaus, thickly wooded, to the summit, falling eastward in abrupt descents to the much lower country along the west shores of Lakes Manitobah and Winnipegoos; presenting towards them a mountainous and lofty aspect.

Rising from the prairie they are covered with a thick growth of wood, chiefly poplar. The table land of the summit of the Riding Mountain is described by Professor Hind as fine land, heavy clay soil supporting a forest of very large white spruce, poplar, birch, aspen, &c. ; the white spruce girthing from five feet six inches to seven feet three inches. In Mr. Dawson's report, the table land forming the summit of Duck Mountain is described, from information obtained, to be of rich soil and heavily wooded. Porcupine Mountain, besides being higher, rises in a more definite form from the plains at its base.

NAVIGATION OF LAKES MANITOBAH AND WINNIPEGOOS AND RIVER LITTLE SASKATCHEWAN.

As the Little Saskatchewan, the outlet of Lake Manitobah, is a fine navigable stream of seven hundred and fifty feet in breadth, and the Waterhen River or Sangisipi, which connects Lakes Manitobah and Winnipegoos, has a broad channel not less than three feet deep at low water, they present together with these lakes an unbroken line of water communication from Fort Garry to Mossy Portage, at the head of Lake Winnipegoos, a distance of about five hundred miles.

Mossy Portage, which is only about four miles and a quarter in length, through low ground, connects the head of Lake Winnipegoos with Cedar Lake on the River Saskatchewan, above its great rapids. A short canal there would unite the navigation by these lakes from Fort Garry with that of the River Saskatchewan, (from Cedar Lake upwards) which for nearly a thousand miles presents no greater obstructions to navigation than are to be found in the River Ohio. This would form a line of water communication of about fifteen hundred miles in length from Fort Garry to the foot of the Rocky Mountains. By ascending the Assiniboine seventy miles to

Prairie Portage, and canalling by the Rat River and White Mud River, about twenty-five miles, to the south end of Lake Manitobah, the distance to the Saskatchewan would be shortened by a hundred miles. A cheaply constructed shallow canal, with a good length and breadth of lock-pit, would be sufficient there for large business. The character of the Saskatchewan, as a navigable river, will be further noticed.

CHAPTER XII.

THE RIVER SASKATCHEWAN AND ITS COUNTRY.

The term country is more properly applicable than valley to the region drained by the Saskatchewan and its tributaries. The country through which the two great arms of the Saskatchewan have their courses, being a portion of the great interior plateau that slopes down eastward from the Rocky Mountains, it does not present the aspect of a valley. The term valley is more appropriately applicable to the deep hollows, in the generally plain country, in which its rivers flow.

The north and south branches of the Saskatchewan, as before mentioned, have their sources in the Rocky Mountains but a few miles apart, about latitude 51° 40' N. ; that is, about a hundred and eighty-five miles north of the United States boundary.

From their nearly common source the North Branch diverges north-eastward, and the South Branch or Bow River south-eastward, till at two hundred and fifty miles due eastward they attain a distance of three hundred miles from each other ; the South Branch being there within forty-five miles of the frontier. Then gradually approaching, they meet at five hundred and fifty miles eastward from their source.

The length of the North Branch, by the manuscript field notes of the survey of it by the North-West Company's astronomer, David Thompson, is seven hundred and seventy-two and a half miles, and that of the South or Main Branch, by the latest maps, is about eight hundred and ten miles.

From their junction, the course of the Main Saskatchewan to Lake Winnipeg is, by Thompson's field notes, two hundred and eighty-two miles. This makes the whole length of the Saskatchewan, from the source of the South Branch, (which is the main stream,) to Lake Winnipeg, a thousand and ninety-two miles. Following the North Branch, as measured by Thompson, the total length to Lake Winnipeg is a thousand and fifty-four and a half miles.

This gives occasion to remark that the length of rivers, and distances generally, are much exaggerated in new countries; and even scientific men are led into error by hearing them so spoken of by the people of the country.   In this manner Capt. Blackiston gives the distance from Lake Winnipeg to Edmonton, on the North Branch, as a thousand miles; but by Thompson's field-book the measured distance is only seven hundred and seventy-two miles. Much of the extraordinary length and size attributed to rivers in the United States is due to this; and errors respecting them from this source have found their way into standard works, such as Johnson's Physical Atlas.

Passing through the north end of Lake Winnipeg, at four hundred and twenty-three miles further, the Saskatchewan falls into Hudson's Bay, making its entire length from its source to the sea, fifteen hundred and fifteen miles.   In this last distance its waters are more than doubled in volume from the large tributaries that feed Lake Winnipeg; and as it descends six hundred and twenty-eight feet, its course is exceedingly obstructed by rapids and falls.

The total area drained by it is five hundred thousand miles, or one-seventh more than the Ganges unwaters.

By the careful measurements of Mr. Fleming, of the Canadian Exploring Expedition, the volume of water passing in the North Branch, in the month of August, was 25,264 cubic feet per second, or one-fifth more than the mean volume of the Rhone, by D'Aubuisson; and that of the South Branch was 34,285, or 585 feet more than the mean of the Rhine, by the same authority.   Measured below the forks, where it is 980 feet wide and 20 feet in average depth, that of the main Saskatchewan was 59,667 cubic feet per second, or nearly three-quarters of the mean discharge of the Ottawa at Grenville.*

The area drained by the South Saskatchewan is greater than that of the Rhine, and the water-shed of the Rocky Mountains drained by it is greater than that of the Alps drained by the Rhine, and the excess of its volume would be much greater were it not for the extent of dry prairie land it passes through.   The River Missouri, which flows through the same description of country, is similarly affected.   Though draining an equal area to that of the St. Lawrence, and nearly as long in direct distance from its source to its mouth, it throws into the Mississippi only about one-fourth of the water the St. Lawrence discharges into the Gulf; and its general width is only five hundred yards.

In considering the character of the Saskatchewan and its country,

* When it is considered that the Ottawa draws its waters from a cold, high and densely-wooded region with innumerable deep lakes, the cause of its great volume will be at once apparent.

as described by the Canadian Exploring Party and others, let us ascend it from Lake Winnipeg.

From its mouth there are over two miles of strong current up to the Grand Rapids, which are nearly three miles in length, with a descent of forty-three and a half feet. The river has there worn its channel, varying from six hundred and sixty to two hundred and twenty yards in width, down through the lips of the horizontal beds of limestone, which form the basis of the level and generally marshy plateau behind.

As to the country in the vicinity of the Grand Rapids, Professor Hind says it is "very favorable for a road, and even for a settlement, as the banks of the river are high, with a considerable depth of good soil, from the second rapid east of Cross Lake to near Lake Winnipeg," about eight miles, and adds, there is also abundance of timber for fuel and building.

The second rapid referred to is at four miles above the head of the Grand Rapid. It is fully a mile long, with a fall of seven and a half feet. From this up to Cedar Lake, which is twenty miles from Lake Winnipeg, there is a succession of rapids and swift currents, which, with the rapids already mentioned, make a total descent of upwards of sixty feet.

Cedar Lake is thirty miles long, and twenty-five miles in greatest width. From the foot of it the river is navigable for steamers, without interruption, up a hundred and eighty miles to Tobern's Rapids.

North of Cedar Lake the country is described as low and flat for a long distance back; the main land and islands well wooded with balsam, spruce, birch, poplar, tamarack, cedar, and Banksean pine. Low beds of horizontal limestone appear in the islands, and "a considerable portion of the land is reported to be swampy and unavailable for agricultural purposes."

From Cedar Lake up to Marshy Lake, about forty miles, the country on each side of the river is not more than eighteen inches over the water, which is skirted by a belt of willows, alders and long grass ; in the rear an extensive marsh, with occasional islands of small poplar and spruce. The floods cover these flats every spring, depositing a very rich mud, which is raising and extending them. Much land has been so formed within the memory of the natives. No high ground is to be seen on either side, and the Indians report that there is nothing but boggy swamps behind for many miles. Up to near the mouth of the Pasquia River, which is about eighty-five miles in direct distance from Lake Winnipeg, the banks continue only from two to three feet above the river, with a nearly similar low marshy country behind.

The Pas Mission is situated at the mouth of the Pasquia, a considerable tributary. The river banks are there ten or twelve feet high, the soil a dark mould over drift clay. Here the exploring party found farm houses and fields of grain. The banks, however, continue low alluvial, with a rather low country behind.

Around Cumberland House (about 116 miles further), the country is low and flat; "the soil in some places is a stiff clay, but in general it consists of a gravelly loam a few feet in thickness, covering a bed of white limestone, supporting a light growth of poplar and birch," with occasional groves of spruce : much of it is submerged in spring floods ; many of the marshes could be drained and improved without much difficulty.

Here we have reached a very favorable country for agriculture. Speaking of the twenty-nine miles above this, Mr. Fleming says :— 'The general character of the country we have passed through to-day is excellent, the soil being rich, and the timber of a fair quality." Of the forty-seven miles succeeding, upwards, he says he "passed through an excellent tract of country all day, the soil on both sides of the river consisting of a very rich alluvial deposit, ten feet in thickness above the water, well wooded with large poplar, balsam, spruce and birch ; some of the poplars measuring two and a half feet in diameter ; and, as far as I was enabled to ascertain, the land continues good for a great distance on either side, but more especially on the south side of the river."

Of the fifty-three miles next above that he says that it is "well adapted for agricultural purposes and settlement, the soil being a rich alluvial loam, of considerable depth, well watered and drained by many fine creeks, and clothed with abundance of timber for fuel, fencing and building."

The country on the banks of the river continues the same for a few miles further, till, approaching Fort à la Corne, the immediate banks become gradually higher, and the bluffs that form the edge of the high plateau behind on each side gradually approach nearer to the river.

From Fort à la Corne, which is a hundred and fifty miles above Cumberland House, up to the forks of the north and south branches, a distance of sixteen miles, the river is described as sweeping, in magnificent curves, in a valley of about a mile in width, and from a hundred and fifty to two hundred feet lower than the general level of the country on each side.

Describing the country on the south side of the Saskatchewan, here, Professor hind says : "The trail from Fort à la Corne to the old track leading from Fort Ellice to Carleton House ascends the hills, forming the banks of the deep eroded valley of the Saskatchewan, in rear of the Fort. It passes through a thick forest of small aspens, until near the summit, when a sandy soil begins, covered with Banksean pine and a few small oak. The sandy soil occupies a narrow strip on the banks of the river varying from half a mile to four miles broad.   South of the sandy strip the soil changes to a rich black mould, distributed over a gently undulating country.   The pine gives way to aspen and willows, in groves, the aspen occupying the crest of the undulations, and the willows the lowest portion of the intervening valleys.   On the slopes the grass is long and luxuriant, affording fine pasturage.   The general aspect of the country is highly favorable for agriculture, the soil deep and uniformly rich, rivalling the low prairies of Red River and the Assiniboine."

Beyond this he speaks of the wooded country that extends southwards to the head of the Assiniboine, which is gradually being converted into open prairie, by the great fires that have done so already over great extents.   He explains that by the term wooded country is to be understood a region in which prairie or grassy areas predominate over the aspen woods.

This favorable country of mixed woodland and prairie, extends southward from the forks of the Saskatchewan, eighty miles, to the treeless prairie region on the northerly waters of the River Qu'Appelle.   South-easterly it extends, including the wooded region on Root River, through to the fertile country on the Assiniboine already described ; making together in that direction a breadth of three hundred and twenty miles of fertile country, interspersed with woodlands, between the forks of the Saskatchewan and the Assiniboine opposite the mouth of the Souris.

ROOT OR CARROT RIVER

Rises in rich lands on the south flank of the Lumpy Hill of the woods, sixty miles south-west from the forks of the Saskatchewan, and thirteen miles from the South Branch, and flows chiefly through what is described as wooded country with many lakes, generally from thirty to forty-five miles south of the Saskatchewan, into which it falls after a course of about two hundred and forty miles. Professor Hind estimates that there are three millions of acres of land of the first quality between it and the Saskatchewan.

CHAPTER XIII.

THE SOUTH BRANCH OF THE SASKATCHEWAN.

Immediately above the Forks the South Branch of the Saskatchewan is only a hundred and eighty yards in width, but the current is swift, $3\frac{1}{2}$ miles an hour, and the average depth seven and a half feet. Professor Hind states it as being less in volume, and not half the width that it is two hundred and twenty miles further up.

For about a hundred and thirty miles up its course, or a hundred miles in direct distance, its valley preserves the same character as that of the main river between the Forks and Fort à la Corne, but the banks, which the prairie plateaus on each side present to the narrow valley of the river, are generally lower, varying from a hundred, to forty feet in height, exposing sand-stone cliffs where cut by the bends of the river. The country on each side is described as having a rich soil, with abundant woods, in clumps and groves, for a great part of the way. It then becomes gradually less wooded and more sandy in parts, especially on the west side, till, after passing the distance last mentioned, it assumes the character of light treeless prairie land.

The river in this distance varies from 180 to 440 yards in breadth, increasing in width in ascending, generally from 10 to 14 feet in depth, the current three and three and a half miles an hour, with a swifter current and whirlpools in a few places.

The generally treeless prairie country, reached at a hundred and thirty miles from the Forks, is the commencement of the great infertile region which has been already described as covering the greater part of the River Qu'Appelle and its tributaries, and which, with some considerable exception, is described by Dr. Hector and Capt. Palliser, as extending westward over the South Saskatchewan and its tributaries, nearly to the hilly country at the base of the Rocky Mountains.

Continuing about seventy miles further in the same south-southwest direction, or nearly a hundred miles by its course, the Elbow of the South Branch is reached at two hundred and ten, or what is usually called two hundred and fifty miles from the Forks. In the commencement of this distance is the "Moose Woods," a rich alluvial expansion of the low valley of the river, partly wooded, with rich glades between : it is twenty-five miles in length, and six or eight miles in breadth, and bounded on each side by sandy crested bluffs. From this to the Elbow the river again assumes its narrow valley, the banks of which gradually ascend to two hundred feet in height.

About thirty-five miles above the Elbow the South Branch approaches the Eyebrow and Thunder-breeding Mountains, and there skirts the salient angle of the Coteau de Missouri, which springs like a vast bastion from the United States boundary ; its east face, which rises six hundred feet above the elevated plain at its foot, is two hundred miles in length, and its western face, called the Cypree Hills, extends a hundred and sixty miles with much greater elevation, being, according to Dr. Hector, four thousand two hundred feet above the sea, and sixteen hundred above the plains, according to Capt. Palliser.

For nearly five hundred miles above the Elbow of the South Saskatchewan, its upward course passes through the great infertile region of light prairie land, the greater part of which is described as consisting of arid wastes; from which, however, there are apparently some large exceptions, for instance, the Cypree Hills, just mentioned, are stated by Capt. Palliser to be " covered in fine timber, abounding in excellent grass, and well watered, and fairly, though not abundantly stocked with game."

The following further extracts from Capt. Palliser's report, together with the above, give a very clear general view of the character of the country on the South Saskatchewan and its chief tributary, the Red Deer River. He says, "the Wachee or Hand Hills, in Lat. 51° 32′ N. Long. 111° 20′, are a plateau elevated about 450 feet above the level of the surrounding prairies. The grass and land were very good, but the timber not of any value, being chiefly willow and poplar. With the exception of very few similar spots, the whole prairie over which we passed, to our crossing place on the Red Deer river, (about forty miles above the forks of Red Deer and Bow rivers,) is a sandy country, the grass very scanty, and no wood."

He proceeds to say, "we crossed Red Deer river, and followed along its south bank, until we arrived opposite the site where the old Fort called Chesterfield House once stood; with the exception of the bed of Red Deer River, the whole of that region is valueless the grass being very scanty and timber very scarce." He does not say how wide the bed or valley of Red Deer River is.

He says further, "there is throughout the whole of this region a great scarcity of rain; but in a few places here and there, where the land rises above the plain to the height of three or four hundred feet, good grass and some timber, as rough bark poplar and willow appear."

Speaking of the South Branch of the Saskatchewan, he says "having now examined all that river, we find the whole region from the Elbow, in longitude 107° 37 W., up to the point where the meridian 112° W. strikes the "line of the woods," by no means a desirable district for settlement."

Red Deer River enters the South Branch about a hundred and thirty miles above the Elbow. It is nearly five hundred miles in length, and is two hundred and fifty yards wide fifty miles above its mouth. The lower half of its course is in the infertile region Above that, a hundred and thirty miles of its course lies in the fertile region towards the North Branch of the Saskatchewan; and the remainder in the wooded region at the base of the Rocky Mountains, and its sources are in their valleys. Coal is noted by Dr. Hector about a hundred and seventy miles up from its mouth, and again a hundred miles further up.

Capt. Blackiston estimates the average descent of the South Branch of the Saskatchewan, from Chesterfield House at the mouth of Red Deer River, down to the Forks, at two feet a mile, but says that those who are acquainted with the river from boating upon it consider it navigable for steamers. The distance is about 340 miles.

FERTILE GROUNDS NEAR SOURCES ON SKIRT OF ROCKY MOUNTAINS.

Beyond the infertile region the upper course of the South Branch to its source, about a hundred and sixty miles, is among the Rocky Mountains and their lower outliers, where the country is generally wooded, and the valleys fertile, but very elevated.

Capt. Blackiston's journal of exploration of a line, of about ninety miles S. S. E. from Bow Fort, on the Bow River, or South Branch, gives a good description of the country on the skirts of the lower mountain ranges.

He speaks of woods of spruce, poplar, aspen, and large rough barked pine; of the track being blocked with fallen timber in parts; of fine prairie bottoms, and others partially covered with scrub and willow, and fine streams; of passing for three days in valleys within the outlying parallel ridges, "less wooded than previously passed, being for considerable part through fine prairie slopes," the main range visible occasionally at a distance of thirty miles, through gaps in the nearer mountains, of undulating prairie; of the trail passing between numerous wooded ridges, and says "the soil of the valleys was usually a deep dark mould, supporting a luxuriant vegetation, of the smaller plants. This was the nature of most of these mountain valleys. Where the strata is upheaved the ground is of course rocky; such, however, is not often the case in the valleys." Continues to say "soon after we gained the height of land between the Speechee and Belly Rivers, and the wide prairie valley of the latter burst upon our view." He then descended a short distance and camped at an elevation of four thousand feet above the sea.

This elevation, which is the same as that of Bow Fort, is doubtless too great to admit of the cultivation of wheat. Coarse grains and vegetables, however, might seemingly be cultivated. Dr. Hector mentions that some of the Indians who have been converted to christianity cultivate little plots of ground at Bow Fort, and that their principal crops are turnips and potatoes.

This speaks little in favor of the climate of this locality, but on the other hand it is to be remarked that even this cold elevated region presents an advantage for cattle feeding that we do not enjoy in Canada, which Dr. Hector especially notices, and describes as extending to this locality.

He says "the most valuable feature of this belt of country, which also stretches from Touchwood Hills, Carleton, and Fort Pitt south of Edmonton to the old Bow Fort at the Rocky Mountains" (he had previously mentioned also the head waters of Red Deer River) " is the immense extent of what I shall term winter pasturage."

" This winter pasturage consists of tracts of country partially wooded with poplar and willow clumps, and bearing a most luxuriant growth of vetches and nutritious grasses. The clumps of wood afford shelter to animals, while the scrubby bush keeps the snow in such a loose state that they find no difficulty in feeding the large tracts of swampy country, when frozen, also afford admirable feeding grounds ; and it is only towards spring, in very severe winters, that horses and cattle cannot be left to feed in well chosen localities throughout this region of country."

Any practical man will see that such advantages, for unlimited cattle feeding, without the labor of clearing land and raising hay crops, combined with the extreme richness of soil in the valleys are weighty offsets against the coolness of the summer climate. As for the winter Dr. Hector says, with reference to the whole region from Bow Fort, along the skirt of the Rocky Mountains, as far north as the River Athabasca, "having travelled the Rocky Mountains at the most unfavorable period of an unusually severe winter, I am enabled to state that whatever may be the amount of snow on the heights of land and their western flank, the valleys of the eastern ranges are actually less encumbered by snow than much of the prairie country."

It is to be observed that these remarks apply to the country on the east flank of the Rocky Mountains for at least three hundred and fifty miles northward from the United States boundary, including the head waters of the North Branch of the Saskatchewan, and the Athabasca.

CHAPTER XIV.

THE NORTH BRANCH OF THE SASKATCHEWAN.

The country drained by the North Branch of the Saskatchewan, and its extensive tributary the Battle River, though incomparably more valuable than the country traversed by the South Branch, does not require to be described so much at length, owing to its more uniform character.

The North Branch, for the greater part of its course, and the Battle River, lie in the great belt of country which the Canadian and the Imperial exploring parties describe as generally fertile land of the first quality.

The North Branch, for five hundred and twenty miles up from the Forks, and the Battle River, for its whole course of four hundred and fifty miles, (excepting a short elbow of it,) traverse a rich prairie country more or less interspersed with woods.

The remaining two hundred and eighty-two miles of the upper course of the North Branch lie in the thick wood country, which, to the commencement of the mountains, about two hundred miles, is represented as abounding in marshes with patches of fine land in parts. In this distance the banks of the river display beds of lignite coal. Beyond it the remaining course of the river lies in the valleys of the mountains, to the glaciers at its source.

The Battle River enters the North Branch about a hundred and seventy miles above the main Forks. It drains a large part of the country between the North and South Branches. It has its source about ten miles from the North Branch, thirty miles above Edmonton, but they are a hundred and thirty miles apart at the middle of its course, and between them the pasturage is described as very rich. Coal presents itself there, in the banks of the stream, two hundred and fifty miles from its mouth.

The rich prairie country which covers the course of the Battle River and the northerly part of Red Deer River, and includes the North Branch from the forks, up to thirty miles above Edmonton, has a breadth of about a hundred miles, at the forks, seventy miles at the mouth of Battle River, a hundred and fifty miles at its middle course, and about seventy at its source; beyond which the belt of fertile prairie country becomes gradually narrower, and turning to the southward, up the course of the Red Deer River, becomes merged in the fertile region on the skirt of the mountains below Bow Fort on the South Branch. It is bounded on the north by the line of the Thick Woods, which sweeps northerly parallel to the course of the North Branch at the distance of forty to twenty miles beyond it, then curving to the southward crosses it about thirty miles above Edmonton, and continuing in that direction strikes the mountains near Bow Fort, making a circuit from the forks of about seven hundred miles.

This circuit of the Thick Woods is the present boundary of the progress of successive fires which are gradually encroaching on the forest, or partly wooded country, and converting it into treeless prairie, unless where clumps of young aspen and poplar, growing up, escape the ravages of succeeding fires.

Without entering into particulars here as to climate, we may observe that Capt. Palliser, who with Dr. Hector explored a greater extent of the valley of Saskatchewan than had been previously visited by any other scientific men, says that the climate of the southern and western parts of it is decidedly milder than that of Red River.

CHAPTER XV.

NAVIGATION OF THE SASKATCHEWAN.

There is a good harbour at the mouth of the Saskatchewan, from which the current is swift up to the foot of the Grand Rapids which are three miles in length, with a fall of forty-three and a half feet. Above them the current is moderate for four miles to a rapid of one mile in length with a fall of seven feet. The ascent of this by a powerful steamer is said to be practicable; but the advantage of it might be questionable.

From it to Cedar Lake, ten miles, the current is strong with several rapids. Captain Munn, of the Steamer "International," and Mr. Hutchison, the pilot of that vessel, who examined the river up to Carleton House, state that a steamer could ascend this distance, with the single improvement of a pier at Cross Lake.

To connect the foot of this reach with Lake Winnepeg, a tram road or railway would be sufficient. There would be no object in canalling past the Grand Rapids, for the vessels employed on Lake Winnipeg would have to be much stronger than what would be suitable on the Saskatchewan, so transhipment would be necessary at any rate.

From the foot of Cedar Lake to "Tobern's Falls," Captain Munn says, the river is uninterrupted by anything to impede navigation the distance is said to be a hundred and eighty miles,—probably not over a hundred and sixty.

Tobern's Rapid, Captain Blackiston says, is certainly not navigable at low, and he doubts much if it be so at high water, but adds that the difference is so great that it is hardly safe to say.

Damming, with lockage, to gorge the rapid would seem necessary there, or a tram road past it.

Above Tobern's Falls, Captain Munn says, that for eight or ten miles the river is wide and shoal, with intermediate rapids, not navigable at low water. Captain Blackiston, R. E., who ascended the river to Edmonton, is of opinion that there are no obstructions from Tobern's Rapids up to Coles' Falls or Rapids above the forks, (a distance of about a hundred miles,) which could not be surmounted by a steamer at high water. Captain Munn, of the steamer "International," in his report to the Hudson's Bay Company says, in summing up, that the Saskatchewan is a good navigable stream from the Grand Rapids up as far as Tobern's Falls, with the improvement suggested by him at Cross Lake. From Tobern's Falls to Carleton House, he did not find the river navigable, the water being low when he examined it, but he was informed by Mr. Pruden, at the latter place, that the water in the river is three and a-half feet higher from the first of June to the middle of September than it then was. He adds, " with this additional water, I am of opinion that light draught steamers could be sent as far as I explored it, without any serious difficulty." He found the river well wooded, affording abundance for steam purposes. In this report his pilot fully concurred.

Coles' Falls, immediately above the Forks, are a succession of rapids, twenty-six in number, from a hundred and fifty to three hundred feet in length each, with slack water between. Captain Munn includes them in the extent passable in the high water period mentioned.

For twenty-two miles above the Forks the ascent per mile is great, and the rapids continue for eighteen miles of that distance; the current is six to seven miles an hour when the water is high, by Professor Hind's observation, a rate of current by no means insurmountable by a steamer of fair power, but for safety to vessels the boulders should be removed from a sufficient width of the channel.

Above this, for the distance of two hundred and eighty miles, the ascent per mile is very much less than in the lower part of the river. It is estimated by Mr. Thompson, who surveyed it, as being from six to nine inches per mile, and for a hundred and eighty miles further, up to Edmonton, at two feet a mile, less than half the rate of descent of the Rhone from Avignon to the sea. From Edmonton to within forty-three miles of Rocky Mountain House, Thompson states the ascent to be four feet to the mile.

Captain Blackiston gives the average descent of the Saskatchewan from Edmonton to Lake Winnipeg as one foot four inches to the mile. To the foot of Cedar Lake it would be one foot three inches to the mile, the same as the descent of the Rhine from Strasbourg to the Sea. As the Rhine is navigated throughout that distance by steamers and vessels of considerable tonnage, the current of the Saskatchewan, excepting at particular points, cannot be such as to present any great obstruction to steamboats. Powerful steamers of two feet draught, such as are used on the Rhine, would navigate it very freely.

From the 1st of June to the end of September, and probably for a longer period, such vessels could ply.

The navigation of the Saskatchewan will probably prove to be nearly as useful as that of the Ohio, but less liable, on account of its greater volume, to interruption from low water, to which the navigation of the Ohio is very subject in the dry months of summer.

CHAPTER XVI.

PROPORTION OF ARABLE LANDS IN SOUTH HALF OF CENTRAL PRAIRIE COUNTRY.

We have now gone over that part of the great territory under consideration, drained by the Saskatchewan and other tributaries of Lake Winnipeg, the area of which, as before stated, is about two hundred and eighty thousand square miles.

Speaking of part of this area, Captain Palliser says : " The extent of surface drained by the Saskatchewan and other tributaries to Lake Winnipeg which we had the opportunity of examining amounts in round numbers to 150,000 square miles. This region is bounded to the north by what is called the ' strong woods, or the southern limit of the great circum-arctic zone of forest which occupies these latitudes in the northern hemisphere. This line which is indicated in the map, sweeps to the north-west from the shore of Lake Winnipeg, and reaches its most northerly limit about 54° 30′ N. and long. 109° W., from whence it again passes to south west, meeting the Rocky Mountains in lat. 51° N., long. 115° W Between this line of the ' strong woods' and the northerly limit of the true prairie country, there is a belt of land varying in width which at one period must have been covered by an extension of the northern forests, but which has been gradually cleared by successive fires.

" It is now a partially wooded country, abounding in lakes, and rich in natural pasturage, in some parts rivalling the finest park scenery of our own country. Throughout this region of country the climate seems to preserve the same character, although it passes through very different latitudes—its form being doubtless determined by the curves of the isothermal line. Its superficial extent embraces about 65,000 square miles (query—geographical or statute If the former, it would be about 85,000 statute, which would agree with the area shown on Professor Hind's map,) of which more than one-third may be considered as at once available for the purposes of the agriculturist. Its elevation increases from 700 to 4,000 feet

5

as we approach the Rocky Mountains, consequently it is not equally adapted throughout to the cultivation of any one crop; nevertheless, at Fort Edmonton, which has an altitude of 3,000 feet, even wheat is sometimes cultivated with success.

"The least valuable portion of the prairie country has an extent of above 80,000 square miles, and is that lying along the southern branch of the Saskatchewan, and southward from thence to the boundary line; while its northern limit is designated in the Indian languages as the 'edge of the woods,' the original line of the woods before invaded by the fire."

The fertile belt thus described by Captain Palliser contains, as represented on Dr. Hector's and Professor Hind's map, an area of about 85,000 statute miles, the equivalent nearly of 65,000 geographical square miles. We have here, then, in the portion of this territory explored by Captain Palliser and his party, an extent of very fertile, mixed prairie and woodlands, three times the size of that part of Upper Canada from Kingston to Sarnia; of which more than one-third is at once ready to receive the plough.

This, however, does not include the very considerable portion of really good prairie land, already described as interspersed in the region classed as infertile country; nor the Cypree Mountains south of the South Branch of the Saskatchewan above the Elbow, described as a range elevated 1,600 feet above the plains, covered with fine timber, abounding in excellent grass and well watered; nor does it include the parts described as good of the wooded country on the west side of Lakes Manitobah and Winnepegoos. If these were included, to say nothing of ground north of the line of "thick woods," not yet converted by fires into prairie, the total would probably amount to one hundred thousand square miles estimated by Mr. Dawson, in his report, as suitable for settlement.

It would be absurd to expect any country in a state of nature to be all equally fit to receive the plough at once. The one-third of the fertile region, estimated by Captain Palliser as being so, is a very fair proportion; the other two-thirds, no doubt, are parts requiring draining or partial clearing. It would also be absurd to suppose it to be all equally fertile. There is a considerable difference between the deep beds of black vegetable mould which prevail chiefly in the Red River valley, and the rich sandy loam spoken of in some other parts; and there are the occasional bad spots and poor sandy ground, which we expect to find in all countries, though there are, apparently, tracts of great extent unusually free from them.

As for the 80,000 square miles (about a hundred thousand statute square miles) which Captain Palliser designates as the least valuable part of the Prairie Country, it will no doubt, as he says,

" be for ever comparatively useless," with the exception of such tract as the Cypress Mountains, and others where there is good grass with wood and water. These, with the richer parts of the vast green treeless plains, will afford great scope for cattle feeding after the great fertile region has become occupied.

Messrs. Cooper and Sucklay, the Naturalists of the U. S. Pacific Railway Exploration, identify the same kind of dry prairie country of Nebraska (of which this is a continuation) with the " perpetual steppes" of Russia in Europe. There the pasturage or green sward is not even continuous, except in very low valleys, as stated by Mr Haxhausen, and it is not uncommon for twenty months to pass without rain. Yet these grounds, he says, afford excellent pasture especially for sheep, and yield, where cultivated, sixfold to one sown of wheat and rye, which he observes is greater than the aver age yield of Russia in Europe.

These steppes are stated to be increasing in population by immi gration from the northern parts of the Empire, now attracted to them. Buckwheat, Indian Corn, Oats, Barley and Beets grow there abundantly.

We have now taken a general view of the south part of the section under consideration, or that part of it which is comonly called Rupert's Land. It is not usual to include more than this in speaking of the capacity of the country for settlement. But it is far from being all that is fit for agricultural occupation. We have still the countries lying on the Athabasca and Peace Rivers, the River of the Mountains, Hay's River and the upper part of Beaver River, suitable for settlement, to go over, to complete the great sec tion of available country under consideration.

In beginning to treat of this great section of territory, it was stated, that in applying the term Central Prairie Land to it, that expression was meant merely to indicate this section as one contain ing prairie land, with the distinction, that prairies prevailed in the southern half, and woods in the northern half, with occasional prairie tracts. It is the latter which we have now to consider under the divisions indicated by its rivers. It contains an area of about two hundred thousand superficial miles.

CHAPTER XVII.

THE BEAVER OR UPPER CHURCHILL RIVER.

The Beaver River has its source about forty miles only from the
orth Saskatchewan at Edmonton, beyond the line of the " strong
oods."

Its course to Hudson's Bay is about eleven hundred miles in
ngth, of which five hundred miles lie within the section under
nsideration.

For two hundred and fifty miles from its source, its course is in
e plain country of Silurian or more recent formations.   It then,
low Isle à la Crosse, enters the great primary or azoic belt, which
vers the remainder of its course within this section.   It may be
nsidered as draining part of the same plain as the Saskatchewan,
eir basins being divided only by rocks a few feet in height.   At
rog Portage, two hundred and thirty miles lower, crossing to a
ibutary of the. Saskatchewan, the waters of the Beaver or
hurchill flow over into it at high flood.

Sir John Richardson says that the Beaver River drains a com-
ratively small extent of prairie land. and Capt. Palliser describes
e country between it and the forks of the Saskatchewan as a
ick wood country, with many lakes abounding in fish.   Lying on
e same formations, it no doubt resembles the fertile belt on the
orth Branch of the Saskatchewan before its prairies were cleared
timber by devastating fires.

Sir Alex. McKenzie speaks favorably of the soil on the upper
rt of the Beaver River, of the buffaloes ranging the partial
tches of prairie along it, and of a garden at Isle à la Crosse,
at well repaid the labor bestowed on it.   He speaks of Lake à la
rosse abounding in " the finest fish in the world," and of the rich-
ss of its surrounding banks and forests in moose and fallow deer,
ith the vast number of the smaller tribes of animals, and the
imerous flocks of wild fowl."

As its Indian name Missinipi, *much water*, implies, the Beaver,
Churchhill as it is called in its lower course, is a river of great
lume.   At Island Portage, above Frog Portage, Sir J. Richardson
eaks of its being five or six hundred yards wide, where pent up
id narrow, with a strong current.   Eastward of Lac à la Crosse,
here it passes through the primary or azoic formation, the soil of
e country is poor, sandy, stony and rocky.   Describing part of it,
r John Richardson says the general aspect of it is like the coun-
y on the north shores of Lake Superior, though the water basin is
it so deeply excavated.

CHAPTER XVIII.

THE RIVER ATHABASCA.

Westward and northward of the Beaver River country lies the greater region drained by the River Athabasca and its tributaries.

The River Athabasca, though not the largest, is the most southerly and far extending branch of the River McKenzie. It has its source between glaciers, among mountains whose highest peaks rise to 15,000 feet, in lat. 52° 20′ N., and long. 118° 25′ W., near the north bend of the Columbia River. It reaches almost across the Rocky Mountains towards the Boat encampment, on a feeder of the Columbia; the narrow valley of its main stream forming there the Athabasca Pass, while that of a more northerly arm is the site of the Leather Pass known as the Tête Jaune or Yellow-Head Pass.

At Jasper House, which stands in a wide valley within the second range, about ninety miles bebow the source of the river, Dr. Hector describes the mountains as rising magnificently to the height of 5,400 feet above its bed, or 7,300 above the sea. Changing from north to north-east, its general direction, at a hundred and eighty miles further, (the greater part of the way among the mountains and their lower ranges,) it receives, on the south, McLeod's River.

At Fort Assiniboine, about three hundred and sixty miles from its source, Dr. Hector describes it as a stream 300 yards in width, flowing in a valley from one to two miles wide, and 250 feet below the level of the surrounding plain. At about forty miles lower, it receives, on the south, the Pembina, a river about two hundred and fifty miles in length; at thirty miles lower the Lesser Slave Lake River from the North:—the lake is a hundred miles in length, the river from it about forty. From this it makes an elbow south-eastward, and then turns nearly north, which general direction it maintains, to its mouth at Lake Athabasca, receiving midway, at a hundred and fifty miles from its mouth, Clear Water River, on the south-east, from Methy Portage. The whole length of the Athabasca is nearly nine hundred miles.

Sir John Richardson describes the Athabasca, at its junction with the Clear Lake River, as a majestic stream, between a quarter and a half mile wide, with a considerable current but without rapids. Sir Alex. McKenzie says it is about three quarters of a mile wide, and runs with a steady current, sometimes contracting but never increasing its channel, till, after receiving several small streams, it discharges itself into the Lake of the Hills (Lake

Athabasca.) He mentions that, about twenty-four miles below the mouth of Clear Water River, there are some bituminous fountains, into which a pole may be inserted without the least resistance.

He mentions that, in 1787, he found Mr. Fond, one of the north-west Traders, residing on the Elk River, (the Athabasca) forty miles from its mouth, where he remained for three years, and had formed as fine a kitchen garden as he (McKenzie) had ever seen in Canada—which is not surprising, as the line of mean summer temperature of Halifax, Nova Scotia, passes through that vicinity.

The bed of the Athabasca is described as being in many places deeply cut below the level of the prairie plateau, which is not separated, by any marked ridge, from the prairie country of the Saskatchewan. Near Lake Athabasca, the high banks of the river's bed sink into the alluvial lands of the delta at its mouth. . From the west end of that lake the combined waters of the Athabasca and the Peace River, under the name of Slave River, flow northward to Great Slave Lake, in what is described as the fracture between the Silurian and primitive rocks.

Mr. David Thompson and Sir John Richardson describe limestone as prevailing throughout the lower course of the Athabasca, generally under beds of sandy soil saturated with bitumen, sometimes of great depth. Thirty miles below Clear Water River the limestone beds are covered with bituminous deposit, upwards of a hundred feet thick. The roots of living trees and herbaceous plants push themselves deep into beds highly impregnated with bitumen, and, Sir John adds, the forest where that mineral is most abundant does not suffer in its growth. He states that below Rivière Rouge, a tributary, a copious spring of mineral pitch issues from a crevice in a cliff, composed of sand and bitumen, in the middle of a thick wood. It seems rather to increase than impair the fertility of the soil. Below Pierre au Calumet, he says : " the whole country, for many miles, is so full of bitumen, that it flows readily into a pit dug a few feet below the surface. Below Clear Water River, he speaks of pretty thick layers of lignite coal appearing in one of the cliffs. On the upper part of the river, above Fort Assiniboine, Dr. Hector states that lignite coal appears in the banks, though not so much as in the Saskatchewan.

The Athabasca country, "from Methy Portage, westward," Sir John Richardson says, "though deeply furrowed by river courses and ravines, and more or less thickly wooded, partakes so much of a prairie character that horsemen may travel over it to Lesser Slave Lake and the Saskatchewan," (three hundred and fifty miles,) and adds that in 1849 a fine body of upwards of forty horses came through early in the season, and in good condition.

The following extracts from Mr. Thompson's journal indicate the nature of the soil and climate of the upper Athabasca, *en rout* from Edmonton to the Forks of the Athabasca. He says " he se off with three men and five horses on 19th April, 1799, rivers open 20th, white frost in the morning, but fine warm day.

" 21st. Very fine day, through thick woods, much wet ground and deep mud, small prairies occasionally—reached the Pembina River in the afternoon in a fine meadow.

" The soil for these three days has been in general a very fin black vegetable mould, with very little sand. It is also the same from Fort George to Fort Augustus in the interior country, thougl intermixed with more sand, and in a few places ridges of san hills."

This description, it is to be observed, refers to a hundred an fifty miles of country. He then descends the River Pembin for three days ; "banks well wooded, with small meadows ; soil sandy earth—woods, birch, aspen pine and poplar."

His Journal continues to say : "April 25th.—Sandy earth, i banks ; they are high near the Athabasca. Enter Athabasca Rive 250 to 350 yards wide ; banks, including inner bank, 80 to 120 fee high. White sandy earth, woods mostly pine ; there is also birch aspen and poplar.

26th. "Always fine weather." Ascends Little Slave River.

27th. "No portaging yet ;" is on west branch of Little Slav River, then on right branch ; high hills in sight—wet grass; meadows, Buffalo and Moose abundant, by tracks.

28th. "Cold blustry frosty morning ; came to Slave Lake ; Lak partly open and part sound ice ;" hills round lake 800 feet high.

29th. "On Main Athabasca, very deep strong current, 220 t 250 yards wide ; banks, 240 to 360 feet over river ; mild cloud; day."

1st May "Clear sharp frosty morning—banks, sinking to lov ones, or valleys, then swelling to hills 200 to 240 feet high witl small pines, mossy surface, the soil is now mostly a bluish cla; mixed with marl."

2nd. "Canoe birch trees, many of them $2\frac{1}{2}$ to 4 feet round found a poplar two fathoms round."

Here we have evidence of a country of varied character, bu presenting in its sandy earth, blue clay, and a hundred and fift; miles of generally rich black mould, a great deal of fair arable land much of it of the best quality imaginable ; and with a spring quit; as early as Lower Canada generally.

But it is important to notice that it presents something, of mucl value, that we have not in Canada. Dr. Hector mentions tha where he crossed the River Pembina " a bed of coal is exposed in ts banks eight feet thick, and at one point has previously been on ire." As the Pembina is a large stream from 90 to 110 yards wide, with a moderately strong current, it may afford the means of transport ; and as there is much good land in the vicinity, as we have seen, this coal, which extends to the main Athabasca, may be useful uel for future settlements, even before the wood, which is not of he best quality, becomes exhausted. The country on the upper waters of the Athabasca, like that around Edmonton on the Saskatchewan, adjoining, is no doubt too elevated to be favorable for he growth of wheat. This is greatly balanced by the extreme fer-ility of much of the land, and the advantages it offers for cattle eeding. The objection of over elevation does not lie against the emainder of the Athabasca country.

Mr. McLean, a gentleman who had resided twenty-five years n the North-west Territory, speaks of the banks of the Athabasca and Slave River as presenting many localities fit for farming, and Ross Cox says of the Athabasca: "It is here a noble river, flowing through a rich pasture country, thinly wooded." A little further on he adds, "For the last one hundred and twenty miles its navigation was uninterrupted by rapids, with a smooth steady current, and the soil on each bank was of the richest description."

Speaking of the valley of Clear Water River, one of its tributaries, towards the eastern side of the section of territory we have under consideration, looking on it from an eminence, Sir Alexander McKenzie says:

"From thence the eye looks down on the course of the little river, by some called the Swan River, and by others the Clear Water and Pelican River, beautifully meandering for thirty miles. The valley, which is at once refreshed and adorned by it, is about three miles in breadth, and is confined by two lofty ridges of equal height, displaying a most delightful intermixture of wood and lawn, and stretching on till the blue mists obscure the prospect ; some parts of the inclining heights are clothed with stately forests, relieved by promontories of the finest verdure, where the elk and buffalo find pasture."

Sir John Richardson describes the scenery as unequalled, the soil as sandy, but on a limestone basis, which is favorable to its warmth as well as to its fertility.

CHAPTER XIX.

THE PEACE RIVER.

The Peace River is the largest branch of the River McKenzie.. Its head waters lie beyond the Rocky Mountains, where its north and south branches drain the great valley to the westward, between. the Rocky Mountains and the Peak Range. Its south branch is about two hundred miles long, and its north branch, the Findlay River, is nearly three hundred.

The Findlay, or Main Peace River, is represented as having its remotest source in a lake beyond the Peak Range, about lat. 56° 30′ N., long. 126° W., about two hundred miles from the Pacific.

A little eastward from the junction of its branches, the Peace River traverses the Rocky Mountains, and enters the section of territory under consideration, through a gap, which forms one of the passes leading to the coast of the Pacific—it was through it that Sir Alex. McKenzie first penetrated to that ocean.

From the Forks the course of the Peace River is nearly due east for two hundred and forty miles, to Fort Dunvegan; passing Rocky Mountain House nearly at half way. From Dunvegan its course is northward for a hundred and forty miles, then nearly east north-east for about three hundred and thirty-five miles, to its mouth. Fort Vermilion is about two hundred and fifty-five miles from its mouth, and the Falls, of about twenty feet in height, are about forty-five miles below it.

The whole length of Peace River, rejecting lesser sinuosities inappreciable on a good map, is about a thousand and fifteen miles; which, when added to the remaining course of the McKenzie, makes the length of that river two thousand four hundred and seventy miles.

The delta of the mouth of Peace River, and the country between it and the mouth of the Athabasca, is a low alluvial flat, formed by the sediment brought down by the high floods, which at some seasons entirely overflow it. McKenzie says further, "The country in general is low from the entrance of the river to the Falls, and with the exception of a few open parts covered with grass, it is clothed with wood. Where the banks are very low, the soil is good, being composed of the sediment of the river and putrefied leaves and vegetables." Where they are more elevated. they display a face of yellowish clay, mixed with small stones. On a line with the Falls, and on either side of the river, there are said to be very extensive plains which afford pasture to numerous herds of buffaloes."

He says, "The banks of the river from the Falls are in general lofty, except at low woody points, accidentally formed in the manner I have mentioned; they also displayed in all their broken parts a face of clay, intermixed with stones; in some places there likewise appeared a black mould." Speaking of cultivation, he says, "There is not the least doubt but the soil would be very productive, if proper attention was given to its preparation."

At low water the Peace River does not exceed a quarter of a mile in breadth below the falls; at the falls it is four hundred yards. Its width up to the Rocky Mountains continues much the same, sometimes attaining eight hundred yards. It has much less descent than the Saskatchewan. From Dunvegan to its mouth, about four hundred and seventy-five miles apparently, but which Capt. Lefroy, probably quoting the reputed distances, calls six hundred and fifty miles, there occur, he says, but the falls mentioned and a few rapids; the bed of the stream preserves a nearly uniform inclination, rising only three hundred and ten feet.

He says the stream is more rapid above Fort Vermilion than below it, and that the depth of the bed of the river, below the surrounding country, increases with great uniformity upwards. About sixty miles above Fort Vermilion, where it has cut through alternating sandstone and limestone cliffs to a bed of shale, it flows at a depth of two hundred feet below their summits.

He adds: "The general elevation of the country, however, still continues to increase, and at Dunvegan it is six hundred feet above the bed of the stream; yet even at this point, except in approaching the deep gorges, through which the tributaries of Peace River join its waters, there is little indication of an elevated country; the Rocky Mountains are not visible, and no range of hills meets the eye."

Captain Lefroy gives 1,600 feet as the elevation of the country about Dunvegan above the sea; and the region in which the river has its sources is probably four times as high, according to Sir J. Richardson.

In latitude and longtitude corresponding with Dunvegan, however, McKenzie speaks of the Deer Mountains being seen, at a distance to the westward, as "an immense ridge of highland or mountains which take an oblique direction from below the falls." He adds, under date December, 1792: "Opposite our present situation are beautiful meadows, with various animals grazing on them, and groves of poplar irregularly scattered over them."

Describing the country immediately above that, on resuming his journey the following spring, on the 10th of May he says:— "From the place which we quitted this morning, the west side of the river displayed a succession of the most beautiful scenery I had ever beheld. The ground rises at intervals to a considerable height, and stretches inwards to a considerable distance; at every interval or pause in the rise there is a gently ascending space or lawn, which is alternate with abrupt precipices to the summit of the whole, or at least as far as the eye could distinguish. This magnificent theatre of nature has all the decorations which the trees and animals of the country can afford it; groves of poplars in every shape enliven the scene; and their intervals are enlivened with vast herds of elks and buffaloes; the former choosing the steep uplands, and the latter preferring the plains. At this time the buffaloes were attended with their young ones, and it appeared that the elks would soon exhibit the same enlivening circumstance. The whole country exhibited an exuberant verdure; the trees that bear a blossom were advancing fast to that delightful appearance." He adds, "the east side of the river consists of a range of highland covered with spruce and soft birch, while the banks abound with the alder and willow."

As it was on the 10th of May that McKenzie found things in this condition, it is evident, not only that it is a fine country, but also that the spring is earlier than in the most favorable parts of Lower Canada.

We might suppose that this was an unusually early spring, were it not that the meteorological observations of Mr. David Thompson, at the same place, give quite as favorable indications as to the climate. Only twice in the month of May, 1803, on the 2nd and 14th, did the thermometer at 5 o'clock A.M. fall to 30°, and only twice was it as low as 36° at that hour, and that never after the 14th of that month. Frost did not occur in the fall till the 27th September. It freezes much later in May in Canada; and at Montreal, for seven years out of the last nine, the first frost occurred between 24th August and 16th September.

Elevated as Dunvegan on Peace River is, nine hundred and ten feet above the sea by Lefroy, seven hundred and seventy-eight by Richardson, and under the high latitude of 56° 6′ N., it may be interesting to compare the mean temperature of the seven months from April to October, inclusively, of the year 1803, with the mean temperature of Halifax, Nova Scotia, lat. 44° 30′ N., as given in the table of temperatures a few pages forward.

It shows the monthly mean temperature at Dunvegan to be fully a degree, and that of the three summer months to be about two degrees, warmer than at Halifax.

The three coldest months in winter are, on the other hand, intensely cold compared with Halifax—an admirable arrangement for utility. The milder winter of Halifax would be comparatively valueless at Dunvegan, but it is of the utmost importance at Halifax, which owes its open winter navigation to it.

Nothing conclusive can be based on one year's observations; but combined with other indications of climate, they afford favorable evidence.

From what McKenzie says of the country about a hundred miles above Dunvegan, it would seem very favorable for cattle-feeding, and for the raising of at least the coarser grains. " Some parts," he says, " offer beautiful scenery in some degree similar to that which we passed on the second day of our voyage, and equally enlivened with elk and buffalo, which were feeding in great numbers."

A little further, twelve miles above Sinew River, he says : " The land above where we camped spreads into an extensive plain, and stretches on to a very high ridge, which in some parts presents a face of rock, but is principally covered with verdure, and varied with the poplar and white birch tree. The country is so crowded with animals as to have the appearance in some places of a stall-yard, from the state of the ground and the quantity of dung that is scattered over it. The soil is black and light."

Two days' journey, by the river, above this, where the country is wooded heavily, McKenzie speaks, in crossing a portage, of the forest being of spruce and birch, and the largest poplars he had ever seen. Further on he speaks of travelling through heavy woods of spruce, red pine, cypress, poplar, white birch and willow, and of travelling through tall pine woods. Soil light, and of a dusty colour over gravelly clay. The river still from 400 to 800 yards wide, diminishing to 200 where confined. It is here passing through the Rocky Mountains, which do not rise apparently more than 1,500 feet above their base—bare of wood in the upper parts, wooded at the base. The bed of the river is limestone, and the mountains solid masses of the same.

On the 27th of May the trees towards the bases of the mountains were, he says, putting forth their leaves. It is worthy of remark, as indicating earliness of spring in these mountain valleys, notwithstanding their great elevation and consequent coldness, that the putting forth of the leaves here spoken of is a day or two earlier than it was with us in the neighbourhood of Ottawa this season, (1867). Towards the Forks of the Findlay and South Branch he speaks of the mountains being covered with wood.

These wooded slopes and valleys of the mountains may be noticed as presenting a supply of timber which may, in future times, be valuable for the use of the prairie regions below.

Speaking of the Peace River country, Sir John Richardson says, " The oaks, the elms, the ashes, the Weymouth pine and the pitch pine, which reach the Saskatchewan basin, are wanting here ; the balsam fir is rare ; but as these trees form no prominent feature of the landscape in the former quarter, no marked change in the woodland scenery takes place, in any part of the McKenzie

River district, until we approach the shores of the Arctic Sea." The white spruce continues to be the predominent tree in dry soils, whether rich or poor; the Banksean pine occupies a few sandy spots; the black spruce skirts the marshes; and the balsam, poplar and aspen, fringe the streams. The white birch attains a good size, even up to latitude 65° in sheltered positions, that is, nearly to six hundred and fifty miles north of Dunvegan.

CHAPTER XX.

SLAVE RIVER.

Slave River, which carries the united waters of the Athabasca and the Peace River, and of Lake Athabasca, from that Lake to Slave Lake, is about two hundred miles in length. It is, properly speaking, a portion of the main River McKenzie. It lies beyond the section of territory we have under consideration, and north-eastward from it. McKenzie describes the country on its west bank as having a soil of rich black mould, covered with a growth of heavy wood towards the river, with extensive plains, immediately behind, frequented by numerous herds of buffalo.

Though stated by Mr. McLean as suitable for farming purposes, the country on Slave River is not included within the limits roughly assumed for the section under consideration, on account of the apparent severity of the climate. Before reaching Slave Lake on the 9th of June, McKenzie found the ground was not thawed beyond the depth of fourteen inches; yet, the leaves of the trees had attained their full growth, which is but little if anything later than in Lower Canada.

THE HAY RIVER.

Hay River, a tributary of Slave Lake, is nearly four hundred miles in length. Three-quarters of its course lie within the section before us, of which it unwaters the north-eastern corner.

It has two branches; the west one rises in Hay Lake; the other rises not far from the banks of Peace River, and flows at no great distance from Fort Vermilion. The country on this branch is described by Sir J. Richardson as an agreeable mixture of prairie and woodland, and frequented by vast bands of buffaloes.

This he says is the limit of those vast prairies which extend from New Mexico. Below the forks of Hay River the country on it is covered with forests, and intersected with swamps.

THE RIVER OF THE MOUNTAINS.

This large tributary of the McKenzie is formed of two great branches beyond the Rocky Mountains, which it traverses about seventy miles below their junction, or nearly four hundred miles from the source of either. It flows for about a hundred and seventy miles through this section, first due east and then due north, to latitude 60° N., and at a hundred and ninety miles further, on the same course, enters the McKenzie, at Fort Simpson, after a course of about seven hundred and fifty miles. It is half a mile wide at its mouth.

Its lower course is through a country of limestone formation; the mountains are composed of it and it appears in the rapids of the river.

Fort Liard is situated on it near latitude 60° N.; below the sharp turn it takes to the north. Speaking of it, Richardson says: "Though this post is more elevated than Fort Simpson, by at least a hundred and fifty feet, and is only two degrees of latitude to the southward, its climate is said to be very superior, and its vegetable productions of better growth and quality. Barley and oats yield good crops, and in favorable seasons wheat ripens well." This place, then he adds, "on the 60th parallel may be considered as the northern limit of the economical culture of wheat." A little further he says, "Mr. McPherson had most kindly set aside for me a cask of excellent corned beef, cured at the fort, and some bags of very fine potatoes raised at Fort Liard, with several other things."

The great elbow of this river, with its eastern branch, which has a course of about a hundred and seventy miles, together with Smith's branch which enters above it, on the north-west side, drain the north-west angle of the section under consideration.

As the outlines of this section were assumed to include, in a general way, the extent of country fit for agricultural occupation, the parallel of latitude 60° was adopted as its northern boundary, from its being apparently the northern limit of the profitable cultivation of wheat.

Such being the climate at that latitude on the River of the Mountains, it may reasonably be assumed to be fully as favorable in the country extending two hundred miles further south, on its eastern branch and on Hay River.

CHAPTER XXI.

CLIMATE AND FITNESS FOR AGRICULTURAL OCCUPATIONS.

We have already noticed, in some degree, the climate of the northern and less favorably situated parts of this great central section, containing more or less prairie land.

We have noted the indications of it at Mr. Pond's settlement, near Lake Athabasca, towards its north-eastern angle, McKenzie's description of the earliness of the spring at Dunvegan, and above it towards the Rocky Mountains, on Peace River, with Mr. David Thompson's highly favorable thermometrical record of that region, though so elevated, and lastly what Richardson has recorded as to the climate and cultivation at Fort Liard, in the north-west corner of this section. We have next to consider the climate of the middle and southern, or more favorable parts of it.

As bearing on the climate of this section, and the other north-west territories, it may be well to repeat a few general observations.

The warm current of the Pacific Ocean, flowing up along the western coast of North America, gives it a comparatively warm and temperate climate, as the Gulf Stream does to the north-western coasts of the old world, accompanied with humidity, in both cases, giving much rain. The temperature of the east coast is, on the contrary, much reduced by the cold current from the Arctic Sea, with its icebergs flowing southward along it.

Thus, Sitka on the Pacific coast, in lat. 57° 03′ N., has an annual mean temperature (45° by Bäer) fully higher than that of Halifax, N. S., in lat. 44° 39′, (which is about 43°). Nor is the difference from this cause confined to the immediate seaboard; Montreal, two hundred miles from the Atlantic, lat. 45° 31′ N., has a mean annual temperature of about 43°, while Fort Dallas in Oregon, lat. 45° 36′ N., two hundred miles from the Pacific, has an annual mean of about 52°.

Hudson's Bay being an expansion of the same cold ice-bearing Arctic waters, has the same cooling effect, not only on the regions adjoining, but also in some degree on the country lying more remotely between it and the River St. Lawrence and its Lakes. Accordingly, it is not till we pass westward of the parallel to which Hudson's Bay extends—and that is half-way between the Straits of Belle Isle and the Pacific—that we find any great change in the direction of the lines of equal mean annual temperature.

Yet, though the mean annual temperature remains nearly the same in going due westward so far, the climate for agricultural purposes improves very much after leaving the sea coast. Thus, Montreal has a mean temperature for three summer months of 68°, while that of Halifax is only 61°, and Green Bay, Lake Michigan, in the same latitude as Halifax, has a summer mean of 69°, though its annual mean is only 44°.*

* It is proper to observe that authorities differ materially as to temperatures, from various causes; partly through actual variety in the years observed, and partly, probably, owing to errors in instruments and oversight as to the position of them.

West of Lake Superior, about long. 94°W., the lines of equal mean
nnual temperature curve to a north-west direction, and maintain it
iagonally, through this section, till deflected again to the south-
vard at the high grounds at the base of the Rocky Mountains,
vhere the rapidly increasing elevation reduces the temperature.

The result of this rapid increase of heat westward towards the
'acific, except where interrupted by the elevation and consequent
old temperature of the Rocky Mountain ranges, is, as would appear
rom the observations of Mr. David Thompson, that Dunvegan, on
'eace River, lat. 56° 17′ N., has a mean annual temperature of 35°
i1′, equal to that of Fort William on Lake Superior, lat. 48° 23′ N.,
vith a mean temperature for four summer months, May to August,
nclusive, of 62° 9′, while that of Fort William for the same months
s only 57° 13′, or 59° 9′ for the warmest three of them ; yet Dunve-
;an is about five hundred and forty miles further north than Fort
Villiam.

Even Fort Simpson, in lat. 61° 41′ N., on the river of the Moun-
ains, about a hundred and fifteen miles north of the assumed out-
ine of the section now before us, has a mean summer temperature
or three months, of 59° 48′, and for five months, from May to Sep-
ember, inclusive, a mean of 55° 15′, nearly the same as that of
?ort William, which for the same months is 55° 32′.   Fort Simpson
s about nine hundred and fifty miles further north than Fort
Villiam.

The following table will afford the means of further compari-
ons :

TABLE OF MEAN TEMPERATURES IN THE NORTH-WEST TERRITORY AND CANADIAN PROVINCES COMPARED.

Months.	Fort William, Lake Superior. Altitude 660 feet above the sea. Lat. 48 23½' N. Long. 89 22' W.	Cumberland House. Altitude 900 feet above the sea. Lat. 53 57' N. Long. 102 13' W.	St. John's, N.B. Altitude 30 feet above the sea. Lat. 45 15' N.	Halifax, Nova Scotia. Altitude 15 feet above the sea. Lat. 44 39' N. Long. 63 35' W.	Dunvegan, on Peace River. Altitude 1000 feet above the sea. Lat. 56 8' N. Long. 117 13' W.	†Quebec. Altitude 250 feet above the sea. Lat. 46 49' N.	Fort Garry, Red River. Altitude 680 feet above the sea. Lat. 49 53' N.	Toronto. Altitude 340 feet above the sea. Lat. 43 40' N. Long. 79 22' W.
	a	b	c	d	e	f	g	l
April	31.42	25	37.5	38	37.6	37.9	39°.83	41°.2
May	48.87	50	47.3	48	64	51.6	58°.46	51°.5
June	55.73	59	54.5	56.3	64.5	63.1	69°.10	61°
July	62.19	70	59.7	62.3	63	67.5	71°.16	66°.3
August	58.84	60	60	63.7	60	65.9	63°.3	65°.7
September	48.16	48	55	57	55	57.6	59°.26	57°.4
October	41.88	39	45.7	47	40	44.6	42°.20	45°.8
Mean	50.01	50.14	51.38	53.18	54.87	55.45	57°.58	55°.44
Do. of three Summer months	59.92	63	58.06	60.76	62.50	65.50	67°.76	64°.33
November	23.43	11	37.5	39.3	14.6	34°.1	21°.19	36°.1
December	18.16	5	25.5	25.7	-4	17°.7	-8°.31	27°
January	5.70	5	18.6	25.0	*7	11°.7	-10°.55	24°.8
February	8.22	2	21.6	24.3	2	14°.8	-18°.71	23°.7
March	22.72	6	28	29.0	22°.5	25°.1	+*9.09	30°.2
Mean	15.64	5.80	26.24	28.66	8.42	20°.68	+1°.94	28°.36
Do. of the year	35.69	31.66	40.90	42.69	35.51	40°.99	34°.29	42°.16

*More correctly about 600 feet.
† Citadel Cape Diamond.

a Sir John Richardson.
b David Thompson, 1789-90.
e   "   "   1803.
c Tables by Mr. J. Murdock, of St. John's.
d From a paper read by Col. Byers at the Nova Scotia Institute of Science.
fh Lieutenant Ashe.
g Professor Hind.

It must be observed that Capt. Blackiston gives the mean ummer temperature at Fort Garry at nearly four degrees less than Mr. Hind, who admits that necessary corrections had not been pplied to the above observations used by him, but says that he hinks the winter observations too low through probable error in hè particular instrument used by the observer who made them; ut as Capt. Blackiston made use in part of observations by the ame person, the inferiority of the instrument might possibly slightly ffect Capt. Blackiston's conclusions. Lorin Blodget, in his climatlogy, gives Fort Garry a mean summer temperature of 65°, which orresponds with that assigned to it by Governor Stevens in his re-ort of Pacific Railway Surveys. Blackiston and Hind, however, gree in the mean annual temperature.

Climatologists, according to the European practice, divide the ear into four seasons of three months each, in their tables. Such ivision is unsuitable in our northern countries for the consideraion of the climate with a view to the practical purposes of agricul-ure. As it is more natural, owing to the suddenness of the transiions from one to the other in Canada, to consider the year under wo great divisions—the frozen and the warm seasons—the mean f seven months for the latter and five for the former are shown in he foregoing table.

Admitting an error of four degrees in Professor Hind's summer emperature, which the corrections would chiefly affect, and deduct-ng one-half of it, as its mean, from the temperature of the seven warm months at Fort Garry, the mean of them would be 55°58, or lly half a degree warmer than the mean of the corresponding even months at Toronto.

As the result of careful observations by Capt. Palliser's assis-ants, Capt. Blackiston assigns the same temperature as that of 'ort Garry to Fort Carleton, on the North Branch of the Saskat-hewan, above the forks. This agrees with the isotherm of mean ummer of 65°, as represented by Governor Stevens. He carries ; from Green Bay, in Wisconsin, to the Little Falls, between St. 'aul's and Fort Ripley, in Minnesota, by Fort Garry, and crossing ake Manitobah, by Fort Pelly, on the Assiniboine, to the Forks of ie Saskatchewan, and thence north-westward to the sources of the ;eaver River. He gives the middle course of the North Saskat-hewan and of the Athabasca, the mean winter temperature of 'ort Ripley, or 10°. Capt. Palliser, who explored the Saskatchewan ɔuntry personally, says its climate is somewhat similar to that of :ed River, but decidedly milder in the southern and western parts.

There is besides conclusive evidence of such a difference. Pro-ssor Hind observed the temperature of the waters of the North nd South Branches of the Saskatchewan, just above their junction, on the 5th of August, and found the latter five degrees warmer than the former. As large rivers change temperature very slowly, this may be taken as the mean result of having flowed for ten or twelve days through a warmer climate than that of the northern branch. But the difference would necessarily be diminished as the rivers approached their junction in a common climate, and consequently must have been originally much greater. The southwestern parts may, therefore, be taken to be 5° to 7° warmer in summer than the country traversed by the North Branch, or that around Fort Garry. This corresponds with what is reported by the Blackfeet Indians.

Professor Hind found a considerable difference in favor of the lower part of the South Branch as to the ripening of wild fruit. A hundred and fifty miles further west, at Chesterfield House, though the elevation there is about two thousand feet above the sea, the mean annual temperature is stated as 39°, or nearly 5° warmer than that of Fort Garry.

DEPTH OF SNOW.

In considering the climate it is proper to notice that the snow does not fall so deep in this section of territory as it does in Canada, which is of considerable importance, as regards the feeding of cattle in winter and facility of travelling, and will be still more so in the use of railways, for which this country is, in other respects, so unusually well adapted.

The ordinary greatest depth of snow in the Red River settlement is about eighteen inches, and people ride freely everywhere through it all winter. Eastward towards the thick wooded country the depth increases, but it decreases in the plains to the westward, though where there are wooded tracts it accumulates to a greater depth.

It is an ordinary well-known fact that dealers in stock, residing in the Red River settlement, who purchase horses from the prairie Indians, for the purpose of selling them in the American markets, winter them at large, in droves of a hundred and upwards, in charge of herdsmen, in the prairies where there are clumps of wood, from ten to forty miles west of Fort Garry. The horses find abundant food there, under the shallow snow, to keep themselves in good condition. Their other cattle the settlers feed at home on hay, which is very abundant.

This present winter of 1867, from the date of its commencement and the suddenness of transition from mild weather to hard frost, resembles a Red River winter.

At the Touchwood Hills, west of the Upper Assiniboine, Professor Hind says that the snow falls two and a half feet deep in the woods, and not unfrequently eighteen inches in the plains where aspen groves are numerous. He says, so rich and abundant is the vegetation here that horses remain in the open glades all winter, and always find plenty of forage to keep themselves in good condition.

Speaking of the country from two hundred and fifty to four hundred and fifty miles westward, Dr. Hector says, the winter of 1858-9 had been unusually severe, as far as the quantity of snow is concerned, and yet the average depth of snow, when undisturbed, as in the woods, was only about eight to twelve inches, throughout a large district between Battle River and North Saskatchewan at Edmonton. Towards the Mountains, in a south-west direction, the quantity is still less ; but during the early part of April, after the snow had nearly disappeared from Edmonton, a series of storms from the North visited the neighborhood of Fort Pitt, so that in the middle of April there were from three to four feet of snow on the ground.

The great quantity of snow at that time, and at that particular point, was no doubt as unusual as the severity of the season. Speaking of the whole region to the Rocky Mountains, and of what he calls the immense extent of winter pasturage that it affords, as being a most valuable feature, he states, as before quoted, that " it is only towards spring, in very severe winters, that cattle and horses cannot be left to feed in well chosen localities throughout this region of country."

From these facts as to climate, it evidently appears that we have, in a very great part of this central prairie country, an open or summer season of seven months, the mean temperature of which is fully as warm as that of Toronto for the same period, with a winter season of five very cold months, but clear and dry—as cold as the northern parts of Minnesota—a winter fully colder than that of Quebec, but without its obstructively deep snow, or the drawback it presents in the difficulty of feeding cattle through it.

Now, in a cold country like ours (where the frost of winter interrupts agricultural labor at any rate), if the seven open summer months be warm enough, it matters little to the profit of agriculture whether the cold of winter be a few degrees more or less, provided it does not increase the cost and difficulty of feeding cattle. But we see that in a great part of this section, that condition at least is highly favorable, and even in the remainder, owing to the great abundance of natural hay ground not requiring the labor of clearing usual with us, it is more favorable than in Canada generally, but especially so to the poor settler, who has, with us, to clear off heavy woods, at much cost or labor, before he can raise hay for his cattle.

It is true that with increasing settlement and density of population, these most valuable winter pastures may cease to be used as such, but that will be only when they have become still more valuable for cultivation, and that condition cannot arise without the settlement of the country being accomplished, which above all things is the object desired. But even then it does not appear that the advantage of winter feeding, which the very shallow snow admits of, need be lost in the country towards the mountains, for there the cattle could feed on clover and turnips on the ground, as they now do on the natural herbage; or the wild vetch, to which it owes its richness, might even be improved by careful cultivation.

While considering the climate of this section of territory, we have to bear in mind that it is not on climate alone that the fitness of a country for the profitable prosecution of agriculture depends. Within certain limits, quality of soil and character of surface have even more to do with it. Abundant crops of coarse grains and hay are more profitable than scanty crops of wheat. But in the rich lands of this central prairie country, the farmer can get wheat crops far heavier than in these provinces.

It is no exaggeration to say that there are vast tracts there, now vacant, where he could have wheat crops more than double the average returns of Lower Canada, and keep a far larger stock of cattle, with far less labor.

The character of the surface is also to be taken into account. When we consider how much the use of machinery is in future to reduce the labor and increase the profit of agriculture, and the favorable nature of the soil and surface of this prairie country for its application, together with its great facility of internal communication, without the heavy expense of opening roads that we have in Canada, and its inexhaustible supply of coal on navigable rivers, with its valuable metals and other minerals, we have every reason to believe that settlement, and the profitable prosecution of agriculture, will be carried northward, to an extent it would never attain in a rugged and less favorable country.

CULTIVATED CROPS AND GREAT RETURNS OF WHEAT.

Little can be said of cultivated crops in the section of territory we have designated as the Central Prairie Country, except in the Red River settlement.

As already stated, Sir John Richardson has given the line of latitude 60° N., (the assumed northern boundary of this section,) as the limit of the economic culture of wheat, and says that at Fort Liard, on the River of the Mountains in that latitude, barley and oats yield good crops, and potatoes are of an excellent quality, and in favorable seasons wheat ripens well, and gives good returns, but that it does not ripen perfectly every year, owing to summer frosts. This is ten degrees, or nearly seven hundred miles, further north than the Red River Settlement; failures of wheat crops from frost might be expected there, as we have them in some of the settlements of Canada.

Sir John says further, that wheat grows freely on the banks of the Saskatchewan, excepting near Hudson's Bay, that is, beyond the limits of this section of territory; and David Thomson, many years ago, the Astronomer of the Hudson's Bay Company, states in his manuscript journal that " wheat comes to perfection" even as far north-eastward as Cumberland House; but from its position so far to the eastward, and the prevalence of marshy ground near it, the climate is much less favorable than further up the Saskatchewan.

As might be expected from the richness of the soil, where settlement has taken place in this territory, on the Red River and the Assiniboine, the cultivation of wheat has been very successful, and the returns very great.

Sir John Richardson, Capt. Blackiston, and our Canadian explorers, and others, inform us that wheat, in these settlements, is sown early in May and reaped in the end of August, and the returns vary from thirty to forty fold, or bushels to the acre, as it is indifferently expressed. They inform us, that in some parts thirty bushels to the acre is an average crop of wheat, and that in others " forty bushels is not only common, but generally expected;" and Professor Hind mentions a settler who had obtained fifty-six bushels of wheat to the acre, simply by judicious ploughing.

If the average were thirty-two and a half, it would be double that of Upper Canada by the census of 1851, and Upper Canada is one of the best wheat-growing countries in the world. Even if a large deduction were made from them for error and exaggeration, as is generally necessary in such cases, the Red River returns would still far exceed those of Upper Canada.

But this superiority is not without apparent causes in the richest of soils and the best of summers for the growth of wheat, which affect, also, the quality of it. The acknowledged superiority in quality of the wheat of Minnesota, adjoining, is attributed to the powerful midsummer heat common to this region.

It has been already mentioned that the climate at Carleton House, on the North Branch of the Saskatchewan, though three degrees further north, is stated by the officers of the Imperial exploring party, from careful thermometrical observation, to be at least equal to that of the Red River Settlement, and they and others agree in stating that the warmth of climate of the valley of the Saskatchewan, southward and westward from Carleton House, is still greater, till neutralized by elevation in approaching the Mountains.

It is proper to observe, that in the colder parts of this Central Prairie Country, where from elevation or extreme northerly position failures of crop from frost may occur, the deficiency may be more than balanced by the extraordinary returns, in all other years, which the richness of the soil may yield.

To return to the Red River Settlement, the richness of the soil is equalled by its durability, crops of wheat for upwards of twenty years being obtained, from the same ground, nearly equal to the first.

Indian corn is sometimes prevented from ripening on rich but *moist* prairie lands, which is attributed by Mr. Lane, of the Hudson's Bay Company, to careless cultivation. On dry grounds it is said to be a sure crop.

Professor Hind and others speak of melons growing luxuriantly and ripening in the open air, in great perfection, and also of the abundance, size and good quality of the potatoes as remarkable ; that beets, turnips, and all other root crops grow well and attain large dimensions ; and that all common garden vegetables cultivated in Canada are equalled, if not surpassed, by those raised in the settlements of the Red River and the Assiniboine.

When we take into consideration the extreme richness of the soil and warmth of the summer, it will be apparent that it could not well be otherwise as to these productions.

The beet may prove a very important one for the manufacture of sugar, which should be more profitable than the importation of it, so far inland, where the transport in, of it, and out of the produce in payment for it, will be expensive.

The cultivation of hemp and flax, which grow of an excellent quality, may be of considerable importance, especially the latter, for domestic use, as well as for exportation, on the introduction of machinery for the preparation of it, and the opening of any even moderately advantageous outlet for such products. Woollen, linen, leather, and other light goods, would be the most advantageous to export from a country situated so far inland.

CHAPTER XXII.

COAL, PETROLEUM, AND BUILDING MATERIALS.

In describing the great Central Prairie Country, or region generally suitable for cultivation, in which prairie land is more or less prevalent, it has been noticed that wood lands more generally prevail in the north half of it, while in the south half of it, on the waters of the Saskatchewan and the Red River and their tributaries, the extent of prairie lands is very much greater than that of wood lands. The eastern parts of the latter, on the lakes Winnipeg, Manitobah and Winnipegoos, and on the Saskatchewan below its forks, and the broad parallel belt of highlands lying to the west of the two last named lakes, known as the Riding Mountains Duck Mountain, Porcupine Hills, and Thunder Mountain, are described as densely and heavily wooded on the highlands while the valleys present about an equal extent of prairie and wood lands; and it is said that the forests of this region are sufficient to supply the inhabitants who may occupy it and the adjoining country, with wood for all purposes, for generations to come.

Towards the Rocky Mountains also, and on the skirts of them on the head waters of the Saskatchewan, there is a broad belt of wooded country, where there is pine and other useful timber of a good growth, from which supplies of building timber may be brought down by the rivers, for the use of the prairie regions, on their lower courses, when the supply from the limited growth of wood there has become exhausted.

When the same necessity arises, the prairie lands on the Assiniboine may be supplied by its eastern tributaries, from the forests of the highlands mentioned, and the prairies of the Red River from the wood lands on its upper course, and when these fail from the wooded country on the eastern tributaries of Lake Winnipeg.

The River Winnipeg, which unwaters a wooded region probably little inferior to the valley of the Ottawa in area, has timber enough of a useful description to form the staple of an extensive lumber trade, for the supply of the prairie country to the westward.

The timber from it will be much smaller, and inferior in kind as well as quality to that from the Ottawa. Considerable quantities of red and white pine are said by our explorers to be found on some of its waters, though of an inferior size.

The greater size of wood, though much in its favor in foreign markets, is really of little importance for home use; and poplar and spruce yield very useful lumber, and are much to be valued in the absence of pine timber.

In the eastern or nearer part of the prairie region lying on the Assiniboine and its tributaries, and on the head waters of lesser western tributaries of Lake Winnipeg, there seems to be a fair proportion of woods, and advancing northward they predominate. Speaking of this region, Mr. Dawson says: " The streams that flow through the prairie are bordered more or less with forests in which oak and elm of a fair size are to be met with, although not in great quantities; in the wooded section, of which, however, less is known, poplar predominates; but on the borders of the lakes and streams, larch, spruce, birch and oak are to be found of a size and quality available for economic purposes." Mr. Dawson is unquestionably a good judge of the subject, from his extensive previous experience in the lumber trade.

Professor Hind speaks of forests in the valley of the Assiniboine, one of which he describes as four miles in width and thirty miles in length, wooded with oak, elm, ash, maple, poplar and aspen, and speaks of the flats and hill-sides of its valley elsewhere being clothed with fine forests, which he describes as extending also from thirty to seventy miles up its western tributaries; and at intervals beyond, on the Qu'appelle, he says, good timber is found as far as the Mission.

In prairie lands, the abundant supply of timber, which entirely wooded countries afford, does not exist; and in the absence of pine, poplar and spruce have to be used for building purposes. They are both inferior to pine in value; but in a great part of Lower Canada spruce only is to be had, and much of it is exported as sawn lumber to Europe. Poplar is undervalued through prejudice in a great degree. Of all the deciduous trees it is one of the best suited to take the place of pine in flooring and finishing houses; and for building the walls of dwellings it is very durable. I have seen a house built of poplar logs, that stood upwards of a hundred years, perfectly sound to the foundation, when cut open. It may not accord with present ideas to say so, but before the pine of the Ottawa becomes exhausted our extensive forests of poplar will be valued for lumbering purposes and brought into use.

In our interior territories spruce timber, on account of its lightness, its straightness and its strength, will take the place of pine, for engineering purposes; and birch, on account of the fineness of its grain and its strength, will be serviceable for furniture and fine wood-work, especially in the northern regions, where oak and maple are not to be found.

The timber of the interior is of a smaller growth than with us, probably owing to the greater dryness of the summer and cold in winter; it is therefore probably stronger and perhaps more durable. In these respects woods of the same kind differ much with the soil and climate. The oak of the Ottawa averages only half the size of that of the western parts of Upper Canada, but is far superior to it in strength; and the timber that grows in parts of Canada near the sea is more durable than timber, of the same kind, of the interior. In bridge building I have found it to last nearly twice as long. We have no data on which to determine the comparative durability and integral strength of the timber of our interior territory for engineering purposes.

Great size gives squared timber an increased value in European markets, but the small dimension into which our large Ottawa timber is invariably cut, in preparing sawn lumber for home use and exportation, shows that great size is of no importance generally for home use, excepting for the greater quantity it gives.

White spruce is harder to saw and work up than pine, and with us it is less durable when exposed, but it is stronger, and its length and straightness make it very suitable for building timbers.

According to Sir John Richardson, oak, ash, white pine and pitch pine, are not to be found north of the valley of the Saskatchewan, and are not prominent there, and white spruce continues to be the predominant tree alike on rich and poor soil. Though of a small growth near the Arctic Sea, it was found in some instances, in sheltered positions, to attain the size of from three to five feet in girth, even there. Balsam, poplar and aspen, skirt the streams, and white birch is found chiefly, though not exclusively, in rocky districts. It attains a fair size as far north as latitude 65° N.

From the foregoing, and the descriptions in detail given of the different parts of the south half of the central prairie country, it will be seen, that for prairie land, the supply of wood, distributed through it, such as it is, seems sufficient for the supply of settlements in it for a long time to come, if carefully used. As for the north half of it, lying beyond the Saskatchewan and the line of the strong woods, the abundance of the supply of timber in it is not questioned.

But in view of the time when the forests and scattered woods, especially of the south half of this central prairie country, may become inadequate for the supplying of fuel for an increasing population, the great deposits of lignite coal in the western and northern parts of this territory are of the greatest importance.

Nor is the supply of peat fuel that may be obtained, by improved methods of preparation, from the bogs in the eastern parts of it, in and near the Red River Settlement, unworthy of consideration. As it has already become more economical to use it than wood as fuel, in the vicinity of Montreal, it is natural to think that it might before long become advantageous to use it as fuel in prairie countries.

In his report upon the Grand Trunk Railway, Capt. Tyler, R. E., says that peat fuel can now be furnished on the cars of the company at $3 20 a ton, which is more serviceable than a cord of wood for use in locomotive engines ; that it can be more conveniently stored and used than wood, and computes that the company will save £40,000 a year by using it. It is to be borne in mind that this is in Canada, possessing the boasted advantage over prairie countries of abundance of wood; and not by a manufacturing establishment located in a city and obliged to pay the high prices current there, but by a company owning a railway traversing nearly the whole of Canada proper, enabling it to supply itself wherever it could do so with most advantage, and the cost of wood fuel to them must necessarily be not the price of it in towns and cities, but the average cost of it in the country places along the line. Apart from the shallow but extensive muskegs or marshes, the deeper bogs, near the Red River Settlement, would seem to present the vegetable matter necessary for the manufacture of this fuel.

LOCALITIES WHERE LIGNITE AND BITUMEN HAVE BEEN OBSERVED.

Proceeding northward from the United States boundary, (lat. 49° N.,) brown coal is shown by Dr. Hector's geological section at La Roche Percée, Coteau du Prairie, about long. 103° W. lat. 49° 30' N. on the Souris or Mouse River, a tributary of the Assiniboine; and in that direction a bed two feet thick was seen by a Mr. Pratt. Brown coal is also shown by Dr. Hector's section, in the Hand Hills.

On the Red Deer branch of the South Saskatchewan, which it enters a hundred and thirty miles above the Elbow, an extensive deposit of coal is noted by Dr. Hector at a hundred and seventy miles from its mouth, and also at a hundred miles further up. Capt. Blackiston says it is there in beds so close, that of twenty feet of strata exposed, twelve feet were of coal. It is also noted on the Battle River adjacent, to the northward, at two hundred and fifty miles above its mouth. The Battle River enters the North Saskatchewan a hundred and seventy miles above the forks of the latter and the South Branch.

On the North Saskatchewan Capt. Blackiston describes coal as prevailing, with little interruption, in beds two and two and a half feet thick, from a little below Edmonton, upwards, for two hundred miles.

Passing northward to the next stream, the Pembina, a fine navigable tributary of the Arthabasca, Dr. Hector found, where he crossed it, a bed of lignite coal exposed, eight feet thick. On the Arthabasca, above their junction, he says coal appears in the banks but not so much as on the Saskatchewan.

The lower course of the Arthabasca is described by Thomson in his manuscript journal of the year 1799, as abounding in bitumen, presenting strata in parts six to twelve feet thick. Sir John

Richardson speaks of deposits of sand on it a hundred feet thick, charged with slaggy mineral pitch. As already mentioned, in the description of the Arthabasca, he says that at Pierre au Calumet, and a few miles further down the river, the whole country, for many miles, is so full of bitumen, that if you dig a pit a few feet below the surface it flows readily into it; and that below Rivière Rouge there is a copious spring of mineral pitch (fluid bitumen or petroleum) that issues from a crevice in a cliff composed of sand and bitumen.

Sir Alexander McKenzie mentions that twenty-four miles below the forks of the Arthabasca there are some fountains of bitumen in a fluid state, in which a pole of twenty feet may be inserted without resistance. It was used along with gum from the spruce and fir for gumming canoes.

Such abundant deposits of petroleum, for the supply of coal oil for the use of these interior countries, and for other economic uses, are of much importance, and enhance the value of this territory.

Below the mouth of Clear Water River, Sir John Richardson notes lignite coal as appearing, in pretty thick layers, in the bank of the Arthabasca.

Proceeding to the next stream to the northward, the Peace River, Sir Alexander McKenzie found coal on it at Edge Coal Creek, and Chief Factor Stewart informed Sir John Richardson that there were beds of coal on fire on Smoky River, a Southern affluent, which joins the Peace River opposite Dunvegan, a hundred and fifty miles further south, and that there were beds of coal on Lesser Slave Lake, a northern tributary of the Upper Arthabasca. As these points are about two hundred miles west from the lower course of the Arthabasca, that, at least, may be taken as the breadth of country in which coal may be found.

Sir Alexander McKenzie mentions that there is bitumen on the shore of Great Slave Lake, near its discharge; and, as already mentioned, he found coal beds on fire on the banks of the McKenzie. Sir John Richardson says, that where the Bear Lake River joins it, there is a tertiary coal deposit of considerable extent, and that the Garry Islands, lying off the mouth of the McKenzie, contain beds of a tertiary coal that takes fire spontaneously.

From the description given by Sir John Richardson and others, there is much variety in the character, quality and condition of lignite. Some is of very recent formation or yet being formed, like that of the vast deposits of drift wood in the conical hills at the mouth of the McKenzie. In some of the beds of lignite the forms of the trunks of trees are preserved. In others, composed of glance coal, the wood-like structure is lost, and pieces taken from the beds split into small rhomboidal fragments, no longer presenting the grain or layers of wood.   Specimens of pitch coal are spoken of by Sir John Richardson as resembling Spanish liquorice, and also of slaty coal from Edmonton on the Saskatchewan, like that gathered from the shale cliffs of the Arthabasca.   This coal of Edmonton, Captain Blackiston says, is preferred to charcoal for smith's work, though it is said to require rather a strong draft, an objection that would not seem to lie against the lignites, subject to spontaneous combustion.   In some cases the lignites were found heavily charged with bitumen, while others are much silicified.

The following table, extracted from a good work on metallurgy, shows the difference in calorific value of several kinds of European lignite and of varieties of peat, compared with some descriptions of wood and Newcastle coals.

It is proper to notice that the lignite coal of the Nanaimo mines of Vancouver's Island is stated by Dr. Hector to be only ten per cent. inferior to the true coal of the carboniferous epoch.   It would seem, therefore, to be much superior to the European lignites given in this table, which, therefore, does not show the highest value of lignite.   By the rates in the table, we might safely estimate the lignites of our interior territories as equal in heating power to five-sevenths of the same weight of good Newcastle coal.

TABLE OF THE CALORIFIC VALUES OF VARIOUS KINDS OF FUEL.

NAME AND LOCALITY.	Pounds of Lead reduced by 1 lb. of Fuel.	Pounds of Water which 1 lb. of Fuel is capable of raising from 32° to 212° Faht.	Observers.
Varieties of Peat. averages.	16.52	37.40	
Peat from Troyes	8. 0	18. 1	
" Ham, Dép. de la Somme	12. 3	27. 9	
" Bassy, Dép. de la Marne	13. 0	29. 2	} Berthier.
" Konigsbrunn Wurtemberg	14. 3	32. 4	
" Framont, Dép. des Voges	15. 4	34. 9	
From Allan in Ireland, Upper	27. 7	62. 7	} Griffiths.
" " " Lower	25. 0	56. 6	
Brown Coal, Lignite. averages	20.79	47.10	
Saint Martin de Vaud (Canton de Vaud)	22. 6	51.20	
Minerme, Dép. de l'Aude	22. 8	51.60	
Faveau	21. 0	47.60	} Berthier.
Koep Fuarch, Lake of Zurich	20. 7	46.90	
Val, Dép. de la Sarthe	19.25	43.60	
Common German	18.40	41.70	
Sinter Coals. averages	30.48	68.88	
Newcastle { Newcastle Hartley	31.86	72.00	
Coals { Carr's Hartley	30.90	69.83	} Philips.
{ Hedley's Hartley	30.36	68.61	
{ Steamboat Wallsend	28.80	65.08	
Wood. averages	13.63	30.57	
Oak Wood	12.50	28.30	Berthier.
Ash "	14.96	32.07	Winkler.
Sycamore Wood	13.10	29.70	Bertheir.
Beech "	13.70	31.00	"
Elm "	14.50	32.84	Winkler.
Poplar "	13.04	29.54	"

CHAPTER XXIII.

INDUCEMENTS OFFERED BY PRAIRIE LANDS TO SETTLERS.

The chief peculiar advantage of our Central Prarie Country as a field for settlement, lies in the combination it offers of prairie and wood lands; the full advantage of which can be appreciated only by those who have had practical experience of the great and continued labour required to clear off and cultivate a new farm in a wooded country, and the obstruction it presents to the making of the roads necessary for the formation of new settlements.

Much is said of the advantage of the superior supply of wood for fuel and fencing, afforded by wooded countries; but these are indefinitely over-estimated by many in comparing the facilities for settlement offered by prairie lands and wooded countries respectively. Such a comparison can be best approximated by reducing the matter to figures as far as possible.

For the benefit of those who are not aquainted with the labour of making a farm in the backwoods, I may go into particulars.

The first and most obvious cause of expense, in money or labour, is the necessity of clearing off the wood before the land can be even imperfectly cultivated, the average cost of which is three pounds five shillings an acre; but as the stumps still remain, an outlay of twenty-five shillings an acre may be set down as to be incurred afterwards in getting rid of them. Where the stumps are of pine or the land stony, the cost will be much greater.

In general, pine stumps, if removed at all, will cost at least five shillings a piece, and some will cost twenty-five shillings.

We have here as one item, at least four pounds ten shillings an acre, of expense, to be incurred, on account of the wood, before the land can be brought thoroughly under the plough. This is the cost to those who can pay for the labour of skilled backwoodsmen, accustomed to the use of the axe, who can do twice as much of that kind of work as the emigrants from Europe, even though accustomed to other kinds of hard labour.

To the farm labourer from Great Britain, whose time and industry, if applied to the cultivation of prairie land, would be even more valuable than that of the backwoodsman, the cost of clearing wood land, in money's worth of his labour, will be twice as much. If he be very young he may learn the use of the axe perfectly; if not, he will never learn to use it so as to be able to do as much work with it as the native backwoodsman.

As by far the greater part of the emigrants who settle in the woods have to clear their farms by their own unskilled labour, admitting even that they become gradually more proficient, the cost to them in their own labour, of clearing their farms and removing the stumps, may, on a low estimate, be set down at five pounds ten shillings an acre.

I do not here speak of the value which their labour in clearing would command. No one would give them such a price for it. I am speaking of the value of the labour unavoidably lost by them on account of the woods.

Here we have, then, to a family clearing a farm of a hundred acres in ten or fifteen years, a loss of five hundred and fifty pounds on account of the woods.

The settler expends all this, and ten or fifteen years of the best of his life, in toilsome struggles to convert his farm into such proportions of open and wooded land as the settler on the partly wooded prairie lands finds his when first he goes to it.

The latter can adopt a regular system of cultivation ten years ·oner than the other. He can put as much land under the plough, and reap the fruit of it, soon after commencing, as the former can do after ten or fifteen years of crushing toil in clearing land, which necessarily consumes much time which he would gladly devote to more extensive cultivation and raising larger crops, were the woods not an obstruction to his doing so.

Besides this relief from heavy toil and time lost in clearing, there is another advantage of prairie land that would operate strongly in the settler's favor, the full value of which can only be appreciated by a man who has made a beginning in the unbroken forest,—an advantage that would tell immediately to the personal comfort and benefit of the settler and his family—that is, the infinite abundance of the rich grass for summer and winter food of cattle, with which he would be surrounded.

The new settler on prairie land can keep as many cows, for the supply of his family with milk and butter and cheese, as it may suit his means to purchase, from the first day of his settlement; for his pasture and meadows are already in abundance before him, and in favourable places the cattle can even find the chief part of their winter food for themselves.

But it may be said all this is far from market, and no money can be made there. That is true of all remote territories, newly opened for settlement, like the United States territory of Nebraska and the remote parts of Minnesota, to which we assuredly know that settlement will flow nevertheless, and create its own outlets. We have also to remember that of the myriads of the industrious poor and unemployed it is evidently the destiny of few only to make money. The million want independence and abundance of food and clothing; and to obtain them easily is much to them; all which, this territory, even in the meantime offers them, with much less toil than they can be had in the backwoods of Canada.

It is not surprising, therefore, that so many European emigrant pass through Canada to seek the prairie lands of the United States Even old and successful settlers in Canada have found it much to their advantage to do so.

But there is another heavy charge against settlement in wooded countries. That is, the obstruction our dense forests present to the spread of settlement, and the expense that has to be incurred in making roads through them. It takes an expenditure of more than a hundred pounds a mile to make a road through the woods as passable as the natural surface of the prairie, by the innumerable routes it offers ; and when a road through our forests is made, i gives access only to the land immediately on the sides of it. When the settlers strike from it to reach the lands in the back conces sions the obstacle is again encountered, and the expense of opening the roads commences anew.

It is a moderate calculation to say that for every square mile'o forest country settled, an expense in money or labour of £100 ha to be incurred ultimately in making roads, or, what is worse, the settlers have to endure in hardship and difficulty of communica tion a much greater loss from the want of them.

Here again the practical man only can duly appreciate the mag nitude of the obstacle and the expense it entails ; I speak from experience, having superintended the making of upwards of three hundred and fifty miles of roads through wooded countries in Canada, within the last thirty-seven years.

The facts mentioned may assist in showing more definitely the loss, or cost of the obstruction, which the forests, in wooded coun tries, entail upon the settler. They will help to explain why many of our own people as well as European emigrants prefer going to the prairie lands of the West to settling in our wooded country especially since the western peninsula of Upper Canada has been all taken up, and we are obliged to fall back on rugged and partially arable territories, inferior in climate, and generally so in soil.

Our forest lands have the advantage in the more abundant sup ply of timber for fencing and fuel, to a certain degree, over the mixed prairie and wood lands ; but it is to be borne in mind tha great districts of our Central Prairie Country have, in their im mense beds of lignite coal, a supply of fuel, for ever, which place them in a far better position than some of the old settlements o Canada, where wood for fuel is already deficient, and is rapidly be coming more so.

7

CHAPTER XXIV.

WHY WE REQUIRE THE NORTH-WEST TERRITORIES.

Apart from the general reasons which make the acquisition of valuable territory desirable, there are some of a special nature which render the acquisition of this North-West Territory, or the great part of it suitable for settlement, of great importance to us.

We are in present need of it as a field for settlement; because our best and most favorably situated lands in Canada are now all surveyed and disposed of; and we have no vacant settling regions left, fit to attract and receive immigration on a large scale, as we formerley had. We require it because there our young men, and immigrants from Europe, may find the rich prairie lands, ready for cultivation, which they have now to seek in a foreign country.

The acquisition of it for that purpose is desirable, also, as a means of preserving our chief staple of trade—our timber, by relieving us from the necessity of converting our most valuable timber forests into comparatively worthless fields, through want of a sufficiency of better lands to place our settlers upon.

The acquisition of it is very desirable in order that the settlement of it, and the development of its resources, in connexion with the present Provinces of the Dominion, may give a wider market and a greater demand for our manufactures, and extension to our commerce in the manufactures of Great Britain, and in the products of her Colonies and of other countries; and give increased employment to our sea-going shipping and internal carrying trade, and to our canals existing and to be made. We want it that the Maritime Provinces of the East may prosper by the trade of the West.

We want all the strength its future population and trade can give in addition to all that which the extension of settlement in our remaining vacant lands, and the development of their resources, may afford us, to render it possible for us to maintain that degree of self-sustaining independence or future nationality which the Mother Country contemplates.

To see our way to part of these conclusions it will be necessary for us briefly to consider the character of the chief regions of country that we now have left for the reception of settlers, and their comparative value. It will also be necessary to consider in a general way the value of the lumber trade to the Provinces.

As regards the commercial and manufacturing advantages, in which the Maritime Provinces may be largely interested, it would seem only to be necessary to look to the United States adjoining us, and to consider how much the settlement of their western states and territories has contributed to the development of the manufactures of New England and the commerce of New York.[*]

As the people of the Maritime Provinces can build vessels so very much cheaper than the American ship builders can afford to do, and can also undoubtedly compete advantageously in navigating them, they are evidently in a position to reap wealth from the development of the agricultural regions of the West, from the large share they will command of the carrying trade and the commerce of these regions.

Their interest therefore is concerned in the development of the resources of these territories, and in every improvement that will tend to draw the trade of them down the St. Lawrence instead of to American ports, where Canadian shipping would compete for the freight of it with less advantage.

CHAPTER XXV.

OUR VACANT TERRITORIES AND SETTLING REGIONS IN CANADA CONSIDERED.

About forty years ago, when the population of Upper Canada was but one-tenth of what it now is, the western half of that Province, between the Great Lakes, presented an almost unbroken field for settlement, of wheat-growing land of the best quality, comparatively even, and arable throughout as a garden.

The stream of immigration flowed strongly to it for many years. Little or no selection was necessary. There was good land in abundance everywhere for all comers. The settlers prospered, and Upper Canada was a favorite colony for the destination of immigrants from Great Britain, including what is called the better class, with considerable capital. Even the high prices at which lands were sold tended to ensure a greater proportion of the latter.

This lasted till all the vacant public lands of the western peninsula and other parts of Upper Canada, south of the Laurentian formation, were surveyed and sold, or very nearly so.

At the same time, after partially successful attemps to attract immigration into the more favorable of the townships of Lower Canada, the French Canadian population, straitened for room in their old seigniories, and having exhausted much of the rich lands

---

* I here quote, as most appropriate, the expressions of an Honorable Senator of New Brunswick.

of the great plain country of the St. Lawrence, by a bad system
of farming and by over cropping, into which the original richness
of their lands had betrayed them, wisely turned their attention to
these townships, which they have since been rapidly occupying.

Having no other of a better quality, or more suitable to open for
the expansion of settlement, it became necessary to turn to the
inferior lands of the Huron and Ottawa Territory, which are in a
region of Laurentian formation, at the outline of which settlement
had long before, as it were instinctively, stopped.

Of these lands, the best parts will not bear comparison with the
peninsula of Canada West or the older settlements of that Province, nor with the rich alluvial lands of the St. Lawrence and its
tributaries on which the old seigneurial settlements of Lower
Canada were formed ; a proportion of them, unequally prevalent, of
about three-quarters on an average of the whole, or one-half in the
better regions, is rocky and unarable, or poor sandy land unfit for
profitable cultivation.

Notwithstanding the opening of several colonization roads to
give access to them, the powerful efforts of Government to direct
settlers to them by agencies to Europe and other means, and the
far more powerful inducement presented in the very high prices
given, in that territory, by lumberers, for farm produce, these lands
have failed to attract immigration in any considerable degree,
especially of the class of settlers possessing capital.

As we have now nothing better to offer, Canada does not attract
immigrants from Great Britain, as formerly, nor retain those from
other European countries arriving at her ports. Nor will she ever
do so till she has again abundance of the best lands to give them ;
not scattered through a rough and rather forbidding country, of
Laurentian formation, but in unbroken continuity or vast tracts,
which can only be obtained in the territory we claim.

Elsewhere, in Canada, even including the Maritime Provinces,
it is vain to look for any field for settlement at all approaching in
extent and value that which Canada West presented in its infancy
as a province ; incomparably less, therefore, do we possess any such
field for expansion as is required to meet our greatly increased
native demand, or to admit of that increase by immigration so
essential to our prosperity and security in the important and
responsible national position in which Federation has placed us.

THE OTTAWA COUNTRY AND HURON AND OTTAWA TERRITORY.

The valley of the River Ottawa, and the country lying between
it and the Georgian Bay or Lake Huron, form together the largest
and best field for settlement remaining in Canada.

The valley of the River Ottawa is reputed to have an area of eighty thousand superficial miles, but it may prove to be scarcely seventy-seven thousand.

The area of the country lying between the sources of the western tributaries of the Ottawa and the Georgian Bay is about nine thousand square miles.

It is of the same Laurentian formation, and being similar in character generally to the adjoining part of the Ottawa country, may be classed with it—making together probably an area of about eighty-six thousand superficial miles ; of which the part lying between the old townships, on the Ottawa, and the Georgian Bay is called the Huron and Ottawa Territory.

The uncertainty as to the extent of the valley of the Ottawa is owing to that river not having been, till now, surveyed beyond four hundred and thirty miles from its mouth ; that is, to the head of Lake Temiscaming. When the surveys of its upper course, at present in progress, are completed, its entire length may prove to be about eight hundred miles.

Eighty-six thousand superficial miles is a great extent of country —but unfortunately the greater part of it is ground unfit for cultivation, which, in proportion to its prevalence in a greater or less degree, obstructs the settlement of the remainder.

The River Ottawa from its tributary, the Bonnechère, down to its mouth, at the foot of the Island of Montreal, a distance of a hundred and eighty miles by its course,—flows through the northern margin of a plain country of Silurian formation, of limestone and calciferous rocks. These with Potsdam sandstone extend with an irregular outline from two to ten miles west of the Brockville and Ottawa Railroad. This Silurian plain includes about seven thousand square miles of the country watered by the Ottawa and its tributaries. It is generally good arable land, much of it equal to the best in the Provinces. It is all organized into old settled seigniories, (including those north of Montreal,) and old townships, in which there are no vacant Crown Lands of any considerable extent remaining.

The remainder of the valley of the Ottawa, with little exception, together with the country between it and Lake Huron, is of the Laurentian formation. If the assumed extent of the Ottawa country be correct, their joint area will be about seventy-nine thousand square miles, apart from the Silurian tract already mentioned.

Of this area about one-sixth part has been surveyed into townships. A further, and considerably larger portion, has been more or less surveyed or explored, and partially occupied as timber locations. With the exception of surveys just completed on the Montreal River and the Upper Ottawa, but little is known of the interior of the remainder, or about one-half of the entire area, even by the agents of the Hudson's Bay Company ; and that little is unfavorable.

From the returns of surveys made of townships and timber berths, and of the courses of rivers, and from what is reported of the unsurveyed parts by the few who have traversed them, it would be unsafe to estimate, at the utmost, more than an average of one quarter of the whole area of this Laurentian country as arable land, fit for cultivation.

It is unequally distributed, in small spots, veins and larger blocks—sometimes in tracts of considerable extent. In some parts the proportion of arable land of a good quality may be one-half, and in less favorable regions, not one-twentieth part, and that in spots too small to be available.

The other three-fourths of the entire area consist of rugged and unarable or poor sandy land, and worthless swamps.

Of these three-fourths, a considerable proportion may, and no doubt will, ultimately be occupied and brought under cultivation, when the pressure of population and scarcity of land cause such an increase in its value, as to render it profitable to incur the expense of removing stones from ground that is now quite unarable.

Such lands are in part occupied now, under what is called hoe and harrow cultivation, where the demand of the lumber trade gives very high prices for produce, or where poor settlers are led to take them, from the good first crops to be had from a rich surface soil, to be afterwards abandoned from being unarable.

It is scarcely necessary to say that it would be heartless iniquity to induce settlers, in search of permanent homesteads, to sink their labor on such lands, when better can be had.

On the other hand, much may be said in favor of the proportion of good arable land mentioned as occurring in the Laurentian Country of the Ottawa, and Huron and Ottawa Territory.

Notwithstanding the repulsive character of the gneiss ridges, stony swamps, and coarse sandy ground, with which it is more or less associated, and the too frequent presence of boulders, a great part of it has a rich warm loamy soil, though frequently light and sandy, or rather stony, and often uneven. Some of it is equal to the best lands in the Eastern Townships, with a better climate,—though inferior in quality and in character of surface to the rich even lands of the western part of the Province. Over a great extent of it durable clay loam or rich alluvial flats are of rare occurrence.

The largest and most favorable tract of country to which this description would generally apply, is in the heart of the Huron and Ottawa Territory, on the head waters of the western tributaries of the Ottawa and rivers falling into Lake Huron and Lake Nippissing.

It embraces an area of about seven thousand square miles. By the returns of surveys about one-half of it, irregularly distributed, is good land fit for settlement. A belt of inferior rocky country intervenes between it and Lake Huron, about thirty miles in breadth, and a band of rugged bad land, about twenty miles in breadth, lying along the height of land dividing the basin of the Ottawa from that of the St. Lawrence, separates it from the old townships in front of it. To the eastward of it lie the more thickly pine timbered lumbering regions of the Ottawa. Hard wood is its predominent timber. Like all countries of primitive or azoic formation, it is thickly interspersed with lakes abounding in fish, and presenting many desirable positions of great beauty and fertility.

The Gatineau, the chief tributary of the Ottawa, drains nearly ten thousand miles, with a course of about four hundred. There is a good deal of rich alluvial land, but already occupied, along its banks, and also in the narrow valleys of its lower tributaries. Lofty precipitous hills of gneiss and crystalline limestone overhang its east bank for nearly a hundred miles up. Crystalline limestone abounds a hundred miles further up, to, and sixty miles up its eastern tributary, the Piscatong. The romantic character of the lower valley of the Gatineau is very much against its agricultural capacity; and though there is much land fit for cultivation in so considerable an extent even of rugged hilly country—as more than the upper half of the valley is in a very unfavorable sterile region— it is probable the arable land fit for cultivation on the Gatineau will, by our present standard of fitness, be considerably less than a quarter of the area it unwaters.

On the other large northern tributaries of the Ottawa, it would be unsafe to estimate that a greater proportion of arable land, fit for settlement, will be found, than on the Gatineau. If the proportion of such land be less on the northern tributaries of the Ottawa than in the Huron and Ottawa territory, rich alluvial ground and deep clay loam may, as on the Gatineau, be more frequently found.

Commencing gradually, about a hundred and forty miles up the Gatineau, a change occurs in the character of the country and its forests. Poplar, fir, birch and pitch pine, become the prevalent woods; white pines become small and scarce, and, at two hundred and nine miles from the mouth of the Gatineau, cease to be found. Rugged hills of gneiss, occasionally bare and precipitous, with a soil of sand or poor sandy loam in the flats and valleys, in parts burned to utter barrenness, are the prevalent characteristics of the upper half of the valley of the Gatineau, as far as it has been explored. This description of country, interspersed with innumerable lakes, extends over the upper courses of the other large northern tributaries of the Ottawa generally.

Such also, with little exception, as far as yet known, is the character of the country and its forests in the upper valley of the main Ottawa, for about three hundred miles of its course above Lake Temiscaming, and extending north-eastwardly from it.* But by far the greater part of it is quite unknown.

It is varied by the circumstance that, in part of this upper course of the Ottawa, the elevation between its waters and those of Hudson's Bay is very slight, and the clay land of Lake Abbitibbi overlaps the northern tributaries of the Ottawa, and approaches it through their valleys; but the rock formation it overlies is Laurentian, not Silurian, as shown by the ridges of gneiss prevailing throughout, on the routes traversed.

This clay, which here presents itself, is white and hard, but very soluble, and destitute of any grit, and seemingly poor and hard to cultivate. But white clay soil admits of much improvement. A gentleman of my acquaintance in Pembroke, on the Upper Ottawa, obtained thirty bushels of wheat to the acre, from a piece of white clay ground, by proper cultivation and manuring.

This clay occurs on the River Blanche, a northern tributary of Lake Temiscaming. On the lower course of that river there is much very rich alluvial land, but it seems to be occasionally flooded.

A blue clay soil extends for fifty miles along the banks of the Montreal River (a large western tributary of that Lake), occupying its immediate valley, which is from one mile to four miles in width. Some blue clay soils in Lower Canada have been cropped for upwards of sixty years, without manure, owing to their durable fertility. The upper course of the Montreal River is in a poor, rough country, unfit for settlement (as ascertained by recent surveys), which extends, with increasing ruggedness, through to the vicinity of Michipicoten, on Lake Superior.

At the upper end of Lake Temiscaming on both sides, and in the interior between the south end of that lake and Lake Nipissing, and north of the latter, there are considerable tracts of land like the better part of the Huron and Ottawa territory. There is a fine

---

* I am of opinion that a larger proportion than is now estimated of the plain country, on the upper course of the Ottawa, north of the Laurentian highlands, will prove to be arable lands, and much of it of a clay soil; and that though remote and valueless now, it will ultimately become occupied; but I have not yet sufficient data to enable me to speak decidedly.

tract in the interior of the north side, extending westward from the River du Moine, in the Province of Quebec.

There are scattering lands of a middling quality on Black River, and less on the River Coulogne. The valley of the Du Lièvre, a northern tributary of three hundred miles in length, below the Gatineau, is less favorable for settlement than that of the latter river. Further down on the north side, the lower part of the valley of the River Rouge is more favorable, and the country between it and the River Petite Nation above it is generally fit for settlement, back to the distance of fifty or sixty miles from the Ottawa, having much good, though light loamy soil, well suited for cultivation. This tract is most advantageously situated to meet the wants of the surplus population of Vaudreuil, which has no vacant lands in rear of it.

It may be necessary to explain, in using the expression "land fit for settlement," I do not mean land of the best or of a superior quality only, but also land of a second or third-rate quality or value, from being more or less stony or broken—arable, or such as in other parts of Canada is commonly made so, with moderate outlay or labor, and on which settlers, with industry and good management, make a comfortable living.

I may also add, that any estimate of what quantity of such land there is in a country, much of which is but little known, is necessarily very vague, and that the proportion of one-fourth, which I have here given, is merely an approximation I have ventured to make, from having had charge of the public forests of the upper sixty thousand square miles of the valley of the Ottawa for many years past. It is based on personal observation, returns of surveys made under my direction, and other sources of information.

One-fourth of eighty thousand square miles of arable land, good enough for cultivation, is a great quantity, but unfortunately all of it is more or less depreciated by intervening bad ground, and a great part of it, from being remotely scattered in small pieces, has to be deducted as valueless for ordinary settlement, because the cost of getting at it would be greater than its worth.

Forty years ago the inhabitants of Canada complained that the Crown and Clergy Reserves, amounting to two-sevenths of the land granted, obstructed the progress of settlement and maintenance of roads; but where one-third or a fourth only of a country can be occupied, and especially where the intervening lands are rugged and unfavorable to road making, the case is very much worse; for there the inhabitants, in addition to maintaining the roads through their own lands, will have to maintain and travel over twice or three times as much more extent of roads, which the ruggedness of the ground will render twice or even six times as expensive to make good, or even passable, as in a more favorable country.

These roads have either to be made or struggled through un-made ; and where such unoccupied lands prevent the consolidation of settlement, there is difficulty in maintaining schools and churches, and the necessary intercourse of society.

Zealous as we Ottawa people are for our locality, we would deceive ourselves and others were we to deny these facts ; and we cannot reasonably expect to attract any great stream of immigration to our country, while the vast extents of better soil, un-broken by such objectionable characteristics, are to be found else-where.

I go into particulars as to this part of public domain, as a set-tling district, because, as it is the largest and the best, if its unfit-ness to attract immigration, in the degree that we require for the increase of our national strength and prosperity, be considered, that of our inferior territories will be evident. In this, it is not the desirableness of settling the Ottawa country, but the fact that it fails to attract immigration, that we have to consider.

But though it does not attract immigration,—and settlement, owing to the same cause, will advance more slowly in it than on more even ground, we should not undervalue the Ottawa country as a field for the industry and enterprise of our native population, who are more capable of developing its resources.

It presents many important advantages. Its climate is agree-able, and the most healthful of any in the interior of Canada. Its winter is more dry and bracing than that of Toronto, and much milder than that of Lower Canada, eastward of it. The summer of the middle parts of the Ottawa country is upwards of one month longer than that of Quebec.* Fall wheat can be grown with ad-vantage, and yields heavy returns, and unusually high prices are paid for farm produce by the lumber trade. Its minerals, lead,

---

* It is here proper to notice an important and very gross error, in a work on "The Influence of Climate in North and South America," by Mr. J. Disturnell, of New York. In a climatic map showing the limits of the cultivation of grains and vegetables, he places the entire valley of the Ottawa beyond the limits of wheat cul-tivation, and the north half beyond the limits of the cultivation of vegetables. If Mr. Disturnell had used the simple precaution of referring to the Census of Canada for 1861, he would have found that the counties of Carleton, Lanark and Renfrew, altogether north of his limit of wheat cultivation, yielded an average of 17 7-10 bushels of wheat to the acre ; that their total yield of wheat for that year was upwards of a million of bushels, or 11 7-10 bushels to each inhabitant. That is fully fifty per cent. more to each person than the State of Ohio yielded per head of its population by the census of 1850, or nearly three times as much as the rate of wheat raised per head in the United States. He would have seen also, that in the township of Pembroke, on the Ottawa, a hundred miles north of his limit of the growth of wheat, the average yield of wheat was the highest, being twenty-four bushels to the acre. A little enquiry would have enabled him to know that the temperature re-quired for the growth of wheat prevails, as ascertained, a hundred miles still further north, and beyond that to a distance not yet determined.

plumbago and iron are commencing to attract attention from their abundance. It has unlimited water power, which is being largely applied to various manufactures ; and above all, its lumber trade, which contributes so much to the wealth and commerce of the Province, and under careful management may do so for ever.

TERRITORY NORTH OF LAKE HURON.

What is here stated as to the comparative inferiority of the Ottawa country, as a settling region, is applicable even in a greater degree to nearly all the vacant territories of Canada, east and west. The territory north of Lake Huron possesses some valuable sites for settlement and mining enterprise in the front parts of it, much enhanced by their favorable position on the navigation of the great lakes ; but it is generally inferior to the Ottawa country for agricultural purposes, and in its timber. The surveys on the line from the Montreal River of the Ottawa, towards Michipicoten on Lake Superior, show the interior to be a very infertile rough country, increasing in ruggedness westward.

THE ST. MAURICE TERRITORY.

Passing eastward we have the St. Maurice territory, upwards of twenty-one thousand square miles in area. It is of the same Laurentian formation as the Upper Ottawa country, but rather more rugged and inferior to it in fitness for cultivation as well as climate —inferior also in its timber, for which, nevertheless, it is chiefly valuable ; its great river, the St. Maurice and its tributaries, presenting everywhere the means of getting that to the market. As very much less of it has been surveyed into townships, it is more difficult to estimate the quantity of arable land fit for cultivation it contains. It has been roughly estimated at upwards of five thousand square miles, unequally distributed. Its value will be enhanced and the settlement of it powerfully encouraged by the manufacture of its timber. The industrious population of seigniories in front of it, will need the best of it with every advantage it may offer for their own expansion. It will never attract any considerable amount of European immigration.

THE SAGUENAY TERRITORY.

Of the twenty-seven thousand square miles drained by the great River Saguenay and its branches, about four thousand seven hundred square miles is the utmost that has been estimated as fit for cultivation, chiefly in the basin of Lake St. John, between the stern barrier of the Laurentide mountains and the still higher range fifty miles to the north of it, and enjoying from its sheltered position a better climate than Quebec. Though much of it is of the richest description of deep clay loam, a great part of the northward of the lake consists of sandy flats. What is fit for settlement is required for the surplus French Canadian population of the old settlements on the lower St. Lawrence. It offers no important scope for European immigration.

THE EASTERN TOWNSHIPS

And those opposite Quebec are, as already stated, being well filled up.

THE SOUTH SIDE OF THE ST. LAWRENCE BELOW QUEBEC.

Behind the old settlements, the slopes and valleys of the Notre Dame Mountains, with much uneven though good land, have a cold climate, from latitude and elevation. (I have seen white frost on the Temiscouata Portage Road in the month of July). They present little or nothing to attract European immigrants.

BONAVENTURE, GASPÉ AND RESTIGOUCHE.

The County of Bonaventure, on the Baie des Chaleurs, and the Restigouche country lying chiefly in the Province of New Brunswick, from their superior soil and climate, but especially on account of their admirable position for communication with Europe, are as advantageous for settlement as the Eastern Townships, and nearly equal to the better parts of the Ottawa Country.

The soil of the County of Bonaventure, and of the north part of New Brunswick on the River Restigouche, is a rich warm loam, free from stones, even on the table lands on the mountains ; and is unarable only where too steep to be ploughed. It yields heavy crops of spring wheat, and of oats and barley, much superior in quantity to the acre, and in quality, to those raised in counties on the St. Lawrence.

The coast of Gaspé is similar in soil, but the summer is often too cold for the profitable growing of wheat. Its fisheries are very valuable.

If a direct trade were opened, in coarse grains, with Great Britain, these countries might, to some extent, be occupied by European immigrants.

I found the interior, through to the St. Lawrence, on the route afterwards adopted by Major Robinson, as a line for the Intercolonial Railroad, to be generally an arable fertile country ; judging from having had a hundred miles of it dug over in road making.

This is the most healthful and romantic land within the compass of the Dominion. It has a winter temperature ten to fifteen degrees warmer than that of Quebec ; and in summer its rich valleys and high swelling hills are fanned by the fresh breezes of the sea.—A land of interesting historical associations, where, three hundred and fifty years ago, the flag of France was first unfurled on this continent, and the cross first planted, and knelt to, by christian men—grim, armed men,—forefathers possibly of men who fought at " Montcontour " and " Ivry,"—before the astonished gaze of the ancient masters of the land, now extinct, who then ruled from Lachine to the Gulf, and to whom the Dominion of Canada owes its name. Further up the banks of the Restigouche, the high trees wave over the graves and ruined hearths of the defenders of La Petite Rochelle. It was bombarded and burned by Admiral Byron a year before the capture of Quebec by Wolfe.

Returning from romance to practical fact—While the stream of immigration continued to find scope in Western Canada, it was natural that countries like this should be passed by ; but now that it classes with the best that there is left in Canada, it is difficult to see why it should be longer disregarded, especially in view of the Intercolonial Railroad, now to be made, being carried through part of it.

Its rivers are uninterruptedly navigable by large scows drawn by horses, from their mouths nearly to their sources ; and freight from its ports to Europe costs about a dollar a ton less even than from Quebec ; and every enterprise of sea and land is open to the settler on its shores.

These advantages belong also, more or less, to the north-east part of New Brunswick. In the County of Restigouche, the proportion of good arable land will be found about equal to that of the Ottawa Country. The southern part of New Brunswick contains much land as valuable as the best parts of Upper Canada, but it is generally already owned and occupied.

INSUFFICIENCY OF OUR REMAINING LANDS TO SECURE IMMIGRATION ON A LARGE SCALE.

This summary view of our remaining public lands shows us that while we have territories, presenting many excellent sites for the industry and enterprise of our native population, and necessary for their use, the best field that we have to offer for the reception of immigration on a large scale, such as flows to the Western States, or even such as formerly flowed to Upper Canada, is the Huron and Ottawa Country, which already, under the most favorable trial, signally failed to attract such immigration ; and that the next best is a small territory on the Baie des Chaleurs and Restigouche, where immigration on a small scale might be successful, provided an export trade in oats and barley could be established with Great Britain, or any adequate market.

Now, it is evident that we cannot attract the immigration we desire to make us a strong people, while we have nothing better than that to offer.

If, when all Canada numbered less than a million of souls, the great and almost unbroken extent of rich lands which Upper Canada presented, was no more than sufficient for our expansion of settlement by native increase and immigration, it is surely absurd to suppose that these inferior lands, in extent, soil and climate, isolated, or broken up by a much greater proportion of rugged unarable land, can be sufficient for our expansion, now that we number four millions, and are called upon, by the position we have attained, to look chiefly to our own strength for the defence by land of our country, and the maintenance of that constitutional independence that has been awarded us.

VALUE OF REMAINING VACANT LANDS AND THEIR RESOURCES.

In speaking of the rugged and hilly regions of our country, as little suited for the reception of European immigration, it is by no means meant to undervalue them.

What good lands they contain, especially in lumber yielding countries, will have an increased value from the ready market and enhanced prices which lumbering operations, mining and other local industries, may give for their produce.

The sons of the "habitants," and the surplus population of the old settlements adjoining, can select at leisure the good lands in our hilly regions, behind the seigniories; and from their being near their homes, with their knowledge of the labor and climate of the country, can settle up these lands with advantage to themselves, while to European immigrants, they would be inaccessible and unavailable. The value of their minerals, which are now but beginning to be worked, can hardly be sufficiently estimated. The prosperity which mere fertility of soil gives a new country, soon attains its maximum, and is ultimately checked by imprudent over-cropping. We see that it has been so, and that mere fertility of soil never made a country great in history. But the prosperity that arises from mineral resources, manufactures and maritime advantages, though slow of being developed, may raise a country to a pre-eminence which mere fertility of soil can never bestow; while the occupations they afford cultivate and develope the intellect and enterprise of a people to a degree that mere agricultural occupations fail ever to do.

Nevertheless, it is rich agricultural countries only that are suitable for the reception of immigration on a large scale, and that become populous with the greatest rapidity.

It is as such a receptacle for immigration, in order to obtain that increase of population, that we want the great prairie land of the North-West.

Our good lands in the Provinces are far from being filled up, but the nearest and best being held by private owners, requiring high prices, they repel instead of attracting immigrants.

CHAPTER XXVI.

THE PRESERVATION OF OUR TIMBER FORESTS AND LUMBER TRADE. A REASON FOR ACQUIRING THE NORTH-WEST PRAIRIE LAND.

Having assigned the preservation of our Timber Forests, which yield our chief staple of trade, from unnecessary and hasty destruction, as a reason for acquiring the North-West Prairie Land, it seems necessary to consider the value of the lumber trade to the country. In doing so it may be sufficient to take a general view of the value of that of Canada before Confederation.

To judge correctly of the importance of the Lumber Trade, it is necessary to consider carefully the benefits arising from the expenditure attending it, and the employment it gives in the country; besides that which it presents in furnishing the chief export of the Province, and the employment it gives in freight to British and Colonial Shipping.

In considering the benefits arising from the expenditure attending it where the timber is manufactured, it will be suitable to commence by estimating the cost of manufacturing the timber produced by the lumber trade of the Ottawa country for one year.

For this purpose it will be sufficient to take the average of the production of square timber on the Ottawa for the five years from 1861 to 1865, and the produce of the saw-logs of last year (1866), in sawn timber, which, owing to the rapid increase of the latter, recently, will go nearer a fair view of the trade than the five years' average would.

Taken together these will show a total yield of about two hundred and sixty-five millions of feet, board measure, of sawn lumber, and very nearly twenty-four millions of cubic feet of square timber; representing nearly eight hundred and seventy thousand trees.

In the manufacture of these quantities of sawn and squared timber, there would be employed about 17,000 men for nine months

)f the year ; the costs attending the manufacture and taking of the imber to ports of shipment would be:

For men's wages	$2,596,747
Teams	346,760
Hay and Oats	544,907
Pork and Flour	990,740
Duty on Crown Timber and price to owners of private timber	325,938
Slide Dues and Boomage to the Crown or owners of private works, and interest on expenditure on River Improvements	134,112
Interest on cost of Saw Mills and their equipments, insurance, &c	269,062
Interest on cost of shanty stock and equipments, tear, wear and casualities	149,052
Total cost incurred by Ottawa Lumberers for one year, apart from further costs before shipment	$5,357,318

Nearly all this large amount, it will be seen, represents employment and profit given in the country to labourers, mechanics and others, in current or original expenditure made.

Of this it will be observed that the second, third and fourth items, amounting to the large sum of $1,882,407 are for farm produce. It is true that part of the provisions is not produced in the locality, which shows that the trade offers a market for more farm produce than the locality as yet furnishes. About $100,000 is paid or realized to the owners, for private timber, in the locality, and a large part of the expenditure for wages also is local, though much of it is paid to labourers from other parts of the Province, chiefly Lower Canada.

These items of cost are given from the application of known rates of necessary expenditure to known quantities of timber, and show the cost with ordinary good management.

From its operations being remote, the lumber trade gives very high prices for farm produce in remote localities, near its works, to save transport of produce into them. The more remote therefore, the higher are the prices given. It thereby creates a highly favourable market for new settlements, where, from the distance and want of good roads, the value of the produce would be consumed in taking it to any other market, if it could be taken out at all. It thus gives encouragement and assistance where they are most wanted; and that on a scale much exceeding what the most liberal arrangements of Government could ever afford.

It is proper to dwell upon these facts, and to look well to the magnitude of the amounts, because through ignorance of this peculiar subject, and prejudice acquired from others, or from limited and unfavorable knowledge, many think that the lumber trade impedes settlement, and is in its nature injurious to the progress and prosperity of the country. Experience throughout British America shows that it is so to the man who divides his attention between lumbering and his farm, to the injury of the latter. It is still more injurious to the man who has been tempted to settle on bad land by the duty on the timber given him as a bounty for doing so, by the Settlers' License system recently in force. But we know well that it is absurdly untrue, that the settler on suitable land, who confines his industry to his proper business, farming, is injured by the trade which gives him higher prices for his produce than he could otherwise obtain.

These remarks are more or less applicable to all regions of the then Province of Canada, where lumbering is carried on, but especially to the Ottawa country.

From the remainder of the Province, the yield of sawn and squared timber, with the addition of staves, estimated in the same manner, may be about one-fifth less than that from the Ottawa and all its tributaries.

When both are added together, they give a total for the whole Province for one year, of upwards of five hundred millions of feet board measure of sawn lumber, and about thirty-nine millions of cubic feet of squared timber, besides staves and other miscellaneous wood goods, in all the produce of upwards of a million and a half of trees, and giving employment for nine months to about 30,600 men, costing in manufacture and transport to ports of shipment :—

For wages of men	$4,661,960
Teams	618,057
Hay and oats	975,915
Pork and flour	1,763,660
Interest on cost of shanty stock, tear and wear, and casualities	274,794
Interest on cost of saw-mills and equipments, repairs and insurance	538,124
Duty to Crown, or price to owners of private timber	571,824
Interest on cost of river improvements, ground rents, boomage and slidage to Crown, and owners of private works	186,688
Total Cost to the Lumberers for one year's operations, for the whole Province, apart from further charges before shipment	$9,591,022

In this estimate, provisions and labour are calculated below the present high rates.

But this total is far from representing the final amount or value of the timber. Wood goods in the form of lathwood, sleepers, knees, oars, &c., to the value of nearly $1,000,000, besides, got out by country people chiefly, have to be added to the quantity and value.

This would increase the amount to $10,591,022, which, compared with $13,009,207, the total value of exports of the forest, shown by the Trade and Navigation Returns for 1865, (less Pot and Pearl ashes) which the above approximation most nearly represents, leaves a difference of $2,418,185 to cover charges at shipping ports, almost entirely at Quebec, consisting of costs for culling, boomage, putting into shipping order, commissions on sales, &c.

Having shown an annual expenditure by the Lumber Trade of over nine and a half millions of dollars, of which upwards of eight millions is for farm produce and men's wages, we come to another important item to be considered in the worth of the Lumber Trade to the Province, that is, what it contributes to the city of Quebec.

It is almost unnecessary to say that it forms the chief trade of that city. The wealth of its merchants is chiefly made by it, directly or indirectly, and a large portion of its inhabitants are maintained by their labour, in receiving and shipping the lumber in summer, and in the ship-building, connected with and dependent on it, in winter.

Besides the greater part of the amount before mentioned for charges and commissions on the timber, which Quebec receives, her merchants benefit largely by the freight of the vessels owned and built by them. The average amount of freight of timber, shared by them and the shipowners in Britain, for the four years from 1860 to 1863, at 30s. a ton, would amount to £1,258,221 sterling, or nearly six and a half millions of dollars.

In 1865 the value of fifty-one ships built and exported, was $1,923,594; their tonnage 47,262. That this trade is dependent for its profits, which are derived chiefly from the freight of the first cargo they take on being sent home for sale, will be at once seen, when it is considered that a ship of 1,000 tons, worth, say $40,000, will make about $7,000 in freight of her cargo, when sent home for sale.

The greater consumption of articles paying duty by men employed in lumbering, over those remaining in their parishes, is not to be overlooked.

As the mother country is largely engaged in this trade with us, it would be decorous to consider her interests in the matter. Upwards of a thousand ships come annually to Quebec for cargoes of timber, earning profit by their freights for their owners, who are chiefly in Britain; the annual value has been already stated.

The cost of the timber when taken home is a little greater than that from the Baltic, but of that cost, the greater part is freight earned by the British shipping ; and Britain obtains a description of timber here which she requires, and cannot obtain from the Baltic.

It is next necessary to consider the value of the Lumber Trade to the Province in furnishing our chief means of remittance to Europe, in return for our imports.

The value of the timber imported from Canada into Great Britain, by the Imperial Trade and Navigation Returns, for the six years, from 1858 to 1863, gives an annual average of £2,750,731, while that of all our other goods is only £1,965,891 sterling, showing the value of our timber exported to Great Britain to be upwards of a third greater than that of all our other exports there ; showing also that the thirty thousand men, then employed in lumbering, furnished more to her, than all the five hundred thousand other men in Canada did in the same time.

In the same manner, on comparing the total exports, for the year to 30th June, 1865, by our own Trade and Navigation Returns, after deducting the ashes, the total value of Timber Exports is $13,009,207, all produced in Canada, and by the labour of only 30,600 men ; while all the other exports, without deducting anything for part of them imported, amount in value to $29,471,944, including all the exports produced by 600,000 other men engaged in agriculture and all other pursuits ; being only about two and a quarter times the value of the timber exported.

This shows that each man engaged in lumbering contributes about ten times as much to the commerce of the country as other men do, besides contributing twice as much as they do to Internal Trade ; for all that he eats, as well as wears, gives employment to others, besides what he produces. A pauper settler on bad land contributes nothing to the country compared with him.

This view is fully sustained by a statement carefully compiled by Allan Gilmour, Esq., from the Returns of Trade and Navigation, showing, that after deducting from the value of agricultural exports, the equivalents of quantities of the same articles imported, the average annual value of farm produce of Canada, exported from 1857 to 1863, was only $7,639,173, while the average annual value of products of the forest, after deducting ashes, was $9,558,962 ; from $6,000,000 to $14,000,000 worth of farm produce being annually imported for exportation, or to take the place of that exported—the returns in that respect making it seem that the surplus agricultural produce of the Province was double what i really was.

On our imports we depend largely for the comforts and neces saries of life ; if our exports, the remittance in payment for then were diminished, our imports also would have to be diminished.

It is vain to say that they could be made up for in agricultura exports, for we see that to make them what they are, we hav generally to import much from the United States. Nor could th labour now employed in lumbering produce equivalent farm pro duce ; we have already seen that it would hardly produce one tenth of it.

It is also vain to say, as some do, that a great part of the com puted value of lumber exported is properly due to agriculture, a merely representing in another form the agricultural produce con sumed in the manufacture of it. On the contrary, it is eviden that it is the lumber trade which gives a value to the agricultura produce which it consumes ; for we know absolutely that if there were no manufactures, or other branches of industry, to purchase and consume the farmers' surplus produce beyond what he can use, it would be as valueless as heaps of sand.

Such being the importance of the lumber trade to the internal industry and external commerce of the Provinces, it is to the general interest of the Dominion that the public forests, on lands unsuitable for cultivation, should be preserved for economic use for ever, if possible.

It is evident also that the destruction of valuable timber yielding forests, by extraordinary efforts to force settlement upon them, while we have, or can have lands more suitable for cultivation, is undesirable, as injurious to the real interest alike of the country and the settlers themselves.

While every facility should be given for the settlement of the lands really fit for cultivation, to be found in our lumbering regions, no inducement should be held out to settlers to take pine timbered lands in preference to others more suitable for successful settlement.

In lumbering territories some lands, most frequently the best for settlement, have very little or no timber of commercial value upon them, and others have a great deal ; some have so much of such timber that the value of it is equal to ten times the ordinary value of land. The latter are generally unfit for settlement.

The holding out of the pine timber as an inducement to settlers leads to pretended settlement, or temporary settlement for the purpose of lumbering on such lands, causing destruction of the forests by extensive running fires, and also over manufacture.

By withdrawing that inducement, and leaving settlement on the lands fit for it, in our lumbering territories to be encouraged by the far more wholesome stimulus of the high prices for farm produce given by lumberers, and especially by opening our Central Prairie Country for settlement, our timber forests, which yield our chief staple of export trade, may be preserved from the precipitate destruction to which they would otherwise be exposed.

It is important to the prosperity of settlements in our lumbering territories that the lumber trade should steadily continue in them, for were the local market it offers to fail, the produce of the remote settlements could not be taken to any other market with profit, especially as the intervening rugged grounds would prevent the maintenance of good roads, and greatly increase the cost of transport.

The simplest way of withdrawing to a great extent the inducements to take up pine timbered lands would be to give the land for nothing to actual settlers, or sell it to them at a much reduced price, under the condition that the timber on it should not be exempt from the usual Crown duties, on being cut and taken to market, by the settler or others.

This would also stop the abuse of taking up lands under the pretence of settlement in order to evade the payment of duties on the timber, and the duties saved to the revenue by it would soon amount to an important sum annually.

CHAPTER XXVII.

ROUTES TO RED RIVER COMPARED.

We have now to consider what way we have of getting into this Central Prairie Country; the character and comparative value of the different routes known, by land and water, and what can be made of them, as means of travel and heavy transport; especially those which the nature of the intervening country affords through our own territory.

HUDSON'S BAY ROUTE.

The route by Hudson's Bay to York Factory by sea, and thence by Hill River and its many portages, to Lake Winnipeg and Red River, may be dismissed without further consideration. As only one voyage can be made in a season into Hudson's Bay, and that with difficulty and danger—with a rough portage navigation of nearly four hundred miles from York Factory to Lake Winnipeg, ascending upwards of six hundred feet—this route can never be an advantageous outlet for the produce of the interior fertile region, and much less can it be an inlet for us. The cost of transport by it from York Factory to Red River is four dollars a hundred pounds.

FORT WILLIAM AND DOG LAKE ROUTE.

We may now turn to the route from Fort William, on Lake Superior, which is being opened by Government.

Commencing near Fort William, the first part of this route is the Dog Portage Road, leading north-westward twenty-five miles to the foot of Dog Lake. This road was projected in the field by the Canadian Exploring Expedition. It is to be a thoroughly made turnpike road, well crowned and graded; six miles of it have been made this last season; and in further pursuance of Mr. Dawson's original project of improvement, material has been prepared for the building of a dam at the outlet of Dog Lake. This dam, by raising the lake, will gorge Dog River, that feeds it, so as to give a navigable reach of about thirty miles to Jourdain's Rapids, The elevation of Jourdain's Rapids above Lake Superior is seven hundred and twenty feet.

At three and a quarter miles further, is the height of land, Prairie Portage, two and a half miles in length, between the waters of Lake Superior and those of Lake Winnipeg. It is eight hundred and eighty-seven feet above the level of Lake Superior.

A good road is to be made over it, eleven miles in length, from Jourdain's Rapids to Savanne River, which is eight hundred and thirty-two feet above Lake Superior.

Savanne River is about sixty-six feet wide and flows sluggishly, with a depth of four feet, for twenty-two miles, to Lac des Mille Lacs, which is thirty-four miles in length, forming, with it, a navigable reach of fifty-six miles, which, by constructing a dam below the outlet of the lake, might be increased in depth, and to about sixty miles in length.

Savanne River is the head of the River Seine, which flows westward from Lac des Mille Lacs, by a course of about a hundred miles to the foot of the Twelve Portages, where its waters reach the level of Rainy Lake; to this River, as a route of communication, we shall have occasion further to refer.

After going forty-two miles by Savanne River and Mille Lacs, the route we are describing leaves the latter at twenty miles from the head of it, on the south side, and passes by a portage of less than a quarter of a mile (seventeen chains) to Baril Lake, which is seven and a half miles in length, and nearly two feet higher than Mille Lacs.

From Baril Lake, Brulé Portage, about a quarter of a mile (twenty-two chains) in length, descends forty-seven feet to Lake Windogoostogoon, seven and three-quarter miles long, and lesser lakes connected with it, which, by a dam at the head of French Portage below them, will give a navigable reach of about eleven and a half miles, in which there is a fall of seven feet now.

From it, a portage of a mile and three-quarters descends a hundred feet to Lac Français, which, with Lake Kaogasica, or Pickerel Lake, makes a slack water navigation of nearly eleven miles and three-quarters.

Then there are two short portages, with a pond of a mile and a half between them, to be passed, by a road of two miles in length, with a descent of a hundred and twenty-four feet, to a fine, deep creek, sixty-six feet wide, which, at a mile and a half further, enters Sturgeon Lake, forming with it a deep navigable reach of sixteen miles. This reach Mr. Dawson proposes to extend downwards to twenty-eight miles, by damming the river at Island Portage, to flood out the rapids below Sturgeon Lake. The head of Sturgeon Lake is three hundred and thirty-three feet lower than the height of land at Prairie Portage, and only a hundred and twenty-five feet above the level of Rainy Lake, and is about forty-eight miles due east of it. By the course of the waters forming the route we are describing, the distance from the head of Sturgeon Lake to Rainy Lake is sixty-five miles.

These facts regarding Sturgeon Lake are worthy of attention, for in view of the proposal to construct a railroad from Fort William, or rather from Point de Meuron to Rainy Lake, which would touch the head of Sturgeon Lake, it is important to consider whether it would not be better to terminate the railroad and adopt the water route there.

As the forty-eight or fifty miles of direct distance from Sturgeon Lake to Rainy Lake would probably, in a rough country full of lakes, require one-fifth more, or sixty miles of railroad, costing, owing to the rocky unevenness of the surface, at least £600,000, the improvement of the river by locks and dams, to overcome a rise which is little more than one-third of that of the Welland Canal, would cost much less ; and we know that the line of water so improved could do more than four times as much business, and carry heavy freight at half the cost per ton. It would be more likely to give us command of the traffic, as it would bring the continuous navigation of the Lake of the Woods and Rainy Lake about fifty miles in direct distance nearer us. The supply of water is sufficient, as Sturgeon River is from three to six chains in width, with abundant lake reservoirs on its course and connected with it. If done on the same scale of dimensions and quality of work, and at the same expensive rate as the Rideau Canal, it would cost only £280,000, or less than half the cost of a railroad, —the lockage being little more than a quarter that of the Rideau.

If this were done, the remainder of the route we are describing would continue permanently to be the line of communication. But the same arguments, besides other reasons, point forcibly to the advantage of canalling the whole route, or that by the River Seine to Lac des Mille Lacs and Dog Lake, so as to reduce the use of railway to the least possible extent.

At Island Rapids, by which Sturgeon River descends ten feet into Pine Lake, a portage road of thirteen chains in length is required, or, in case of canalling, lockage of forty-five feet to overcome that fall, and flood out the small rapids on the twenty-eight and a half miles above it.

Pine Lake is an expansion of the River Nameaukan or Macan, a deep and powerful stream, the main branch of the Rainy River or Winnipeg. This lake presents a navigable reach of ten miles to its outlet, the Macan River, and extends further westward.

Then there are two miles of strong current terminating in Snake Falls, which may render a portage road of that length necessary; or in case of canalling a dam and double lock making seventeen feet lift, besides the additional height required in this and all other lockages mentioned, to meet the difference between high and low water.

Then after three miles of slack water, Crow Portage requires a road of nine chains in length, or a lock of ten feet lift.

Then follows a reach of eight and a half miles to the Great Falls, with shoals and two small rapids, which should be flooded out by damming up the water a few feet at the head of the falls, in case of canalling.

The Great Falls, sixteen feet in height, are now passed by a portage six chains in length. In the distance of four and a half miles from the Falls to Cross Lake, there is one rapid which descends ten feet, and another of seven feet fall, run by canoes. These, with the falls, would require thirty-six feet lockage, or a good portage road of four and a half miles. By following the south channel (the U. S. boundary), or the portage of two miles from the west extremity of Pine Lake to the level of Cross Lake, the difficulty here would be less, or the portages be reduced to one.

Then follows the navigable reach of Cross Lake, eight and a half miles long to Bare Portage, where a portage road of nearly a quarter of a mile in length is required, to the entrance of Rainy Lake, or a lock of eight and a half feet lift.

We have then thirty-six and three-quarter miles of deep navigation along Rainy Lake and Rainy River to its Great Falls, two miles beyond the lake. They are twenty-three feet in height, requiring a double lock at least.

Professor Hind says that Rainy Lake freezes over about 1st of December, and is open about 1st May.

The boundary line of the United States passes through Pine Lake, Cross Lake, Rainy Lake and River, and the Lake of the Woods.

Rainy River, which the route now follows, is a large, deep, navigable stream, averaging six hundred feet in width. Its course, from the Great Falls to the Lake of the Woods, is about seventy-four and a half miles. In this distance there are two small rapids; the Manitou, at thirty-one and a half miles down, falls two and a half feet in three chains of length, and the Long Rapid, at seven and a half miles further, falls three feet in five chains. It is said that as they are so short, a good steamer by getting under strong headway could ascend them. They have a fair depth of water, but may require improvement.

Leaving Rainy River, the route originally proposed traverses the Lake of the Woods and Lac Platte, connected with it, to its western extremity, a distance of eighty-four miles, forming, with Rainy River, an unbroken reach of navigation a hundred and fifty-eight and a half miles in length. From the west end of Lac Platte the distance to the Red River at Fort Garry, by the exploring line measured, is ninety-one and a half miles.

But on further examination, it was found that the best site for a road was to be had by leaving the Lake of the Woods at the extremity of its north-west arm, a long inlet extending south of Lac Platte. By doing so the route over the Lake of the Woods is reduced to fifty miles, and the land route from it to Fort Garry is nearly a hundred miles in length. This land route was traversed on horseback, and is an exceedingly favorable site for a railroad.

We may here make a few general remarks on the route from Lake Superior to Red River, which we have been describing. It naturally presents itself for consideration in two great divisions. The first part, from Fort William on Lake Superior to Rainy Lake, two hundred and six and a half miles in length by computation, consisting of eleven portage roads, varying from the ninth part of a mile to twenty-five miles in length—amounting together to forty-seven and a quarter miles of land road—and ten reaches of slack water, which, with the exception of one short piece of three miles, vary from seven and a half to forty miles in length, making together a hundred and fifty-nine and a quarter miles of water conveyance.

The second part, from the east end of Rainy Lake to Fort Garry on Red River, two hundred and sixty-one and a quarter miles in length by computation, consisting of a hundred and sixty-one and a quarter miles of unbroken navigation, excepting at Rainy River Falls, and a hundred miles of land road, from the north-west arm of the Lake of the Woods to Fort Garry.

Making a total distance by this route of four hundred and sixty-seven and three-quarter miles from Fort William to Fort Garry, of which there are a hundred and forty-seven and a quarter miles of land route, and three hundred and twenty and a half miles of water communication; the latter in twelve divisions, if no canalling be done.

Such is the line of boat and waggon communication with Red River which this route would afford, on the simple scale of improvement already commenced—by making the hundred and forty-seven miles of road required, one hundred of which is over an even and inexpensive site, partly prairie ground—and constructing three or perhaps four wooden dams, which would cost less than what some Ottawa lumberers would spend in improvements on a single river.

As to the character of the roads and navigable reaches so obtained, the roads, though costly to make, from their remoteness, and the frequently rocky or swampy character of the ground, would be as favorable for transport as good roads in Canada usually are; for the ascents and descents are not such as to render them otherwise.

The navigable reaches, though sometimes short, being deep lakes, flooded streams and large rivers, would, even without canalling, admit of boats drawing upwards of three feet of water in the shallowest portions of the line. The tonnage of such boats might be considerable; and in the greater waters, others of a larger size might be used as preferable. Large row-boats and barges with sails might be used on the short reaches, and steamboats on the longer ones. At first, no doubt boats like those of the Hudson's Bay Company, that could be drawn over the portages, would be used, till suitable boats were established on each reach.

It is to be observed that this navigation would not be subject to interruption from droughts, or obstruction from sand bars, like that of the shallow and swift tributaries of the Missouri, or even the Red River in Minnesota.

As soon as the portage roads were opened, there are plenty of enterprising men who would settle on them at the landings, and keep teams and waggons to do the transport on them, as on the Ottawa portages.

Such is the communication this route would afford if opened in an economical way for immediate use.

In the forgoing, by following the Macan River between Pine Lake and Cross Lake, for the purpose of connected description of the main stream, instead of the two mile portage between them adopted by Mr. Dawson, two portages are unnecessarily added, making together nearly five miles over-estimated as land carriage in all my calculations of this route, wherever they occur, in tables or otherwise.

CHAPTER XXVIII.

DESCRIPTION OF ROUTES CONTINUED.—CAPACITY OF ROUTE BY STURGEON LAKE COMBINED WITH RAILROAD.

Before proceeding further, it is well to consider the ultimate capacity of this route, if improved by lockage past the portages, from the head of Sturgeon Lake westward, with a railroad from that point to Fort William, as already mentioned, and another from the north-west arm of the Lake of the Woods to Fort Garry.

This route, so modified, presents three naturally distinct parts : First,—a line of a railroad from Point de Meuron, on the Kammisti-quoia, eight miles west of Fort William, to the head of Sturgeon Lake, which with one-fifth added to the direct distance for una-voidable sinuosities, due to the nature of the country, would be one hundred and twenty-two miles in length.

Second,—a water communication of two hundred and twenty-six miles in length from the head of Sturgeon Lake to the extremity of the north-west arm of the Lake of the Woods, to be rendered continously navigable throughout, on a scale much exceeding that of the original Erie Canal, by the construction of sixteen locks, equal to about a hundred and forty feet of lockage.

Third,—a railroad of a hundred miles in length from the Lake of the Woods to Fort Garry, including only one-tenth additional on the direct distance for sinuosities—the ground being highly favorable.

Making a total distance to Fort Garry, of four hundred and forty-eight miles, of which nearly one-half would be unbroken navigation.

To assist in judging of the natural advantages and capacity of this water system, it is to be observed that Sturgeon River, a strong stream from three to six chains wide, would, with its lakes, be converted into a level sheet of water twenty-eight miles in length ; and that the Nameaukan, next, followed through its expansions to Rainy Lake, is equal to fully twice the River Rideau in passing volume of water. At and below its great falls, where the principal works on it are required, its waters can be turned off by the south side of the island and the bed laid nearly bare for the construction of the locks, if the river be followed.

As Mr. Dawson's and Mr. Napier's separate levellings very nearly agree, though depending on estimation in parts, in making the head of Strugeon Lake a hundred and twenty-five feet higer than Rainy Lake, if we allow for the descent of the river in parts on the sixty-five miles of distance, a lockage downwards of a hundred and seventeen feet in fourteen locks, as described, would seem sufficient. The remaining two locks would be required at the Falls of Rainy River, as already mentioned.

As Rainy Lake is said to open about the first of May, we may assume that the waters of Sturgeon River, within fifty miles of it, and not much higher, will be open for navigation nearly as soon as it, though they may not remain open, like it, so late as the first of December.

Wooden dams would be by far the most economical and most suitable on such a route. The tenacity and strength of wood work is much greater than stone, and under water it never decays. It would do well enough also for the lock walls if well secured, backed solidly with stones, earth and brushwood, in broken layers. The parts that could not be kept generally wet or under water could be easily repaired.

LINE OF RAILROAD FROM FORT WILLIAM TO STURGEON LAKE.

Of the character of the country between Fort William, on Lake Superior, and Sturgeon Lake, we are not entirely ignorant. An exploration was made through it sixty miles westward, though not with a view to a railway. Though rough and rocky, it was found to be lower and less rugged than the country towards Lake Superior, which is mountainous, very rough and precipitous.

As the height of the water-shed to be traversed is probably about a thousand feet, its elevation is not such as necessarily to present an unsurmountable obstacle in a distance of a hundred and twenty-two miles. Without an adequate exploration for the purpose, nothing can be said with certainty as to the quality of the railway line it might afford. It is believed that a practicable railway could be made by sufficient expenditure. On such terms it would be well worth making, if we could do no better. But even if a line of favorable general grades be found, yet, owing to the unarable character of the country generally, the frequent out-cropping of beds of primitive rock, and unevenness of surface, the cost will probably be at least thirty per cent. greater than in an even arable country.

The conditions presented by the country to be traversed are all unfavorable to a railway, which would besides be destitute of the usual advantage of being useful in winter, being subsidiary to a water communication.

For water communication, on the other hand, the conditions are unusually favorable—abundant summit supply—rivers and chains of deep lakes nearly in the line desired, offering extensive sheets of slack water, with the difference of level, accumulated so as to be most advantageously dealt with by lockage.

LINE OF RAILROAD FROM THE LAKE OF THE WOODS TO RED RIVER.

For the line of Railroad from the Lake of the Woods to Red River, on the other hand, the conditions are in the highest degree favorable—an alluvial plain country, where the bridging and grading required will be very unusually little. Some low embankments, in shallow swamps with hard bottoms, will, however, be required. The road will not be useless in winter; there will be sawn lumber to be carried to the prairie settlements from the forests on the Lake of the Woods and its tributaries, and fuel from the extensive beds of excellent peat that abound; and the line will be in the proper position to form part of a direct interior railroad to Montreal.

These details are given so fully respecting this route, involving the construction of a railway to Sturgeon Lake, not for the purpose of setting it forth as the best we have, which is very questionable, but because we are already in possession of sufficient information respecting it to give us reason to believe that, such as it is, if we had no better, its natural capacity and advantages are such, notwithstanding the disadvantage of a very expensive piece of railway, as to give us, through our own territory, a highway for the heavy traffic of our north-west prairie lands, decidedly superior to any other known, not within our territory, as will immediately more clearly appear.

SUPERIOR CHARACTER OF THE WATER COMMUNICATION.

Continuing to speak of the water communication, as it would be, if improved by lockage from the head of Sturgeon Lake westward, it divides itself into two parts, distinctly different in character and condition.

First, the waters of the Sturgeon River and the Nameaukan to Rainy Lake, sixty-five miles, where nearly all the lockage is required; secondly, the remaining hundred and sixty-one miles, from the east end of Rainy Lake to the end of the north-west arm of the Lake of the Woods. As the latter is already a magnificent stretch of inland navigation, of great capacity, requiring lockage only at Rainy Falls, it is to the Sturgeon and Nameaukan part only that the term canalling can properly be applied.

To engineers, the favorable character of the navigation it would seemingly afford, will be sufficiently apparent from what has been already stated respecting it. To enable those who are not familiar with such subjects, to judge of it, and of the economy in rendering it available, and in the after use of it, it may be necessary to explain that the comparative value of such a navigation depends on the length of it, compared with the amount of lockage, alike as regards the cost of making the locks and works connected with them, and the maintaining and working of them; and on account of the delay to vessels in passing through them; and also upon the capacity of the navigation obtained, as the economy of transport by it will be in proportion to the size of the vessels that can use it.

The least favorable, the Sturgeon and Nameaukan section, compares very advantageously with other river and canal navigations of the best description.

The Erie Canal, which has been so exceedingly useful and beneficial, has a total lockage of 692 feet in 363 miles of length, or about $1\frac{9}{100}$ feet of average lockage to the mile.

The Rideau Canal, which was exceedingly useful till superseded by the St. Lawrence Canals, has a total lockage of $446\frac{1}{4}$ feet, (or by adding the lift of the locks in detail 454 feet 11 inches,) in its length of $126\frac{3}{4}$ miles or $3\frac{51}{100}$ feet per mile.

The Sturgeon and Nameaukan section of this route, with 117 feet of lockage on its length of 65 miles, would have an average lockage of only $1\frac{80}{100}$ feet per mile.

As to its capacity, it would be, as stated, much greater than that of the Erie Canal as originally made, the depth of which was four feet, its locks ninety feet in length and fifteen feet in width.

The Sturgeon and Nameaukan section, according to published and unpublished information, apparently will afford, when improved by lockage, a depth of at least five feet, which is that of the Rideau Canal; and were it desirable the locks might be a hundred and eighty feet long and thirty-five feet wide, that is to say, equal to five times the original capacity of the Erie Canal; or greater if required.

Besides the greater capacity, this navigation would admit of the use of steamboats, and of their going at full speed, as there would be no artificial banks to be injured by the swell they occasioned.

Mr. McAlpine, a high authority, in his report of the Erie Canal, states that from 1848 to 1852, the proportion of tonnage transported on the Erie Canal and the New York Central Railroad, was as 32 on the Canal to 1 on the Railroad, and still more favorable to the Canal as to heavy articles.

Now, as a Canal of greater capacity admits of freight being carried at a lower rate, it seems grossly evident, that, even the Sturgeon and Nameaukan section of our route, with less lockage and five times the capacity—and obtained at no cost for canalling, excepting the locks—would have a much greater advantage over railroads for transport than the Erie Canal possessed.

It is equally evident, that if we apply the comparison to the whole line of 226 miles of water communication on this route, when so improved, with only 140 feet of lockage, or only $\frac{62}{100}$ of a foot to the mile,.the superiority over any railroad of equal length will be much greater still.

These details and comparative views are gone over for the purpose of establishing a basis of comparison, in considering what advantage we possess as to routes of access to our interior territory, a question of much importance to us in relation to it, and one on which conclusions against the practicability of our maintaining communication advantageously with that territory have been drawn hastily, and I would venture to say, in error.

The details given may seem prolix, but no opinion of value on this important question can be formed without some reference to them ; and I beg to remark, generally, that these and other details on the subject of communication are quoted from the reports of our explorers, with no pretension in using them beyond that of roughly approaching such an opinion or suggesting investigation.

As the information we have of the Baril Portage and Sturgeon Lake route is a great deal more ample than that before the public, respecting the route by the River Seine, the opportunity is taken of using it to show the character of the navigation that would be afforded by either of these routes.

It is necessary to explain, that in setting forth a line of railroad to Sturgeon Lake, as more advantageous than one to Rainy Lake, it is by no means meant to show that to be the best means of communication we can have. On the contrary, the Sturgeon Lake route admits of being canalled throughout, with facility from Lac des Mille Lacs ; its deep lakes being highly favorable, and Lac des Mille Lacs affording an abundant summit supply of water. It would admit of the water communication being carried through even to Dog Lake, corresponding in that respect with the Seine route, presenting, like it, the advantage of greater economy, alike in the construction of necessary works and in the cost of transport on it.

ROUTE BY THE RIVER SEINE.

The Seine route corresponds with that now under improvement, as far as Lac des Mille Lacs, which is common to both, together with the slack water reach of Dog Lake, already described.

The distances here given do not exactly agree with Mr. Dawson's tables. I have used those stated in Mr. Napier's tables,— not as being more correct, but because they are least favorable, in order to avoid seeming to desire to over-estimate the comparative value of our interior route of water communication.

The difference arises from the length of most of the slack water reaches having been necessarily determined merely by estimation or cursory survey.

On this route, Savanne River and Lac des Mille Lacs form together fifty-six miles of navigable water, which might be increased in length and depth by damming.

Lac des Mille Lacs is about eight hundred and thirty-two feet above Lake Superior—fifty-five feet lower than the height of land and four hundred and three feet higher than Rainy Lake, the level of which is attained by the Seine about a hundred miles, by its course, below Lac des Mille Lacs.

In that distance the Seine presents thirteen short reaches of navigable water, of from about three to twelve miles in length, separated by rapids or falls; the last and greatest being at the Twelve Portages, where it falls seventy-two feet in twelve miles, to the level of Rainy Lake.

To render this river navigable from Rainy Lake to the head of Savanne River, near the height of land, say a hundred and sixty miles, with a small allowance for the descent of the stream, about three hundred and eighty feet of lockage would be required; making an average of about $2\frac{37}{100}$ feet per mile, or less than two-thirds of the rate of lockage per mile on the Rideau Canal. To state the matter more simply, a navigation thirty-four miles longer than the Rideau Canal would be obtained, with sixty feet less of lockage than it has.

As the head of this navigation is, by the route now being opened, only sixty-six miles from Thunder Bay, near Fort William, it might be connected by a railroad of about that length.

Or, (though a better way could most probably be found by the water courses,) as the height of land is only fifty-five feet higher than Lac des Mille Lacs, and is described as a sandy flat,—by a dam of thirty-five feet in height at the outlet of Mille Lacs, and a cutting of from thirteen to twenty-five feet in depth, over a length of five miles, the waters of that lake would be carried over the height of land, with a depth of five feet, by a downward lockage of a hundred and nineteen feet in that distance, to the head of the slack water of Dog Lake, which a dam of thirty-four feet in height at its outlet would obtain; using Mr. Napier's levels as least favorable.

This would extend the navigation thirty-seven miles further, and bring it within twenty-five miles of the landing of Thunder Bay, on Lake Superior.*

On the distance of a hundred and ninety-seven miles, from the foot of Dog Lake to Rainy Lake, the amount of ascent and descent to be overcome by lockage would be five hundred and twenty-nine feet, (that is a hundred and sixty-three feet less than the Erie Canal,) making an average of $2\frac{63}{100}$ feet per mile, or about one quarter less per mile than the Rideau Canal.

As the Seine drains an area of about three thousand superficial miles, or more than double what the River Rideau does, and Lac des Mille Lacs, which would be the summit reservoir of this route, receives the waters of upwards of seven hundred superficial miles of a proverbially rainy country, or more than double the area that the Rideau has to furnish its summit supply, there is little reason to doubt the sufficiency of it. The capacity of the route to afford a sufficient depth of channel seems unquestionable, as twenty-four feet additional lockage would apparently flood the river to levels throughout.

The practicability of this route, therefore, resolves itself into a mere question of cost. The works required on it are not of a nature to render the expense extraordinary, and the commerce of the interior may, at no very remote period, be such as to render the opening of the route in this manner profitable.

It would then consist of three hundred and fifty-eight miles of continuous navigation, from the lower end of Dog Lake to the extremity of the north-west arm of the Lake of the Woods, the average lockage on which would be only $1\frac{57}{100}$ feet per mile, and a hundred and twenty-five miles of railroad, that is, twenty-five from Thunder Bay, on Lake Superior, to Dog Lake, and a hundred from the Lake of the Woods to Fort Garry, on the Red River,—making the total length of the route four hundred and eighty-three miles.

The continuous navigation would be nine miles longer than the

* Since the above was written, Mr. Dawson, by further survey this summer, (1868), has found a new and more favorable route by which the navigable water of Lac des Mille Lacs can be carried through the height of land and brought within about forty miles of Lake Superior, at a cost so small as to admit of the route being made immediately available in connection with the greater part of the Dog Portage Road already commenced.

This important improvement dispenses with the interruption of the ten or eleven miles of portage road at the height of land, which is crossed at a thirty feet lower level, through a ravine, by which the waters of Lake Shebandowan on the River Matawin, a branch of the Kaministiquoia, can be flooded through, in an unbroken reach of thirty miles, to Lac des Mille Lacs. It shortens the route to Rainy Lake twenty-five miles—reduces the obstructions on it to a few short portages, amounting in all to about six-and-a-half miles ; and in case of future canalling will not require the five miles of deep cutting and about a hundred and fifty feet of lockage necessary in crossing the height of land from Lac des Mille Lacs to Dog Lake by the old route.

main trunk of the Erie Canal, but would have forty feet less lockage, the average of which would be only $1\frac{57}{100}$ per mile on the whole.

As steamers of a good size could be used on it, and often at full speed, it would be superior to a canal. Possessing even more than the usual advantage that a canal has, in capacity and economy of transport, over a railroad, and reducing the extent of the latter necessary to a minimum, it would render this route better than any other known for heavy freight, and therefore for that of the interior generally.*

In relation to our routes of water communication to Red River, the following remarks on the neglect of canal and slack water navigation, contained in an article in the "Scientific American" for January, 1868, may not be out of place.

The writer says "this neglect is in a great measure due to the mania for building railroads, which has for many years past absorbed the attention and capital of the American people, without yielding a return at all proportionate to the outlay."

After speaking of the disproportionately small outlay, in rendering streams completely navigable that are already partly so, he says, "It is not at all essential that streams should be large or deep to obtain sufficient depth of channel for barges or small steam-boats, as a few feet of water would amply suffice for vessels of the requisite tonnage for inland trade, steam propulsion being perfectly admissable (there being no artificial banks to be washed as with canals); the cost of transport would be so low as to permit the carrying of all available freights, and the employment of fast steam-packets would provide a means of travel more pleasant, and quite as rapid, as the accommodation trains on many railroads."

These remarks would seem to be applicable, with much more force, to the generally large and deep waters of our route to Red River. We may appropriately add to them the opinion of Mr. Jarvis, an Engineer of great experience in such matters, expressed in his report to the Canadian Government, on the proposed Caughnawaga Canal. He says that many persons suppose that Railroads will in a great measure supersede Canals, but that it is evident that this conclusion has been reached without consideration, *especially when applied to channels of great trade.* Speaking

---

* I have obtained much valuable information on this and other subjects of this pamphlet, verbally, beyond what appears in his Report, from Mr. Dawson, whose opinion on such matters is of great value, from his ability as an Engineer, and his experience in River Work in new countries. As such information, though exceedingly copious and valuable, cannot be quoted in detail, being unpublished, it is only in this manner that it can be adequately acknowledged. Mr. Dawson, however, is not committed to any error in fact or in judgment I may have made in using it.

A. J. R.

of the trade of the West, he says, "In regard to the trade under
consideration, it may be remarked, that the great mass is composed of bulky and heavy articles, of such general value as materially feels the weight of transport charges, especially if the distance moved be great, and cannot under the general condition of
the market afford to pay much additional, to save a few days' time
in transit."

Now, as a remoteness which will place even lighter articles of
commerce at the disadvantage spoken of by Mr. Jarvis is unquestionably the greatest drawback which the prosperity of our
interior prairie land will be subject to, and as there will be many
articles, products of agricultural and other industry, the bare pos-
sibility of exporting which will depend on even the slightest difference in cost of freight, it is evident that we should avail ourselves to the utmost degree of water communication, wherever
cheaper transport can be obtained by it, even if at greater original
cost in utilizing it; much more therefore should we do so where it
can be made available at less expense.

It cannot be argued that water communication being shut for
a long winter is a reason for not doing so; for as long as water
communication is to form a great part of the route to Red River
not only beyond Fort William, but also in getting there, it will
necessarily govern the utility of the Railways depending upon it
and the great depth of snow that falls in the slope towards Lake
Superior is somewhat against the utility of any Railroad there in
winter.

COST OF IMPROVING OR CANALLING RIVERS.

Having assumed $40,000 a mile,* or say thirty per cent. over
the cost of our cheapest railways in Canada, as the least possible
cost of a railroad from Lake Superior to the Rainy Lake waters
$30,000 would be in proportion a very ample rate at which to
estimate the railroad from the Lake of the Woods to Red River
Together with these rates it is necessary to form some idea of the
cost of improving or canalling rivers, in order to form any opinion
of the comparative economy of each as available means of com
munication. Difficult as it may at first sight appear, we have the
means of approximating the probable limit of cost of such improve
ment, in a general way it is true, but in such a way as may be
accepted as reliable.

Such river work is widely different from ordinary canalling
The length of the navigation throws no light whatever on the cost

* The average cost of Railways already made in Upper and Lower Canada i
$66,222$\frac{71}{100}$ per mile.

it is the difference of level—the dams and locks required to overcome it—that determine the cost.

We have for data as to that, a case of the same kind, the Rideau Canal, on which the lockage is 455 feet, or only one-sixth less than that required to make a continuous navigation like that of the Rideau, from Dog Lake, twenty-five miles from Lake Superior, through to Rainy Lake. The Rideau Canal is also a system of rivers and lakes. Its locks are 134 feet long, 33 wide, and 5 feet depth of water. The ordinary width of canal excavated is seventy-five feet. There are forty-seven locks. Twenty-four dams, varying from 5 to 60 feet in height, amounting in total length to 15,472 feet; and of excavated canal the total length is 16½ miles. By an official synopsis of the Royal Engineer Department, for it, the total expenditure for works (including £23,141 6s. 10¾d. for gates), was £648,686 13s. 3¾d. stg.; for establishment, i. e., management, £110,279 19s. 8d.; total for works, not including land damages,* £758,966 12s. 11¾d. stg.; equal to currency, £923,409 1s. 8¼d.

As the cost of management was rather greater than we would feel necessary, we may put the worth of the work for our purpose at £900,000 currency.

Those who have seen the stupendous stone dam, sixty feet in height, that was built at Jones' Falls,—the bridge and locks at Ottawa, and the 6,024 feet of dam built at Kingston Mills, will be satisfied that the magnitude and style of the works are more than the utmost we require for our Red River Route. Speaking from having served on the Rideau at the time, some of the work, at least, was extravagantly paid for; yet even at that high rate and style of work, water communication would cost less in construction than a railroad.

Thus, canalling from Dog Lake to Rainy Lake, requiring one-sixth more lockage than the Rideau Canal, would cost one-sixth more, or...	£1,050,000 cy.
Add Railroad from Lake Superior to Dog Lake, 25 miles, at £10,000 a mile	250,000 cy.
	£1,300,000 cy.
Railroad from Fort William to Rainy Lake at £10,000 a mile, 180 miles.......................	1,800,000 cy.
Difference gained by canalling rivers	£500,000 cy.

But as canalling on the scale of the Rideau, with a capacity of

* I am indebted to Wm. Clegg, Esquire, late of that Department, who compiled t, for correct information as to these details.

transport equal to many railroads taken together, would be out of all proportion with the one railroad, to be worked in conjunction with it, canalling on the small scale of the Erie Canal as first made would be quite sufficient for many years. But if the locks were made nearly equal to those of the Rideau, say with four feet depth of water, and their walls and the dams built of wood, of which the supply is said by Mr. Dawson to be abundant, the rate of cost might be much under two-thirds of that of the Rideau, making the whole cost of the route about £900,000 cy., from Fort William on Lake Superior to Rainy Lake, or half the cost of a railway between the same points.

The top timbers over water only, would, say after ten years, require repair, those under water would not decay. A railroad would be useless until completed through. The water communication would be serviceable in the meantime, with the improvements already commenced; and its usefulness would be increased as the works advanced.

CHAPTER XXIX.

COMPARISON OF KNOWN ROUTES TO RED RIVER.

Having considered the character of the Dog Lake Route, now under improvement, and the capacity of that part of it from Sturgeon Lake westward, as a separate route, in connexion with a railroad from Fort William to it, and also the Seine route, we can now compare them with other known or proposed routes to Red River Settlement.

For that purpose, the routes described are exhibited in the following table, together with the route by Chicago and St. Paul's, and a proposed route by Superior City and Crow Wing, in Minnesota, and also a practicable direct railroad line, by the valley of the Ottawa and Montreal River, and thence westward through the interior.

APPROXIMATE COMPARATIVE TABLE of known and proposed routes from Montreal to Red River Settlement.

	1	2	3	4	5	6	7
	By direct rail: By railroad to the port: route: to lake Pries: route: by Proposed railroad: By Dog Lake and: By Dog Lake and: road route up the Chicago and: St. by Fort William railroad: in Fort route from Supe-: River Settle- can-: River Settle-: Ottawa and Mon-: Paul's, thence by and Rainy Lake William to Star: rior city, by low-: aled to Rainy: Mouth and Bot-: treal River, and thence to Fort: as now: being from Lake canal: Wina through: Lake, with rail-: Lake, and so and: toin Lake of the: through the in-Garry, or partly open-: with road ing Stage-on-La Rive: road to lake of the: Woods by White: Garry.: ferior: to Fort by imperfect: tran-: from Lake of the Saskatchewan Rive: Woods by White: Mouth and Bot-: ficial of Red Woods to Fort: or St. to Rainy Lake: Garry.: and Bot River: River in Minne. Garry, Red River, and railroad and from: to Root River:: sota.: Lake of the Woods: : to Fort Garry					
	Miles.	Miles.	Miles.	Miles.	Miles.	Miles.	Miles.
On Lakes Huron and Superior (from Collingwood)	......	......	54	54	654	54	54
On large or continuous inland navigation, (with small lockage)	......	......	......	(a) 164	......	......	......
On do. with moderate do.	......	......	(a) 164	(a) 64	......	(f) 164	(i) 164
On do. with great lockage.	......	530	......	......	......	412	(i) 157 (i)
On imperfect or small do. connected by portage roads	......	......	(b) 124	......	......	......	(i) 100
Continuous land road and portages	......	......	(c) 164	(d) 92	348	125	25
Railroad	1,367	1,257	442	412	412	412	412
Total distances	1,367	1,787	1,463	1,434	1,611	1,454	1,454

(a) One double lock required on this.

(b) In ten pieces, connected by portages.

(c) 100 miles in one piece, and 47¼ in 11 portages.

(d) From Montreal to Collingwood by rail.

* Area of the locks, say one-half greater than those of Rideau Canal, with same depth.

(e) Continuous—average lockage 1$\frac{82}{100}$ of a foot per mile.

(f) Continuous—average lockage 1$\frac{57}{100}$ do. do. or 1$\frac{34}{100}$ less than the Erie Canal.

(g) 2$\frac{69}{100}$ feet per mile, or ¼ less than the Rideau Canal.

(h) Average lockage 3$\frac{61}{100}$ feet per mile, or 1$\frac{49}{100}$ more than Rideau Canal.

Total Fall to Lake Winnipeg, 361 feet, or 31 feet more than Welland Canal.

(i) Continuous—connecting with all the navigable waters of Red River, Lake Winnipeg and River Saskatchewan, to the Rocky Mountains.

To form a comparitive estimate of the value of these routes, fe
the transport of heavy freight, we may apply to them the followin
rates of transport, per ton, per mile, given by Mr. McAlpine in hi
report on the canals of the State of New York, which are considere
of high authority by Engineers :

On the Lakes, long voyage............................... 2 mills.
    Do.   short do. .... 3 to 4 mills.
St. Lawrence and Mississippi........................... 3   "
Tributaries, Mississippi................................ 5 to 10 mills
Canals, Erie enlargement............................... 4   "
Other canals but shorter............................... 5 to 6   "
Erie Canal, ordinary size.............................. 5   "
Canals with great lockage.............................. 6 to 8   "
Railroads transporting coal............................ 6 to 10 "
    Do.   not for coal, favorable grades and lines. 12½   "
    Do.   steep grades.................................... 15 to 25 "

These rates include nothing for tolls on canals, or to cover co
of construction of railroads.   Mr. Jervis, in his report on the pro
posed Caughnawaga Canal, says the actual cost of transporting
ton of freight from Ogdensburg to Rouse's Point, on the railroae
by the report of the State Engineer, was 11 and 7-10 mills a mil
allowing no profit on capital expended in construction.

How much more would have to be added, in the form of tol
on the canalled rivers, or additional rates on railroads, to cover th
costs of construction, no practical man would like to say, withou
deliberate estimation, based on specific survey. But we ma
safely assume, that on the improved river reaches, where the
was little lockage, it would be small, compared with what
would be on a railroad, especially if wooden dams and lock
were used, and that on the great central reach of Rainy Lake an
River, and the Lake of the Woods, it would be next to nothing.

We have to bear in mind also, in judging of the comparativ
value of these routes, that where railroads are proposed to b
used, in connexion with reaches of water communication, the
usefulness, in that way, will be limited to the period of open nav
gation, and that therefore their usefulness in winter, which und
ordinary circumstances gives them a great advantage over canal
cannot be reckoned in their favor in this comparison.

Applying the foregoing rates to the approximate table of length
we have the bare cost of moving a ton of goods from Montreal t
Red River Settlement, by the respective routes, as follows :

By the Grand Trunk and other railways, *via* Chicago and S
Paul's, if railway communication were completed from St. Paul
530 miles to Fort Garry :

1,767 miles of railway transport at 12½ mills
    a ton, per mile..................................... $22.09

By proposed direct route up the Ottawa and
Montreal River valleys and through the
interior to Fort Garry—
1,110 miles, at 12½ mills a ton, per mile..... $13.87
  257 " at 15 " on account of
         probable steeper grades........... 3.86
1,367 $17.73

By proposed route of railway from Fort William to Sturgeon Lake, canalling Sturgeon
and Nameaukan Rivers to Rainy Lake,
and railroad from the Lake of the Woods
to Fort Garry—
442 miles by rail from Montreal to Collingwood, at 12½ mills a ton, per mile.... $ 5.52
534 miles by the Lakes to Fort William, at 2
  mills a ton, per mile..................... 1.07
122 miles by rail to Sturgeon Lake, at 15
  mills a ton, per mile..................... 1.83
226 miles River and Lake navigation, at 4
  mills a ton, per mile..................... 0.90
100 miles railway, Lake of the Woods to
  Fort Garry, at 12½ mills a ton per mile 1.25
1,424 $10.57

It will be at once seen that as there is so much Lake and other
natural navigation on this last route, the additional charges to cover
"costs of construction" on it must be small, compared with either
of the preceding.

By proposed Railway route from Superior City to Crow Wing.
through Minnesota, and thence to Fort Garry if constructed:
442 miles by rail to Collingwood,
548 miles Superior City to Fort Garry.

990 miles at 12½ mills.......................... $12.37
654 miles by Lakes from Collingwood to
  Superior Dity, at 2 mills.............. 1.31
1,644 $13.68

By proposed route by Dog Lake and River
Seine, if canalled through from Dog
Lake to Rainy Lake—
442 miles rail to Collingwood.................. $ 5.52
534 miles Lakes to Fort William.............. 1.07
25 miles rail to Dog Lake, at 20 mills, on
  account of steeper grades.............. 0.50

358 miles River and Lakes from Dog Lake
    to end of north-west arm of Lake of
    the Woods, at 4 mills.................... 1.43
100 miles rail to Fort Garry, at 12½ mills... 1.25
————   ————— $ 9.77
1,459 miles.

If 100 miles of canal were made from the Lake of
    the Woods to Fort Garry, instead of railway, there
    would be a reduction of 55 cents a ton, reducing
    the above to... $ 9.22
And the cost by Sturgeon Lake route to.............. 10.02

As already mentioned, these rates are very far from showing the total cost of transport on canals and railroads; but being adopted by Engineers as indicating the bare cost of movement of freight, they may be considered as sufficient to enable us to form a general idea of the comparative advantage that the routes respectively offer, as ultimate highways for the transport of heavy freight to and from our interior territories.

The difference shown by them in favor of the routes through our own territory, is such as to warrant our believing that they possess that advantage in a greater degree than any other known routes.

CHAPTER XXX.

DIRECT RAILROAD ROUTE TO RED RIVER BY THE VALLEY OF THE OTTAWA.

The probability of a direct railroad route being found by the valley of the Ottawa, to Red River, has been to a great degree confirmed, as already mentioned, by the recent survey of the Montreal River, a tributary which joins the Ottawa in Lake Temiscaming.

This route for a railway to the Pacific was, I believe, first proposed by Col. Carmichael Smith, probably from information obtained from officers of the Hudson's Bay Company.

From Pembroke, the contemplated termination of the Brockville and Ottawa Railroad, there is a favorable site for it along the Ottawa to the Matawan, though the soil is there generally too poor for settlement. It might, with little loss of distance, be carried more to the West, through the interior, where the land is not so unfavorable for cultivation.

Beyond this, the best ground would be found, alike for the road and settlement, by passing near the head of the Matawan, and thence directly to the Montreal River, about two hundred and eighty-five miles by this route from the City of Ottawa.

Thence, north-westward about ninety-nine miles by a very direct and highly favorable course, along the Montreal River, over a flat country, suitable for settlement for two-thirds of the distance, to the north elbow of that river, and the northern extremity, in lat. 48° N., of the long lake that receives it, to the water-shed; immediately beyond which commences the level clay country, which extends to Hudson's Bay.

Thence, in a west-north-west course, in the edge of the clay country, say a hundred and twelve miles, including sinuosities, to the meridian of the termination of Provincial Surveyor D. Sinclair's west line, run from the Montreal River.

So far the country is now known; the level clay country, which is here twenty miles north of Mr. Sinclair's line, continues north-westward; how far is not definitely known. This nearly direct line proposed would pass fifty or sixty miles north of the termination of Mr. Sinclair's line; his line is a hundred and five miles in length. It lies altogether in a country which, though presenting no serious obstacle to the passing of a railway line through it, is exceedingly poor, sandy and rocky soil, unfit for cultivation. The clay country north of it is at least superior in that respect. It is worthy of remark here, that New Brunswick House, where Mr. Gladman resided, and describes the cultivation of grain, including wheat, to have been successful, lies about a hundred and ten miles northward, and a little to the west of the termination of Mr. Sinclair's line, which is from thirty to forty miles north of the water-shed, from which the branches of Moose River descend towards Hudson's Bay. Our proposed line would therefore be about ninety miles north of the water-shed here.

From the meridian of the termination of Mr. Sinclair's line, to long. 86° W., a hundred and sixty-eight miles, and even to long. 88° W., a hundred and eight miles further westward, including one-fifth for sinuosities, we have but little knowledge of the country over which our direct route would pass. Strictly speaking, a straight line from Montreal to Fort Garry, would touch the northerly bays of Lake Superior, near Pic Island; and the country along the shore of the lake is well known to be mountainous and unsuitable for a railway line; but as it is known that the country behind is more favorable, and as the length of the line would not be increased in any appreciable degree by carrying it forty miles further north, but on the contrary probably be slightly diminished, by having much fewer minor sinuosities, from being in better ground, it is assumed that our route would be carried there.

What little we do know is definite and favorable; the line would be situated nearly altogether, if not quite so, in the level clay country, north of the height of land, on waters flowing to Hudson's Bay, till it approaches Lake Nipigon, near long. 88° W.

This character of the country, which has long been well known to the officers of the Hudson's Bay Company, and has been confirmed as far as recent surveys of the northerly waters of the Ottawa have extended, is referred to by Provincial Surveyor Herric, in his report of his exploratory survey, in the country north of Lake Superior.

He says: "From inquiries made amongst the Indians, as well as from the officers of the Hudson's Bay Company who have travelled much through the country, I am informed, that after from thirty to fifty miles of hilly country, round Lake Superior, is passed, a level country is reached, which extends from the height of land, between Lake Superior and the Red River Settlement, east, for several hundred miles and along the north of the sources of the tributaries of the Ottawa. If, then, at any future period it may be proposed to connect Canada with the Red River Settlement by railroad, it does not appear that much difficulty will be experienced on this part of the route." The same description of the intervening country has long been given by officers of the Hudson's Bay Company, stationed on the northern waters of the Ottawa.

Passing south of Lake Nipigon, and crossing the River Nipigon at 18 miles from long. 88° W., difficulty would be encountered on this line from the rugged and hilly nature of the country, but from the character of the valleys no doubt a fair passage could be obtained.

Before proceeding further we may notice a few facts as to the elevation of the country.

The ridge of maximum elevation, between Lake Huron and Hudson's Bay, is a continuation of the anticlinal axis which traverses Lake Temiscaming on the Ottawa, at the mouth of the Montreal River, about lat. 47° 07′ N. It continues westward, a little to the north of that parallel, till approaching Lake Superior it turns up towards Michipicoten. Mr. Murray, the Asst. Prov. Geologist, traced the waters of the Sturgeon River of Lake Nipissing, and the Wahnapetec, which flows to Lake Huron, up to an elevation of more than 930 feet above the level of the sea, with lofty hills to the northward rising 700 feet higher, or 1,630 feet above the sea.

From this high range the head waters of Moose River, as ascertained by recent survey, flow northward to Hudson's Bay, and even the Montreal River flows from it northward to near lat. 48° N., whence it turns abruptly and flows southward a hundred miles to Lake Temiscaming.

So much does the country fall to the northward of this range that the height of land, between Lac La Quinze on the Ottawa above Lake Temiscaming, and the tributaries of Hudson's Bay is scarcely fifty feet higher than the surface of the main Ottawa or only about 830 above the level of the sea; * and it is over a similar low level that the proposed line of railway, by the valley of the Ottawa and Montreal River, passes the Laurentides, and enters the level clay country of the north.

Traversing the branches of Moose River from forty to ninety miles north of their sources, which are in the high range mentioned the line would still be in a comparatively low country. In long 87° W., it would cross a branch of the Albany River on Hudson's Bay, which has its source within six miles of Lake Superior; so near does the trough of Hudson's Bay there approach the lake.

Passing south of Lake Nipigon it would be again necessary to enter the trough of the St. Lawrence, but at no great elevation Lake Nipigon being only four hundred feet above Lake Superior

Lake Nipigon is the last and the most romantic of the lakes o the St. Lawrence. By the highly interesting though brief repor of Mr. Armstrong, it is ninety-five miles long and sixty-five mile wide, but full of islands. Its south end is about fifty miles nortl from Nipigon Bay.

Towards Lake Superior the mountains or high grounds rise to a thousand feet above that lake; at the south end of Lake Nipigon they are noted as being less elevated, and there is much good land in the valleys.

From the River Nipigon, a hundred and ninety-three mile: westward, to the meridian of the south end of Lac Seul, little i: known of the country through which a direct route would pass.

As to the elevation of the water-shed to be traversed, we may safely assume that it is no higher than Prairie Portage on the Savanne River route, which is 887 feet above Lake Superior; fo the western feeder of Lake Nipigon, and the Fire Steel River, a branch of the Seine, head together in the same water-shed a littl north of Prairie Portage.

As a general characteristic, the country is known to become lower and more even northward from the high ground toward: Lake Superior.

From the meridian of Lac Seul westward, to the outlet of the Lake of the Woods, a hundred and thirty-four miles, the ground over which the direct route would pass is reported, by those who know it, to be of such a nature as to present no important obsta cles of elevation, though the lakes to be avoided would cause

* Survey of the Upper Ottawa from Lac La Quinze to Grand Lac, and of La Abbitibbi and Canoe Route connecting them, by Prov. Surveyor L. Russell.

ncreased sinuosity, and the roughness of the surface might give ncreased expense in grading.

From the outlet of the Lake of the Woods, to the west end of he part of it called Lac Platte, forty miles, the ground is known o be such as to admit of a fair line of railway being found hrough it.

Thence to Fort Garry, a hundred miles, including sinuosities, he country, as already described, is unusually favorable for the construction of a railway.

The foregoing detailed distances make a total of thirteen hundred and sixty-seven miles from Montreal to Fort Garry, by this direct route.

The total length, by the distances given, of the part of it passing hrough unsurveyed country, between the northerly extremity of he waters of the Montreal River, a tributary of the Ottawa, and he west end of Lac Platte, a part of the Lake of the Woods, is 773 miles, while the direct distance, on the line of the route, is by calculation by meridians, 650¾, the difference being the allowance for sinuosities on the straight line assumed.

Great extents of this line will be comparatively level, and will afford favorable grades. The least favorable parts in that respect will probably be found in the valley of the Ottawa, within the distance to which lumbering operations and surveys extend, and where we have sufficient knowledge to be sure that a fair line of railroad can be carried, notwithstanding.

In the unsurveyed region before mentioned, the greatest difficulty will probably be encountered between the River Nipigon and Lac Seul, in the rise to the water-shed; but that is necessarily less han five hundred feet, or not more than will be met on the Intercolonial Railway before getting twenty miles from the St. Lawrence.

These details are gone into so fully because it is not generally known that we have a favorable and most direct route to Red River, shorter than any other possibly can be. It is in a position that is rendered exceedingly unassailable by the rugged mountainous country in front of it, and by the lakes, forests and extensive marshes, to the westward, between it and the frontier; so much so that an invading force, of any considerable strength, would ake more time to move twenty miles in the intervening country han to advance two hundred in the prairies beyond it.

Therefore, if we do not have a railway through our own territory to Red River, it certainly will not be because we have not a favorable route for it, but for want of sufficient inducement or necessity for making it.

This is of some importance; and it is desirable that the fact should be known, that when the making of it becomes a national requirement, for the purposes of defence or commerce, we command the best and shortest railway route to the interior and to the Pacific.

The level clay country of the north, through which this route passes, seemingly for four hundred miles, presents, as yet, no inducement whatever for opening it up. But when the navigation of the Ottawa is improved as far as the Matawan, two hundred miles above the capital, a comparatively small expenditure will carry it a hundred miles further, to the head of Lake Temiscaming. This will entirely change the prospect of settlement, not only of the good lands there, but also eventually of the clay country beyond it, should the soil of that great extent, of entirely arable land, prove as capable of improvement by cultivation as other clay soils are.

To be safe, we must reserve our judgment on the subject till more ample information, carefully collected, is before us. But this much we know, that clay soils, though stubborn and hard to cultivate in extremely dry or wet weather, are in the end the most rich and durable; and that tracts where grain can be raised, if well watered, generally become occupied, when land becomes valuable by the increase of population and the progress of improvement.

The period may be remote when such causes will operate in this particular region, but when we consider that, apart from its own requirements under such advanced circumstances, it offers a railway route to Red River and the Pacific four hundred miles shorter for winter travel than any other yet known to be practicable, in view of the vast development of improvements during the term of the past generation, it would really not be irrational to suppose that this route may be opened before the lapse of another.

This will appear the more reasonable when we consider that this route would traverse the most habitable part of this Territory south of Hudson's Bay, which, as before stated, is larger, and apparently fully as suitable for cultivation as Finland, that sustains nearly two millions of inhabitants; and that Lake Superior, and Lake Temiscaming on the Ottawa, are the only possible outlets for the best part of this territory, which would be opened up in the most favorable manner by this proposed route, and placed by it in immediate connection with Lake Temiscaming.

It is difficult to conceive that a country fully equal to Finland, with the great water system of the Ottawa leading directly to it, should remain for ever valueless and uninhabited.

CHAPTER XXXI.

ROUTE TO THE PACIFIC THROUGH BRITISH COLUMBIA.

The subject of communication with the Pacific, through British Columbia, is more immediately and urgently important than the preceding.

It is the opinion of many, that if it be of any importance that Great Britain, the greatest commercial power in the world, should have a highway to the Pacific, for commercial and other purposes,. through her own territory, one that could not be barred against her by any other power; if it be desirable that the solid freedom of British institutions should be maintained on this continent; and if the fair programme of national life, in close connexion with the mother country, set forth in the British North America Act, is to be realized, and this edifice of Confederated British Dominion is to be anything more than a temporary expedient, the Confederation should be completed by the addition of Vancouver's Island and British Columbia, and the opening of a line of commmunication with them, without delay.

Looking to the interest of the Central Prairie Country alone, as British territory, when inhabited, it is as important for it to have a way to the Pacific without being exposed to all the conceivable disadvantages of having its means of communication controlled by a foreign power, and, under very possible circumstances, a hostile one, as it is for us to have communication through our own territory with the Atlantic.

To render the comparison a fair one, we must conceive what it would be if there were no St. Lawrence, and we were dependent on land transport alone.

It is unnecessary to follow the line of evidence adopted by philosophical writers, showing that the importance and prosperity of civilized countries is limited by their extent of frontage on seas open to commerce; it is demonstrated in the history of nations, and the importance of that advantage is acknowledged in their struggles to obtain it.

But whatever power may in future hold British Columbia, a free outlet through it is of the greatest importance to the prosperity of our interior teritory adjoining it; and would have a powerful influence in encouraging settlement there, and in ensuring its success.

It would be to our advantage, as well as to its own, and also greatly to the advantage of British Columbia, that the interior prairie country should be a prosperous one; and its prosperity would be very much restricted if its commerce were limited to the St. Lawrence and Mississippi. It would be a great drawback for it to have its teas and other products of Eastern Asia and the Pacific imported by routes so circuitous, or to be obstructed in exporting its own products to that ocean.

It will assist us in judging of the importance of a route through British Columbia, if we compare the distance by it from the Upper Sasketchewan to the Pacific, with what it would be by the Red River and Mississippi to St. Louis, and thence by the Pacific railroad to San Francisco, now in progress, and which might be supposed to be in some degree useful to our territory.

By the practically good route, though necessarily tortuous one, through a mountainous country, described by Mr. Waddington, (from personal exploration,) in his valuable pamphlet on the subject, the distance, from Edmonton on the north Saskatchewan, to the head of Bute Inlet, a port on the waters of the Pacific, is 841 miles, of which 389 are navigable waters. By substituting his shorter railway route for the navigable water, the distance would be 654 miles.

By St. Louis and the Pacific Railroad the distance would be 1,060 miles from Edmonton to Fort Garry, 532 to St. Paul's, 817 to Omaha, thence to San Francisco 2,032 miles, (by U.S. Sec. at War's Report); in all 4,442 miles, or 3,601 miles longer to the Pacific than the route through British Columbia, or possibly 3,788.

Supposing even that Gov. Stevens' northern route, by the Missouri in lat. 47° N., were opened and 600 miles of road were made to join it at the Rocky Mountains, that is at 750 miles from the Pacific, the total distance would be 1,350 miles against 654 through British Columbia by rail.

Even from Fort Garry on Red River, the difference would be nearly the same on comparison, for we have 1,060 from Fort Garry to Edmonton by water, and 645 further to Bute Inlet by rail, against 532 miles to St. Paul's, and 1,864 thence to the Pacific, by Gov. Stevens' line, making 2,396 miles by it, against 1,705 by Edmonton to Bute Inlet, the latter being 691 miles shorter.

Very little reflection will be sufficient to enable us to see what a powerful inducement the opening of such a route through British Columbia would be, even if at first imperfectly, for the encouragement of settlement in our central prairie country, with the certainty there would be of its being completed as a line of railroad. Instead of being in an isolated "Cul de Sac" the settlers on the Saskatchewan would have the assurance of being, before long, on one of the great highways of the world's commerce.

The route advocated by Mr. Waddington, through the interior, by the valley of the North Saskatchewan, the River Athabasca and the Yellow Head or Leather Pass to the upper Fraser River, and descending it to its tributary, the Quesnelle River, and from it across to Bute Inlet, is unquestionably by far the best as regards this side of the Rocky Mountains, and the passage through them; and there is no room to doubt its being so also to the westward through British Columbia.

The Leather Pass was long known and used by the Hudson's Bay Company. It is singular that Capt. Palliser, Dr. Hector and Capt. Blackiston, were never informed of it. The advantageous nature of it, however, was made apparent in 1862 by the passage of a party of a hundred and fifty Canadian emigrants, including a woman and three children. They gathered at Fort Garry in June, and got through to the settlements on the Fraser River in good time. They took through with them about seventy horses and a hundred and thirty oxen, excepting such of the latter as they killed or sold by the way. So gentle was the ascent, that they did not know that they had passed the ridge of the Rocky Mountains, till they found the waters flowing westward. Lord Milton and Dr. Cheadle, also, in their journal say, of this pass, that they had unconsciously passed the height of land, and that until they had the evidence of the water flow, they had no suspicion that they were even near the dividing ridge.

The height of the summit of this pass, which is in lat. 52°54′ N., is given by Mr. Waddington as 3,760 feet over the sea, being nearly the same level as the elevated sloping plain, on the east side, from which the Rocky Mountains rise.

The elevation of the other generally known passes are as follows:—Howse Pass, 6,347; Kicking Horse Pass, 5,420; Vermilion, 4,944; Kanauski Pass, (recommended by Captain Palliser, but requiring a tunnel,) 4,600; British Kootanie Pass, near U. S. Boundary, 5,960 feet above the sea. This last is recommended by Captain Blackiston, who thought he was the first white man that had entered it. Mr. David Thompson, Astronomer of the North-West Company, in his manuscript journal, now before me, gives interesting accounts of his exploratory journeys through this and other passes of the Rocky Mountains, occasionally with horses, about the beginning of this century.

In the U. S. Secretary at War's Report on the Pacific Railway lines, the elevation of the passes through the Rocky Mountains in the United States are given as follows: Route near lat. 47° and 49° N., 6,044 feet; at lat. 41° and 42° N., 8,373 feet; at lat. 38° and 39° N., 10,032 feet; lat. 35° N., 7,472 feet; at lat. 32° N., 5,717 feet above the sea; and the extent of land generally unfit for cultivation on these routes, is given, in the above succession, as 1,490, 1,400, 1,460 ,1,476 and 1,210 miles respectively, or about two thirds of their length.

On our route by the North Saskatchewan and Yellow Head Pass, we have a continuously and pre-eminently fertile country for 1,300, from the commencement of the Red River prairies to the base of the Rocky Mountains at Jasper House ; and of the remaining 761 miles to the head of Bute Inlet, nearly one-half apparently is cultivable land.   Mr. Waddington's description of the country, between the mouth of Quesnelle River and the coast range, agrees with the favorable account of that plateau quoted from Mr. Barnston's report in Commander Mayne's work on British Columbia; and the unusual favorable character, in that very mountainous country, which he gives of the great region extending northward to the River Skeena, the boundary of British Columbia, corresponds with the description given of parts of it intersected, in reports of extensive explorations referred to in the same work, and published in Imperial Parliamentary papers.

We see, therefore, that we possess a route to the Pacific, through our central prairie country and British Columbia, that besides traversing the Rocky Mountains far more favorably, at half the elevation of the lines through the United States, is as remarkable for passing through a great extent of well watered fertile country, as they are for the general aridity and uninhabitable barrenness of a great part of the country they traverse.

The superiority of our route across to the Pacific, over any other on the continent, is still more evident, when we consider that it has, in addition to the foregoing, the further advantage of consisting chiefly of navigable waters.

This advantage is, in its nature, a double one.   First, the much lower rate of cost of transport by the navigable waters, where on a large scale, like the St. Lawrence and its lakes, and even much of the interior lake and river navigation ; secondly, what to us is of great importance, especially in the commencement, that in the navigable waters we have the greater part of the route ready, without cost of construction, except on a very small proportion of it.

Taking the route, No. 4, in the foregoing table, in connexion with that advocated by Mr. Waddington, we would have, with the improvements mentioned, between Lake Superior and Red River, 226 miles (out of 448½) of continuous navigation, on a large scale for inland waters, and 1,060 from Fort Garry to Edmonton of a similar class, by Lake Winnipeg and the Saskatchewan, requiring lockage, or short portages, only at three places on the latter.   Between Edmonton and Port Waddington, on Bute inlet, a harbour of the Pacific, Mr. Waddington counts 309 miles of steamboat navi-

gation ; making in all 1,595 miles of steamboat navigation, and only
754½ miles of land travel or railroad, in the whole distance of
2,349½ miles by this route from Lake Superior to the Pacific.

If the railway route proposed by Mr. Waddington were adopted,
instead of the navigation of Fraser River, in part, reducing the
distance from Bute Inlet to Edmonton to 654 miles, and if 825
miles of railway were made from Edmonton to Fort Garry, the total
distance from the Pacific to Lake Superior would be reduced to
1,927½ miles; which with 976 miles to Montreal, *vià* Collingwood,
and 843 to Halifax, would give a total distance from that city to
the Pacific of 3,746½ miles.

If a line of railroad throughout were ultimately required, to
ensure rapid communication at all seasons, we could have from
Bute Inlet to Edmonton, 654 miles, and to Fort Garry, 825 more,
and then the direct route, No. 1, of the table, from Fort Garry to
Montreal, by the Ottawa, 1,367 miles, making 2,846 from the
Pacific to Montreal; which, with 843 to Halifax, would make a
total from the Pacific of 3,689 miles, to which adding the distance
to Liverpool, 2,467, would give a total from the Pacific to Liverpool
of 6,156 miles.

By the Report of United States Secretary at War, already
referred to, the distances from New York to the Pacific are, to
Council Bluffs, at the mouth of the River Platte, 1,252 miles;
thence, to the Pacific by the railroad now in progress on both sides
of the Rocky Mountains, and nearly made to them, 2,032 miles,
making together 3,284 miles, to which add, from Liverpool to New
York, 3,073, gives a total by this line of 6,357 miles, or 201 more
than the route through British America.

CHAPTER XXXII.

IMPORTANCE TO BRITISH COLUMBIA OF UNION AND INTERIOR COMMUNICATION WITH THE DOMINION.

Were British Columbia united to the Dominion, and an adequate
line of communication opened through that Province from Lake
Superior to the Pacific, all the commerce of the vast interior of
British America, with the Pacific and Eastern Asia, and the carrying trade of it on the high seas, would be drawn to her ports; and
her route across the continent would be a successful rival of the
Pacific Railway from San Francisco, not only for traffic and communication between the Pacific and the present Provinces of Canada,
and parts of the United States adjoining, but also for that of European countries through this continent. The great proportion of

water conveyance on our route, would render transport by it so much more economical, as to admit of freight being carried of kinds that could not be sent by the San Francisco route, on account of the greater expense of transport entirely by railroad.

Our route through British Columbia would have the advantage also of being shorter to China and Japan ; the distance from any port in these countries to Bute Inlet being upwards of 550 miles less than to San Francisco. This is best seen by measurement on a terrestrial globe ; for the ordinary projections of the hemispheres in charts and atlases give rise to a very erroneous idea as to distances between the continents.

Taking this 550 miles into account, the distance from any port in China or Japan to Liverpool would be 751 miles shorter by our route, through British Columbia, than by the American Pacific Railroad.

United to the Dominion, British Columbia would enjoy these advantages in relation to the interior, and communication through it, which would be lost to her by annexation to the United States. If the Americans held British Columbia, they would be little disposed to use it for the purpose of establishing a line of communication, nearly altogether through British territory, to rival their own Pacific Railroad, and carry trade to Canadian ports.

In this respect, British Columbia, including Vancouver's Island with it, and Nova Scotia, are in a great degree similarly situated, in relation to the interior of British America and its development ; and the similarity goes further, for they are much alike in some other respects. They are both comparatively rather unfavorable generally for cultivation, but on the other hand possess alike extraordinary advantages for commerce and manufactures, in their favorable maritime position and numerous harbours, their metals and their coal beds.

With these advantages, and situated on the eastern and western outlets of the great fertile interior of British America, it seems reasonable to say that they are in a position to enjoy, in the greatest degree, every advantage in the extension of their commerce and increased employment for their shipping and manufactures, to be derived from the development of the resources of the interior, and the opening of a line of communication through it from the Atlantic to the Pacific.

In position with relation to the interior, however, it must be admitted, that British Columbia surpasses Nova Scotia and New Brunswick, the coast of the continent, southward from it, not being studded with rival ports and harbours, reaching close in towards the interior like the Atlantic coast. In the command of communication from the Pacific to the interior, British Columbia has no competitor.

IMPORTANCE OF THE OTTAWA SHIP CANAL TO THESE NORTH-WEST TERRITORIES, &c.

To judge correctly of the ultimate advantage which a route through our own territories presents, alike as a means of communication with them and through them to the Pacific, and in view of the superiority which the greater economy of water transport gives us in the comparison, we should take into account the reduction of distance and of cost which the improvement of our inland navigation may afford.

As presenting the greatest prospective advantage in that respect, the proposed improvement of the Ottawa and French Rivers, or what is called the construction of the Ottawa Ship Canal, may be referred to.

It may be sufficient to remind the reader, that in the distance by this route of four hundred and thirty miles from Montreal to Lake Huron, canalling for 21½ miles only is required, in addition to the Lachine Canal already constructed, according to the report of Mr. Thos. C. Clarke, who completed the survey of it for Government ; and that according to the report of Mr. W. Shanly, his predecessor in charge, the cost of movement of freight per ton, from Chicago to Montreal, by the Ottawa Ship Canal, would be $2 89, while by the St. Lawrence and Welland Canal route, and by the Toronto and Georgian Bay Canal, it would be $3 26 and $3 27 respectively; that the distances by the two latter routes would be 1,348 and 1,050 miles, but by the Ottawa only 973, that is, 375 miles shorter than the St. Lawrence and Welland route now used.

It is proper to observe that the reduction of distance by it to Lake Superior, and consequently to the interior and the Pacific, is 40 miles greater than to Lake Michigan, or 415 miles.

Apart from the advantages claimed for it of being the most favorable route for the trade of what has hitherto been designated the " Great West," and for attracting it to Canadian ports, and as vastly increasing the strength of the Provinces as a work of defence, the Ottawa Ship Canal, inasmuch as it would diminish the distance and the cost of transport, especially of heavy freight, to and from our interior territories, would tend to remove the greatest drawback to the successful settlement of them. It would benefit Lower Canada, now the Province of Quebec, in a manner that no other work would do, for it would, in connexion with Lake Temiscaming, and the navigable waters of its tributary, the River Blanche, develope the south-western frontier of that province for four hundred and fifty miles, and render available the considerable extent of country fit for settlement at the head of that lake, which is now too remote ; and it would facilitate communication with Hudson's Bay, and through the country south of it to Red River, as already mentioned, were that ultimately found desirable.

CHAPTER XXXIII.

THE INTERESTS OF CANADA, THE HUDSON'S BAY COMPANY AND THE INDIANS.

We are at issue with the Hudson's Bay Company. We deny the justice and validity of their title to the territory most valuable to us—the Central Prairie Country—claimed by them under their Charter from King Charles the Second, in 1670, granting them the exclusive right of trade in Hudson's Bay and its waters, and all the lands and territories on their "*Confines*," not "possessed by the subjects of any other Christian Prince or State."

Far from giving the Hudson's Bay Company the interior country on the Red River and the Saskatchewa, their Charter, restricted by this exception, did not even give them that part of the coast of Hudson's Bay in front of it.

These regions were commonly known as French territory, and were virtually recognized as such by the Treaty of St. Germains en Laye, of 1632, which restored to the King of France Canada or "La Nouvelle France," of which they formed part ;—and they had already, in 1627, been chartered to "La Compagnie de la Nouvelle France."

The occupation of Hudson's Bay by the French before the date of the Hudson's Bay Company's Charter is unquestionable, for not only had their trade been established there in 1656 and 1663, by Jean Bourdon and La Couture, and Missions been planted in the interior, but it is also historically notorious that the Hudson's Bay Company originated in two disaffected Canadians, who had been engaged in the trade of the Bay (De Grozelier and Radison), inducing English adventurers to join them in a trading voyage there,* the success of which led to the formation of the Hudson's Bay Company and the granting of its Charter in 1670.

After a protracted struggle the Hudson's Bay Company's people were, in 1686, expelled as trespassers from the posts they had established in the Bay. The justice of this expulsion and the prior rightful possession of France is acknowledged in the treaty of Ryswick, of 1697, which provides for the restitution to France of these posts in particular, as well as of all others taken in the war then terminated, that had formerly belonged to France.

Therefore, without entering into the seemingly well grounded objections made, by able legists, to the fundamentally illegal character of that Charter, we see that in simple equity, (though that

* See Charlevoix, Vol. 1, p. 476.

may probably be disregarded) King Charles could not give—and by the exception evidently did not intend to give—the Company all the territory they now claim, simply because it was not his to give.

We see also that the completeness of the title given by the Charter is vitiated by an exception well grounded on known fact,—a fact affirmed and sustained by the high authority of international treaty ; and that, therefore, the Hudson's Bay Company would probably, under it, be unable, in a Court of Law, to prove perfect title, as required, for the ejectment of adverse possessors.

Previous to the cession of Canada, Canadian traders had long been in undisputed possession of the interior country now in dispute—holding there the forts of Maurepas on Lake Winnipeg, Fort Rouge on Red River, De la Reine on Lake Manitoba, and Forts Bourbon, Pasquiæ and Nippeween on the Saskatchewan. Under the Articles of capitulation of Canada their occupation and property there would be secured to them. After the cession of the country, British and Canadians, following in their track, maintained the right, by trading there, before and after the Hudson's Bay Company entered the same grounds ;—and they continued to do so for upwards of forty years before the Hudson's Bay Company asserted —and in 1814 first attempted—to enforce their exclusive claim.*

Then, after the protracted and sanguinary struggle between them and the Canadian North-west Company, during which the exclusive pretensions of either were expressly and carefully ignored by the Imperial and Provincial authorities†—the Hudson's Bay Company, finding that they could not enforce their Charter, united with the North-west Company, so that they might jointly secure the exclusion of all other traders.

As to the Hudson's Bay Company's claim to the right of soil— how can Canada be asked to entertain it ? The soil, with most insignificant exception, is still the unalienated property of the native Indians.

---

* The great explorations of Sir Alexander McKenzie, up to the Arctic Sea and through to the Pacific Ocean, and the scarcely less important exploratory surveys of David Thompson, after May, 1797, including the discovery and survey of the River Columbia and Thompson's River and the surveys of the Arthabasca and Peace Rivers, Beaver River and Upper Saskatchewan, and of several passages through the Rocky Mountains, were operations of the Canadian North-West Company, of whom McKenzie was a leader, and to whom Thompson transferred his services, in 1799, as stated in his manuscript Journal, after serving the Hudson's Bay Company from October, 1789.

† See Earl Bathurst's despatch of 6th February, 1817, enjoining the maintenance of "the full and free permission for all persons to pursue their usual and accustomed trade without hindrance or molestation."

In Canada, the Mother Country recognized their right by purchasing their lands and paying annuities for them. Before the Union these payments had to be refunded to the Imperial Government by Upper Canada. These annuities are now paid directly by the Canadian Goverment.

Seeing, therefore, that we have to pay for all lands acquired for us, or by us, from Indians, are we to be compelled to recognize the right of the Hudson's Bay Company to lands they never purchased or paid for? And is it consistent with that justice to the Aborigines, which we hear so much spoken about in England, that, in acquiring their lands, instead of paying them the whole price, we are to give part of it to the Hudson's Bay Company,—who never acquired any right to it from the owners? *

The grounds of claim to the territory in dispute are too obscure, hypothetical and conflicting, to be conclusive in favor of either Canada or the Company: it is for the Crown, in whom the absolute right still remains, to deal with it as it sees fit.

Besides that of the native Indians, the only indefeasible right is that of mankind to have the obstruction to its lawful occupation by settlers removed. All that the Company can justly be entitled to is indemnity for any injury to their trade which settlement may occasion, when it takes place.

That, in the large portion of prairie land nearest to us, which is exhausted as a fur-bearing country, must be comparatively little.

In considering this question, we have to bear in mind that it is only such part of the territory, sending waters to Hudson's Bay, as their Charter may, under the restricting exception be found to cover, that the Company can have any permanent right to :—the remainder of the territory they occupy, they held merely temporarily by lease, on the termination of which their rights become extint, without claim to indemnity.

We claim that the Red River and Saskatchewan country comes under the latter description. We should therefore avoid being led into calling it Rupert's Land, for as that was the name given by King Charles to the land he gave the Company, we in a manner admit the Red River and Saskatchewan Country to be the property of the Company if we call it Rupert's Land.

But though our interests are opposed to theirs as to territorial right, we should be careful to be just to the Company, and consider well the particulars in which their interests and ours may agree.

---

* I am led to make these remarks from its having been my duty, for seven years, to keep the accounts of these transactions, between the Imperial Commissariat, the Local Government, and the Indian Department.

We must acknowledge that their admirable system, good management and good faith in dealing with the Indians, are highly creditable to them, and have maintained tranquillity in the vast territories under their sway, and peace on our borders, and respect for the British name and power in the minds of the natives; and that their officers and agents are proverbially honourable men.

If the Company were broken up and their officers withdrawn from these territories, and the trade of them thrown open to all, it might, no doubt, give a few enterprising men in Canada the opportunity of seeking, probably with some success, to amass wealth like that of the old North-West Company of Montreal. But when the irregular, and too often unscrupulous trading of the adventurers was substituted for the well regulated and reliable system of the Hudson's Bay Company, it would probably have, with the free use of spirits that would no doubt attend it, a most injurious and demoralizing effect upon the Indians; and coupled with the many causes of provocation accompanying the advance of settlement, would, almost certainly, lead to difficulties and border warfare with them, as in the adjoining States.

It would therefore probably be better, on the whole, that the fur trade of these territories should remain in the hands of the Hudson's Bay Company, under lease from the Dominion, especially if such an arrangement gave Canada more favourable terms in settlement with the Company. The importance of economy effected in this way will be seen when it is considered that it might be sufficient to defray the expense of opening a serviceable line of communication for the ingress of settlers.

Or it might be better for the Goverment of the Dominion to step into the shoes of the Company, and continue the trade, through the agents and others now employed, retaining their services by giving them the same interest in the trade as they now hold, or equivalent advantage.

By doing so, Government would have thoroughly competent Indian agents throughout the whole of these territories, and by maintaining the same policy of management as heretofore, would prevent an important influence over the native tribes from being impaired or falling into foreign hands, and could use it for the preservation of that tranquillity which would be doubly necessary in the face of advancing settlement.

If we have to buy the improvements or business stands of the Company, it would be reasonable to turn them to some account; and the abrupt withdrawal of that trade on which the natives now depend for ammunition and other things, now become necessaries to them, would be a calamity to the Indians, which it would be the duty of Canada, in extending her dominion over them, to avert.

The exclusive reservation of the fur trade in the hands of Government, for the good of all, would be less obnoxious than its being held by a company. It would enable Government to check the use of spirits in the trade. The agents might be useful in allaying difficulties and watching over the feelings of the natives and their movements, as well as their interests and wants; but there are, no doubt, some obvious objections to the trade being carried on by Government.

But whatever the arrangements as to trade may be, the security of settlement will lie in good faith with the Indians, in all arrangements with them being honorably and liberally maintained. With ultimate advantage to ourselves we might even exceed that. Were the Government of the Dominion, on acquiring these territories, or any part of them, to establish in the settlements, asylums, at a few points, for the helpless and infirm, and orphans of such tribes as any arrangement as to territory or otherwise was made with; and were it also provided that any Indian of any such tribe might, at any time forever thereafter and anywhere, obtain a free grant of two hundred acres of land, on his choosing to become a settler, as an inalienable homestead, and be entitled to admission into any hospital, or to medical assistance in case of illness or injury, to be paid for by Government on the certificate of any magistrate, a strong and favorable impression would be made on the feelings of the Indians. The Indian would have it constantly before him that if he became helpless there was a home ever ready for him under the roof of the Dominion.

The liability to expense which this would entail may be objected to, but when it is considered how little this exceeds what Christian charity would dictate, under such circumstances, and the small number of the Indians,—the benefit to them and the moral influence in our favor,—the liability of cost may be found moderate compared with the general advantage obtained.

By adopting such a system of attaching the Indians, and either obtaining the cordial co-operation of the Hudson's Bay Company, by duly considering their interest, or otherwise by occupying their place, which would be still more effective, the security of orderly settlement, on just principles, would be provided for, and the strength of the Indian nations would be knit to ours for common defence if necessary, at less cost in the end than by bad faith and aggression and bloody wars with them.

CHAPTER XXXIV.

COMPARATIVE VALUE OF THE SEVERAL TERRITORIES TO CANADA, AND CONCLUSION.

Having passed in review the Hudson's Bay and North-West Territories, in naturally distinct sections, we may now consider which, or how many of them we may require; and in what degree they are respectively of value to us.

First and chiefly, as generally admitted, and for reasons already shown, we want the central prairie country on the Red River, Saskatchewan, Athabasca and Peace Rivers, as a favorable site for the immediate extension of settlement and reception of European immigration. We see that it much exceeds Canada in extent, that it has on an average as suitable a climate for agricultural occupation ; while it greatly exceeds Canada in the proportion of arable land it contains; much of which is of the richest quality known.

The next in value to us, though very much inferior to the preceding, is that here described as the South Hudson's Bay Territory, or that part of it, at least, up to the line of latitude 52° 30′ N. from a little above the mouth of the Albany River, on Hudson's Bay, across to Lake Winnipeg. It is a habitable country, with much fertile arable land, admitting of the cultivation of coarse grains in the north, and, as we have seen, is as suitable, in some of the south parts of it, for the growth of wheat, as Lower Canada. We require it in connection with the preceding, because the southern part of it contains the best lines of communication with Red River, and which being chiefly by water, are the most advantageous for the heavy freight of the interior; and also because through it we can have a most direct and favorable line of railroad to Red River and the Pacific.

Next, but in a lesser degree, the Pelly River or Mountain Country would be valuable to us ; chiefly as a defence. Were it in the hands of a power owning the seaboard, with strongholds in commanding positions, at the eastern outlets of the passes through it, our central prairie country would be exposed to being, at any time, suddenly overrun. But with that three hundred and fifty miles in breadth of Alpine country occupied by our fur traders, with posts on all the leading passes, and "couriers du bois" and trappers scattered over it, in friendly communication with the natives, an enemy, without foothold, on attempting to pass, in such insignificant force as it would under such circumstances be practicable to lead, would easily be detected and destroyed before having made much way ; or if by extraordinary fortune they did pass unnoticed, the result to such small force as could so pass, would be as disastrous as Arnold's attempt on Canada by the valley of the Chaudière.

The valleys of the Pelly River and Mountain Country will seemingly admit of the cultivation of coarse grains, and cattle feeding throughout its whole extent, and it is a valuable fish and fur yielding country.

East Main and the remainder of what is here designated as South Hudson's Bay Territory, might be valuable to us for their seal fisheries and fur trade; and the McKenzie River country for its furs and minerals, and for the navigable highway to the most valuable of Arctic whale fisheries, which that river offers; but these territories are of little value to us compared with the first three mentioned—all of which are habitable countries, the first eminently so. As to the North Hudson's Bay, or Barren Ground Territory, it seems to have no conceivable value.

South Hudson's Bay Territory and the Pelly River or Mountain Country, though unsuitable for occupation by our present standard of estimation, will undoubtedly become inhabited. European countries, not more suitable, are occupied by civilized and enlightened nations, and have acquired considerable political and commercial importance.

CONCLUSION.

Some will argue that, in desiring to acquire the North-west Territory, we allow our ambition to override our judgment; that the organizing of it, and the maintenance of jurisdiction over it, are a task beyond the ability of Canada; that it is absurd to incur expense in the development of remote territories, while we have already so much waste land, requiring the making of more roads than we are able to accomplish for the opening of it, to say nothing of the canals and railroads nearer home, which all admit to be desirable for the prosperity of the country.

One might argue interminably in this manner; but there is a shorter and a surer way to a conclusion in this matter. We have only to look south of us, and see what has been done by the people there.

We see that they acquired territory after territory, in the face of obstacles that we have not to encounter.

When they were far weaker than we are, instead of acquiring territories in the easy way that we may do, they had to fight for them. They had to combat fierce and powerful tribes, backed by the power of France; but still they extended their frontier.

When they entered on the career of national existence, they were but three millions; but we are four. And then, in addition to continual wars with the Indians, they had to fight with the mother country, once and again, in wars ruinously expensive to them. But that did not prevent their continuing to extend their jurisdiction over vast territories, which they acquired from European Powers, and had to fight for afterwards.

They had indeed vast regions nearer home of unsettled lands, requiring roads and other improvements to open them up, while we in fact have comparatively none of great value; but instead of the extension of their dominion leading them to neglect improvements in their older states, the very reverse seems to be the case.

Who will say that the acquisition and development of their western territories, which one after the other have grown into thriving and populous states, has retarded the prosperity of their older eastern states and cities? On the contrary, we find them remarkable for their works and improvements; and what is more, we find them enriched by their manufactures for the markets of the western territories, which they acquired and developed into power-

ful states, and that their chief seaports are swollen with the com
merce arising from them.

Now, we are not only greater than they were in population, bu
also exceed them in a much greater degree in wealth, and in th
command of wealth unknown to them, in their beginnings. W
have no Indian wars; and instead of their expensive wars with th
mother country, we enjoy her powerful protection and pecuniar
assistance, and have the immense additional advantage of stear
and railroads in our favor.

With all these advantages, it is evidently preposterous to say
that it is beyond our power to do what they did, unless we adop
the plea that we are intrinsically so inferior to the people of th
United States, in capacity, energy and patriotism, that with ever
advantage in our favor, and obstacles removed which they had t
encounter, we have neither the courage nor ability to imitate thei
successful example.

But some will say, what is the real good of aspiring to nationa
power and greatness? The answer is a simple one. Men ii
general are what the institutions of their country make them. Th
security of these institutions depends on the power of the people t
defend them. Civil liberty depends upon political independence
and that, it is needless to say, depends on the power to maintain it
Where would have been the civil liberty of England had she suc
cumbed to the Armada, or the stability of her institutions had sh
been conquered by France under Napoleon?

The mother country has placed in our hands the national banner
and the institutions of which it is the symbol, under which she ha:
attained her pre-eminent, moral and material greatness; th
standard of responsible constitutional government and law-abiding
liberty; and she expects us, with her assistance, and for our owr
good, to maintain it, and them, honorably, over these broac
dominions of which she endows us with the inheritance. May
there be no failure on our part through short-sighted unpatriotic
pusillanimity.

REPORT

ON THE

LINE OF ROUTE BETWEEN LAKE SUPERIOR

AND

THE RED RIVER SETTLEMENT.

OTTAWA, 20th April, 1868.

SIR,—I have the honor herewith to submit to your consideration a Report on the Line of Route between Lake Superior and the Red River Settlement, with an Estimate of the cost of opening the communication in the manner therein suggested.

I have the honor to be, sir,

Your most obedient servant,

(Signed,)   S. J. DAWSON,

Hon. Wm. McDougall, C.B.,   *Civil Engineer.*
    Minister of Public Works, &c., &c.,
        Ottawa.

REPORT

ON

THE LINE OF ROUTE

BETWEEN

LAKE SUPERIOR AND THE RED RIVER SETTLEMENT.

~~~~~~~~~~~~

In reporting as to the best means of opening a line of communication between Lake Superior and the Red River Settlement, I beg to be permitted, in the first place, to refer briefly to the operations of the Red River Expedition, carried on for several years under my direction, as it will, I doubt not, be satisfactory to the Government to know that the suggestions which I have the honor to submit are not the expression of mere theoretical views, but the result of long-continued investigation, under official instructions from the Canadian Government.

The earlier Reports of the Expedition were printed by order of the Legislature, but those sent in during the last year of its operations have never been published. The present Report will contain all that is believed to be of immediate importance in these documents ; that is, in regard to the subject under consideration.

The following Maps are annexed for convenience of reference :—

1. A Plan, on a scale of two miles to one inch, showing the country between Thunder Bay and Lac des Mille Lacs, Dog Lake line of road, position of dam, &c.

2. A Plan of the Lake Region, on a scale of four miles to one inch, showing the country between the Height of Land and Fort Frances.

3. A Plan on a scale of ten miles to one inch, showing the country between Fort Frances and Fort Garry.

4. A Map, in profile, showing the relative altitude of the Routes by Pigeon River and the Kaministaquia.

Plan No. 3 might be lithographed at small cost, and I think it would be advisable to have it published, as it is the only correct one of the section which it exhibits.

The Red River Expedition consisted at its outset of three distinct parties, receiving their instructions from three different Departments of Government. One of these was under my direction, one under Mr. Napier's, while Mr. Gladman, a retired officer of the

Hudson's Bay Company, who had the guidance of the Expedition on the journey to Red River, had a separate party of his own.

The parties thus organized set out in July, 1857, and proceeding by the usual canoe route from Fort William, made numerous explorations, determined the levels as they went, and eventually arrived at the Red River Settlement in the fall of the same year.

Mr. Gladman, after a short stay, returned by the way he had come to Toronto, where his connection with the Expedition soon afterwards ceased, while Professor Hind, who I should have mentioned had been attached to the party as geologist, proceeded by way of the Red River over the prairies to St. Paul.

My assistants at this time were Mr. Lindsay A. Russell, Mr. J. F. Gaudet, Mr. Alex. W. Wells and Col. C. de Salaberry. The three first-named gentlemen were surveyors, all of whom are of high standing in their profession, while Col. de Salaberry acted chiefly as Commissary—an important office in a region where provisions were not always very abundant.

The winter of 1857-58 was chiefly occupied in exploring the country between the Lake of the Woods and Red River, a region at that time but little known, and reported to be impassable in summer, on account of swamps which were said to cover the greater portion of its area. At the same time, an instrumental survey was made, so as to connect Fort Garry with the survey made many years previously by the Boundary Commissioners, under the treaty of Ghent. This enabled us to establish with accuracy the longitude of Fort Garry, which, on the maps then in use, was set down as much as twenty-one minutes too far to the west.

The party were also able, before the opening of navigation, to explore the Rosseau River and make an instrumental survey of the Red River and Lake Winnipeg, between Fort Alexander, at the mouth of the Winnepeg River, and the Boundary Line at Pembina.

Immediately after the opening of the navigation, having organized a party of half-breed Indians and procured canoes, we proceeded by way of the Manitoba and Winnepegoos Lakes to the great Saskatchewan River, and examined the rapids and impediments to the navigation between Lac Bourbon and Lake Winnipeg. The levels were determined with care, and the "Track Survey" which we had made of the Lake Coasts, as we proceeded, was corrected as often as possible by observations for latitude and longitude.

Separating our party at the Mossy Portage, the name by which the path between Lake Winnepegoos and Lac Bourbon is called, I sent Mr. Wells to explore Lac Dauphin and survey the route by way of the Little Saskatchewan and Lake Winnepeg to the mouth of the Red River, appointing the 1st of July following to meet him at the settlement.

Taking with me my assistants, Mr. Gaudet, and Mr. de Salaberry, and a few Indians, I ascended Swan River, crossed from thence to Fort Pelly, and descended by the Assiniboine to Fort Garry, having on this excursion obtained much information, as to the soil and climate of a very extensive district, and made such observations as enabled us to delineate its geography with tolerable accuracy.

Throughout the entire period during which our head quarters were at the Red River Settlement, a Meteorological Register was kept, regularly, under the supervision of Mr. Russell, and it has since been of considerable value, as, taken in connection with some reliable observations made by others, it has served not a little to dispel the absurd ideas which at one time prevailed in regard to the severity of the climate and the duration of the winters.

On the 4th of July, 1858, our party was once more assembled at the Red River Settlement, and having with some difficulty procured supplies, we set out, with all possible dispatch, for a more thorough exploration of the country between Rainy Lake and Lake Superior. Among the instructions received from the Government at this time were the following :—

"Secretary's Office,
"Toronto, 16th April, 1858.

" Sir,—Adverting to the last paragraph in my letter to you this day, I have the honor to inform you, that it is not thought necessary to make any alterations in the instructions for your future operations, contained in the Order in Council of 29th January last.

" You will therefore consider these instructions, so far as your explorations are concerned, still in force.

" I am to add, however, that if time allows it, you will endeavor to survey the road between Gun Flint Lake and Pointe de Meuron, and when returning from the North-west Corner of the Lake of the Woods and passing through Rainy Lake, make occasional traverses when practicable, with a view to ascertain the extent of arable land in that locality.

" I am further to state that His Excellency, having every confidence in your judgment, does not think it right to trammel your movements by detailed instructions, and that you are therefore at liberty to make any other explorations in addition to those particularly mentioned in the instructions already conveyed to you, should you, upon the information obtained in the locality, deem it desirable you should do so.

" I have the honor to be, Sir,
" Your obedient servant,
(Signed,)   " T. J. J. Loranger,
" Secretary."

" S. J. Dawson, Esq.,
    " Civil Engineer in command,
     " of the Red River Expedition."

From that time forward, for the remainder of the season, and during the winter of 1858–59, our explorations were confined chiefly, I may say exclusively, to the country between Rainy Lake and Lake Superior. Two well appointed parties were kept constantly at work, and sometimes three. Instrumental surveys were carried from Lake Superior, westward, through Dog Lake, Dog River, Lac des Mille Lacs and the Seine, to within a short distance of Rainy Lake. The levels were taken from Jourdain's Rapid to Dog Lake, and from that Lake across, by the line laid out as a road, to Lake Superior.

In the spring of 1859, having learned that a party fitted out by the people of Red River, who at that time took a great deal of interest in promoting the development of the country, had been baffled in an attempt to take horses through to the Lake of the Woods, had in fact got bewildered in swamps, from which they had experienced much difficulty in extricating themselves, and as the impression as to that section of the country being impracticable for roads was thus gaining confirmation, I hastened to the Lake of the Woods, with the most active of my assistants, and proceeding to its western extremity had the good fortune to secure the services of an Indian Chief, who undertook to show us ground on which the country could be crossed.

Leaving my assistants to find their way across with the Chief, I proceeded by way of the Winnipeg to the Red River Settlement, where I had not long to wait for their arrival. They reported that the Chief had led them to a gravelly ridge which extended, with but few breaks, for a long distance across the most swampy parts of the country, and that the remains of Indian encampments showed that it had been much used as a pathway, in times long past.

A number of men were immediately engaged in the Settlement and sent to open the line which had been traced, in such a way as to render it passable for horses; and over this line *our party rode clear through to the Lake of the Woods, on horseback.*

The line thus opened was used afterwards as a Post road for the conveyance of Mails on *horseback*, and it requires but slight knowledge of engineering to understand that ground, over which horses can be ridden, is not so swampy as to be impracticable for roads.

Returning again to Rainy Lake, we made a more thorough examination of the Lakes, by the old canoe route, than we had previously had an opportunity of doing, and the result led me to the conclusion that, considering the long reaches of navigable water on that route, it could be rendered available, in the first instance, to greater advantage and at less outlay than the line by the Seine, which had been examined and reported on the previous year.

Arriving at Lake Superior, I was joined by my assistant, Mr.

Wells, who had spent the whole summer in examining the country about the Height of Land and Lac des Mille Lacs. The fall being now far advanced, the parties were gradually withdrawn, such of them as we had left at the Lake of the Woods returning only in the beginning of November.

To sum up, the explorations and surveys were thus continued, uninterruptedly, for three summers and two winters. There were generally three well-appointed parties simultaneously at work, in different sections, and, whether at Lake Superior or the Lake of the Woods —the one a swampy and the other a hilly region—they always availed themselves of the aid of the natives, whose occupation of hunting, pursued from youth to age, within particular areas, rendered their local knowledge of the greatest value.

A considerable period of time has now elapsed since the operations of the Red River expedition were brought to a close, and since that time there has been no further exploration whatever in the country between Lake Superior and the Red River Settlement, so that such of our preliminary Reports as have been published are the only sources of information generally available.

Having thus briefly alluded to the surveys and explorations made by me, or under my direction, I proceed to describe the different sections of the country in detail, pointing out, as concisely as possible, the works and improvements required, and the reasons for adopting particular lines of route or starting points.

For the sake of convenience, in description, the country between Lake Superior and the Red River Settlement may properly be regarded as forming four divisions.

The first, embracing the region to the east of the water-shed, or Height of Land, will be referred to as the " Lake Superior Section."

The next, extending from the Height of Land to Fort Frances, I propose to designate as the " Lake Region."

The navigable reach, extending from Fort Frances to the north-west angle of the Lake of the Woods, will be called the " Lake of the Woods Division."

While that between the north-west angle and the Red River Settlement may not inappropriately be known as the " Fort Garry Section."

LAKE SUPERIOR SECTION.

The country between the Boundary Line, at Pigeon River, and the head or eastern end of Thunder Bay, was carefully examined with the view of finding a practical route from Lake Superior to some one of the water systems leading from the Height of Land westward, to Rainy Lake.

On all the routes, proposed or suggested, I had at various times during the progress of the expedition, reported to the Government so that, here, I need only state the leading advantages or objections which attach, respectively, to each.

THE PIGEON RIVER ROUTE.

The nature of this route, and the objections to it, will be found pretty fully stated in my preliminary reports, printed by order of the Legislature.—Pages 7 and 27.

The starting point is entirely within the United States territory and, for a distance of one hundred and fifty miles, the canoe route forms the Boundary Line. But this is far from being the only objection. The ascent from Lake Superior is very rapid and steep and at the Height of Land, and far to the westward thereof, the route leads over a very high and broken region. The lakes at the summit of the water-shed are 1,058 feet above the level of Lake Superior, and, even at that elevation, are embosomed in rocky hills which rise to the height of several hundreds of feet around them. Moreover, the supply of water is so inadequate as to forbid the idea of improving the navigation, and there is no source from whence a supply can be obtained. The route itself is at the summit of supply, and touches in its course on the head waters of no less than four different rivers.

Between Pigeon River and the Kaministaquia, there are several good harbours on the coast, but from these access to the interior would be exceedingly difficult, and could only be provided at enormous outlay.

It was at one time suggested that a practicable line might be found by which to cross the country from Pointe de Meuron, so as to join the Pigeon River Route, to the westward of the Height of Land. This point I was instructed to investigate, and accordingly despatched Mr. L. A. Russell, with a well-appointed party, to explore in the direction which had been indicated. He ran a line from Pointe de Meuron to Gun Flint Lake, a distance of some fifty-four miles, and examined the ground on either side thereof, but his report and field notes show that the country which he traversed was too rough and impracticable to admit of an available line of communication.

In concluding my notice of this route, I may say that, for a distance of one hundred and thirty miles from Lake Superior, westward, it cannot be made in any way available as a line of water communication, except for small canoes; that the country being for a great part of the distance rugged, mountainous and cut up with lakes, it is next to impracticable for roads, and, finally, that there being a much better route to the eastward, entirely within British territory, there would be no object in attempting to open this line, or spending further sums in its exploration.

KAMINISTAQUIA ROUTE.

This is the old canoe route of the North-west and Hudson's Bay Companies. On this line the supply of water is ample, and the elevation of the country at the summit of the water-shed less, by some two hundred feet, than on the Pigeon River Route, while it is at the same time, that is, at the turn of the water-shed, comparatively level and practicable for roads. Dog Lake, a large sheet of water on the Kaministaquia, twenty-four miles inland from Lake Superior, extends for a distance of some twenty miles in a direction nearly parallel to the western coast of Thunder Bay. To the westward of this lake, the principal stream which supplies it with water —Dog River—can be made navigable nearly to the Height of Land (and it will be so when a dam now in progress of construction is completed), so that, between river and lake, an available reach of some thirty-five miles could be commanded. It became, therefore, a matter of importance to find access to this navigable reach, and with this end in view, the levels of the Kaministaquia were determined, and the country between Dog Lake and Lake Superior explored.

Dog Lake was found to be at an elevation of 718 feet above the level of Lake Superior, and the intervening country proved to be extremely mountainous and rough, while the difficulties by water were of a still more formidable character.

The Kaministaquia, after leaving Dog Lake, runs nearly south to its confluence with Fish River, then eastwardly to Pointe de Meuron, and thence north-east to its discharge, making a sweep of sixty miles before it reaches Lake Superior ; and as it has in that distance to get down a declivity of 718 feet, its character, in regard to its capacity for navigation, may be easily imagined. It affords, however, an available, although a difficult route for canoes ; but, for large craft, it could only be made navigable at an outlay which no circumstances likely to arise would warrant.

A land road to Dog Lake, therefore, became indispensable, and, after much careful investigation and exploration, an available pass was found and a line laid out, and on this line during the past summer a fair commencement was made, and six miles of road, reckoning from Thunder Bay, completed.

The starting point is at a place called the Depôt, on Thunder Bay, about three miles to the eastward of the mouth of the Kaministaquia, and at this point there is, in my opinion, every facility for constructing wharves and forming a perfectly safe harbour.

The Kaministaquia, itself, has been strongly recommended as a harbour, but, in its present state, it is inaccessible to vessels drawing more than five and a half feet of water, on account of a bar or shoal of great extent at its mouth. Its adoption would involve the dredging of a channel, and the construction of extensive piers or walls of heavy crib work, on either side thereof, to prevent it from being filled up by the action of the ice which, at certain seasons, ploughs over the bar. Another consideration, which should not be lost sight of, is that the causes which produced the shoal are still in operation. Quantities of sediment are brought down with every freshet, more especially in the spring, and the dredging would have to be repeated at intervals to keep the channel, once formed, open.

Everything considered, therefore, I would not for the present recommend the Government to undertake the dredging of the Kaministaquia, and the construction of extensive works to keep the channel so formed from filling up. The first great object is to open the communication with Fort Garry; and, when that is accomplished, there will be no lack of means, from private sources, or of enterprise, to render the Kaministaquia an accessible harbour. In the meantime, it might seriously affect the enterprise if large sums were to be expended at its very outset *on merely local works*.

Fort William is, however, even at present, accessible to the smaller class of schooners or fishing vessels which navigate Lake Superior. It is, besides, a place of importance as being the centre of such trade as is carried on, and it will gradually become of increased consequence, as the mines in the vicinity are developed, and the fertile portion of the valley of the Kaministaquia fills up with settlement. For these reasons, it is expedient to connect it by a branch line with the Dog Lake Road, as shown on the accompanying plan, and for this purpose I have included a sum of seven thousand dollars ($7,000) in the estimate, which I have now the honor to submit.

Before concluding this subject, I would call attention to the fact that many persons who take a deep interest in that part of the country are under the impression that by going up the Kaministaquia to Pointe de Meuron, or as far as the navigable water extends —a distance of some ten or twelve miles—the length of land road, which would then be required to reach Dog Lake, would be by so much shortened. But this is a mistake. Pointe de Meuron is, in an air line, somewhat further than either Fort William or the Depôt from Dog Lake, and there would, consequently, be no object in taking cargoes up a narrow channel to a point which brought them no nearer to their destination. The branch line should, therefore, start from Fort William and not from Pointe de Meuron. From the former place the Dog Lake Road can be reached in six or seven miles, while, from the latter, ten at least would be required, with corresponding increase in the outlay. A glance at the map will show clearly what I have endeavoured to explain.

It has been objected to the Depôt as a starting point, that it is shelterless, and that the ice will tear away any wharves that can be built.

Now, on reference to the map, it will be seen that Thunder Bay is itself a harbour, although of somewhat large dimensions, completely land-locked and sheltered from every wind; any swell therefore, which can be felt must arise within the Bay itself. The huge surges of Lake Superior do not roll into it at all, and it may be regarded for all practical purposes, in relation to the subject under consideration, as an inland lake. Looking upon it in this light, the starting point at the Depôt is in a Bay of moderate depth, completely sheltered from the prevailing winds, which are westerly. A glance at the map will show that it is safe from winds blowing from the west, south-west, north and north-west; and, I may add, that a wind blowing from a direction fifteen or twenty points to the east of north, would not affect it. East, or south-easterly winds, alone, would blow in upon the harbour, but the extent of their sweep would be limited to the width of Thunder Bay, and the surge which could arise in that distance may easily be guarded against. That the swell has no great effect in Thunder Bay, at any time, is demonstrated by the fact, that the trees grow clear down almost to the level of the water, indeed, in some places, dipping their branches into it; whereas, in exposed parts of Lake Superior, the wave-lashed shores are destitute of vegetation.

It has been said, moreover, that the ice would carry wharves away, and, as convincing proof of this, a boulder was pointed out to me which had been shoved ashore by the ice. I merely notice this to show the sort of arguments which have been advanced to disparage Thunder Bay and promote the Kaministaquia. If wharves cannot stand in the tranquil waters of a land-locked bay they can stand nowhere, and those who object to them in Thunder Bay, on the score of ice, can have had but little experience of such a river as the St. Lawrence, where wharves are built to resist ice rushing against them in immense fields, with the full force of the spring floods, as is the case at Three Rivers when Lake St. Peter is breaking up.

Among the advantages which the Depôt at Thunder Bay possesses, may be mentioned the facility of approach or departure to sailing vessels, as they would have ample sea-room to beat in or out, which they could not have in a narrow river like the Kaministaquia, with a shoal at its mouth extending a full mile from the coast; and a very important point to be considered is that Thunder Bay, as compared to the Kaministaquia, opens earlier in the spring and remains open later in the fall. As an instance of this, it may be remarked that, in the fall of 1866, when the steamer *Algoma* made her last trip, the Kaministaquia is said to have been frozen over, and that so strongly that the people of Fort William were skating on the ice.

From the Depôt, eastward along the shore of Thunder Bay, the ground for a distance of several miles is practicable for a road, and there are facilities for the construction of wharves, in various places more especially at a point a little to the eastward of Current River where there is a small natural harbor, which, by means of piers might be sufficiently extended.

It was at one time believed that the upper or eastern end of Thunder Bay, affording as it does an excellent natural harbor, would have been a favorable point from which to run a line of road to Dog Lake, but a careful examination showed such a line to be impracticable, within any reasonable limit of expenditure, on account of the rugged nature of the country over which it would have had to pass. Moreover, to have adopted the head of the bay would have increased the distance to be navigated by some forty miles that is, including the addition both in Dog Lake and the bay.

Referring again to the locality which has been chosen as the starting point at Thunder Bay, it is admirably adapted for the construction of wharves. The water deepens uniformly and gradually from the shore, until, at a distance of five hundred feet, it has a depth of three fathoms and a half. Timber suitable for the work is very abundant on the Kaministaquia, whence it could be easily floated down, and on various parts of the shores there is abundance of loose stone for filling the piers, and the fixed rock, close at hand, is of a nature to be easily blasted.

At present, it is proposed merely to sink an isolated pier or breakwater, at which vessels can discharge their loads, doing in fact no more than is necessary to facilitate the landing of material and supplies for the works, leaving it to a future consideration whether the wharves shall be extended at the public cost, or left to private enterprise.

I conclude this part of the subject by noticing still another route which has been advocated, namely: the

NIPEGON BAY ROUTE.

Among the many schemes recommended for opening the Northwest Territories, the head of this bay has been suggested as a point of departure, chiefly on the ground that it affords an excellent harbour, and that, by its adoption, the distance to be navigated in Lake Superior would be somewhat shortened.

It is not, however, without its objections, and a conclusive one will be found in the fact that it is too far to the eastward of the line which it is proposed to open to render its adoption in any way expedient. It would, in fact, involve at the outset a land road of ninety or a hundred miles to reach the nearest point beyond the water-shed, without any compensating advantage. Moreover, Nipegon Bay, being completely land-locked, is said to be very late of opening in the spring, and the access to it is reported to be so intricate as to require light-houses and beacons to render it safe ; whereas, Thunder Bay is remarkably easy of access, and has been for many years approached, night and day, without the occurrence of an accident.

I may further state that a road from Nipegon Bay, to connect with the proposed line west of the water-shed, would pass over a region as yet unexplored, and only known to be exceedingly mountainous and rough, and as it would run in a direction transverse to the valleys, more than one mountain range would have to be crossed and several considerable rivers bridged.

THE LAKE REGION.

Westward of the Height of Land, on the streams tributary to Rainy Lake, there is a section of country remarkable from the fact that a very considerable portion of its area is occupied by lakes. Those on the various routes which have been followed, are set down on the annexed map, but these give only a faint idea of their number. Every river and rivulet has its lakes. Go in whatever direction he will, the explorer, on passing over a mountain range, is sure to stumble on a lake. The Indians, with their little canoes, seem by means of these lakes to travel in almost any and every direction. So numerous are they, that it would be difficult to say whether the country would be better described as one vast lake with ridges of land running through it, or as land intersected by water. On ascending any of the bare rocky bluffs frequent in the country, mountains are seen stretching away in tumultuous and broken ridges to the horizon, with lakes gleaming from every valley which the eye can reach.

Such a region is but ill adapted for railways, but nature has made up for the deficiency, by providing such means for canals as exist in but few regions of so mountainous a character. Between the hills and mountain ranges there are long reaches of tranquil water which could be connected together by means of lock and dam, with but little excavation. The country, however, in its present state, is not in a condition to admit of such projects as either railways or canals, but, even if it were, the very primitive and moderate way in which I propose to open the communication would still be necessary, as a preliminary step, to render the different points accessible.

A very marked characteristic of the region is that the streams are not subject to sudden or considerable floods, and this is a feature which the engineer, who has to provide for water-works of whatever description, will look upon with unmixed satisfaction.

This very favorable circumstance is due, primarily, to the lakes which serve as reservoirs, rising slowly during freshets, and subsiding gradually when they have passed. It is in part produced also by the character of the country, which is, in general, densely wooded.

The rain fall is excessive, and as a consequence the streams carry a very heavy volume, as compared to the area which they drain.

The lakes are everywhere studded with wooded islands, and so sheltered that the smallest canoes are rarely wind-bound.

The first considerable sheet of water westward of Height of Land, on the route which it is proposed to follow, is

LAC DES MILLE LACS.

To render this Lake accessible from Dog River, all that is required is a road of ten miles across the water-shed, between Jourdain's Rapid and the navigable water of the *Savane* River.

This line would pass over very easy ground, presenting no engineering difficulty whatever, except for about two miles near the *Savane* River, where the ground is low and swampy, requiring to be well ditched and fascined.

Two routes have been followed from Lac des Mille Lacs to Rainy Lake; one by its discharge, the River Seine, and the other by the old canoe route. A description of the former will be found in my printed report, pages 28 and 29. Subsequent to the publication of that report, the old canoe route, marked in yellow on the accompanying plan, was more thoroughly surveyed than it had been before.

Either route can be made practicable in the way I have recommended for the Seine, at a moderate outlay, but, after weighing duly their respective advantages, I am satisfied that the old canoe route will be, both as to economy of work in rendering it available, and facility of managing and navigating it afterwards, the best.

THE CANOE ROUTE.

The canoe route, to describe it more particularly, leaves Lac des Mille Lacs at Baril Bay, by a portage of sixteen chains leading to Baril Lake, which is eight miles and a half in length.

This Lake is again left by the Brulé Portage (of twenty-one chains), leading to Windegoostegoun—a series of Lakes connected by a small stream, and having an aggregate length of twelve miles. The water is in some places shallow, but it can easily be rendered of sufficient depth.

Then comes the Great French Portage of one mile and sixty chains, the descent in that distance being $99\frac{71}{100}$ feet; succeeding which the Kaogassikok Lake presents an unbroken reach of fifteen miles, ending at the Pine Portage.

Then follow two portages in close succession—the Pine and the Deux Rivières—in length, respectively, twenty-six and thirty chains; but a road of two miles, to the navigable water leading to Sturgeon Lake, would pass them both, and a small pond between them.

Sturgeon Lake, with a pond above it, presents sixteen miles of navigable water, but the river below it, for eleven miles downwards to Island Portage, makes a descent of only $32\frac{50}{100}$ feet; a dam of sufficient height at Island Portage would, therefore, add eleven miles of navigable water to its length, making a reach of full twenty-seven miles.

Island Portage is about thirteen chains in length, with, in its present state, a fall of $10\frac{6}{100}$ feet. Immediately below it the Sturgeon River is somewhat shallow, but navigable, nevertheless, and at two miles from the Portage, Nequaquon Lake presents a magnificent expanse, navigable for fifteen miles, making, with the river at its inlet, a reach of seventeen miles.

From the Lake just named to the Nameukan Lake, there are three routes; the northern one, by Snake Falls, always followed at low water, is considered dangerous, as may be inferred from its name, the "*Maligne.*"

The southern, or high water route, is easy of navigation for canoes, the total fall being overcome in three short portages. The third, at present only used with light canoes, avoids all the rapids by a portage of two miles into Nameukan, as shown on the plan, overcoming in that distance a descent of about seventy-two feet.

Then follows a traverse of ten miles, through Nameukan Lake, to the Bare Portage, which is but eleven chains in length, with a fall of $8\frac{55}{100}$ feet to Rainy Lake.

The following table shows the distances, with the fall, at each carrying place, in a more concise form :—

TABLE showing Portages and Navigable Reaches between Height of Land and Fort Frances.

PORTAGES	Land Carriage		Difference in level in feet	Navigable Branches.	Miles Navigable.
	Miles	Chains			
... ...	......	....	....	Savane River and Lac des Mille Lacs Baril Portage	42
Baril Portage	......	16	+ 1.86	Baril Lake	8¾
Brule Portage	......	21	−47.02	Windegoostegoon Lakes...	12
Descent in Windegoostegoon lakes to ts and stream	......	....	.9.50		
French Portage	1	60	−98.71	Little French Lake and Kaogassikok Lake.....	15
Pine and Deux Rivières Portages........	2	......	124.12	Sturgeon Lake and River	27
			(110.06		
Island Portage and Fall, Sturgeon River	......	13	132.50	} Nequaquon Lake......	17
Portage between Nequaquon Lake and Namenkan Lake...	2	....	72.00	Namenkan Lake.........	10
Bare Portage...	......	11	8.55	Rainy Lake and River...	46
Land Carriage...	6	41	403.46	Navigable......	177½
Off + ...	......	....	1.86	Land Carriage..........	6½
Diff. level between Lac des Mille Lacs and Rainy Lake...	......	....	401.60	....	184

Thus, between the head of the *Savane* River and Fort Frances, the extent of navigable water would be one hundred and seventy-seven and a-half miles, in eight reaches, divided by seven portages, the latter having an aggregate length of six miles and forty-one chains; in round numbers, six miles and a half. At a very little outlay, however, over what I am about to propose, the navigable reaches could be somewhat extended, and the number of carrying-places reduced to five.

For example, the difference in level between Lac des Mille Lacs and Baril Lake is hardly two feet, the latter being so much the highest. If, therefore, Lac des Mille Lacs were raised by means of a dam to the level of Baril Lake, and a cut made between the two, eight miles and a half would be added to the navigable reach of Mille Lacs, and one portage done away with.

In like manner, the difference in level between Nameukan and Rainy Lakes is but $8\frac{55}{100}$ feet, which might be overcome by a wooden lock, thus adding some ten miles to the navigable water of Rainy Lake, and avoiding another trans-shipment. There would then remain only five portages, in a distance of one hundred and eighty-four miles—one hundred and seventy-seven and a half miles being by water and a little over six by land. On three of the portages, averaging about two miles each, horses or oxen would have to be maintained, while, on the remaining two, namely: Brulé and Island

Portages, being respectively but twenty-one and thirteen chains in length, wooden-ways might be so constructed as to admit of hand-cars being drawn over them with facility. I point this out, but would not recommend, for the present, either a cut at Baril Lake or a lock to connect Nameukan and Rainy Lake.

The following are the works which I consider of the most pressing and immediate importance in this division :

DAM AT LITTLE FALLS, RIVIERE LA SEINE.

A dam at this point, if of sufficient height, say forty-two feet, would have the effect of raising the water of Lac des Mille Lacs to a level equal with, or a little higher than Baril Lake, the latter being $1\frac{88}{100}$ feet above the level of Mille Lacs; so that, by a mere cut, the two could be connected, and, in the event of more extensive works being undertaken at some future period, it would be no small matter to have the water of Mille Lacs at command, for, until after passing French Portage, the supply of water on the canoe route, although ample for the works now proposed, is not sufficient for the more extensive improvements which will doubtless be required in the future.

Among the further advantages of this dam would be the additional depth which it would give over an extensive shoal just at the mouth of the *Savane* River.

Moreover, in the event of a land road all the way between Lac des Mille Lacs and Rainy Lake becoming necessary, a dam at the Little Falls would extend the navigable waters of Mille Lacs to a distance of seventy miles on Rainy Lake. The construction of such a road has been strongly urged by various parties who have manifested a deep interest in opening the communication, chiefly under the idea that it would greatly expedite the conveyance of mails.

It must be borne in mind, however, that taking into account the character of the country, seventy miles of road made in such a way as to be really useful, in a region so remote, would cost not less than one hundred and twenty thousand dollars. It is therefore a matter for consideration whether for the present the less expensive way would not be the best, and whether if such a sum, instead of being applied to making a road, were expended on the construction of locks to extend the navigable reaches, it would not have a better effect, even as regards the transport of mails, inasmuch as steamers might then be placed to advantage on reaches now too short to admit of their being used.

The situation at the Little Falls is admirably adapted for a dam, the river at that point passing through a cut in the rock with high rocky banks on either side. To have the desired effect of raising the water of Lac des Mille Lacs to the extent of about three feet above its present level, the dam would require to be forty-two feet in height. From a rough estimate by me when on the ground, I have set down its cost at twenty thousand dollars. If, however, the mere raising of Lac des Mille Lacs were the only object in view, it could be attained by a much less costly structure at its immediate outlet.

Taking the works proposed in their regular order from the Lac des Mille Lacs to Rainy Lake, the improvement next required would be at

BARIL PORTAGE.

This is the portage or carrying place, between Lac des Mille Lacs and Baril Lake, in length sixteen chains, For the present it is merely proposed to improve the portage and place a tramway upon it for hand-cars. Baril Lake is, as stated, $1\frac{85}{100}$ feet above the level of Mille Lacs, and when the latter is raised by means of the dam proposed, a cut might easily be made to connect the two lakes and do away with the portage, as already said.

BRULE PORTAGE.

Here, also, it is proposed to place a tramway. The present length of the portage is twenty-one chains, but the brook forming the discharge of Baril Lake can be so improved as to reduce the distance to ten chains. The difference of level between the water of Baril Lake and the lower end of the portage is 47 $\frac{2}{100}$ feet.

DAM AT HEAD OF FRENCH PORTAGE.

The effect of this dam would be to raise the water of the Windegoostegoon Lakes, which is in some places shallow, and do away with a little rapid where there is a fall of three feet. The channel, where the dam is to be built, is of solid rock, eighty feet in width, with rocky banks on each side. The structure would be an ordinary flat dam, built of unhewn timber, and covered in front with timbers hewn to six inches, raised to the height of twelve feet, with a flood-gate fifteen feet in width, provided with stop logs and the means of raising them, in the same manner as at the head gates of a slide. A work of this extent would cost in ordinary circumstances about twelve hundred dollars, but considering the remoteness of the situation and the cost of getting men, supplies, etc., I have set it down at sixteen hundred dollars.

FRENCH PORTAGE.

This carrying place is one mile and sixty chains in length, and the fall from its eastern end to the Little Lake at its western extremity $90\frac{7}{100}$ feet, a difference of level which forbids any attempt to encounter the river for the present. There is nothing for it, therefore, but a road, and for this the ground, although somewhat hilly, is not unfavorable. French Portage is succeeded by a navigable reach of fifteen miles, embracing Kaogassikok Lake and ending at Pine Portage.

PINE PORTAGE AND DEUX RIVIERES PORTAGES.

These two portages may be considered as one, and have to be passed by a land road of two miles, as at French Portage, as the river could only be rendered available at an outlay which must form a subject for consideration in the future, the fall being $124\frac{12}{100}$ feet. At present, a land road, of the required distance (two miles) can be made over ground somewhat rough, but on the whole favorable. This road would end at the navigable water leading to Sturgeon Lake, and the next work required would be the

DAM AT ISLAND PORTAGE.

This is one of the most important works on the whole line of route, as its construction would give an unbroken reach of twenty-seven miles of navigable water, through the very roughest section of the Lake Region. Sturgeon Lake, which would form a link in this stretch, is sixteen miles in length, navigable throughout. From its discharge to Island Portage, the distance is eleven miles, and the aggregate fall $32\frac{50}{100}$. The carrying place is on an island just at the brow of a fall of ten feet. Sturgeon River is, at this point, three hundred and thirty feet wide, with a bottom of solid rock, and rocky banks on either side rising with a moderate ascent. Here it is proposed to construct a flat dam of the simplest form, but at the same time the strongest; and, in this instance, I see no object in going to the expense of making flood gates. The height of the dam would be not less than thirty-five feet. The quantity of timber used in its construction will reach eighty thousand lineal feet, and timber of the finest description, both red and white pine, is available; but, considering the remoteness of the locality, its cost, built into the work, cannot be reckoned at less than seventeen cents per foot, equal to fourteen thousand four hundred dollars, add to which for filling, &c., three thousand six hundred dollars, making eighteen thousand dollars, as set down in the estimate.

DAMS AT NEQUAQUON.

Immediately below Island Portage, Sturgeon River is shallow, but deepens gradually, till, at a distance of some two miles, it

12

opens out in Nequaquon Lake. The main, or northern outlet of this lake, is over a rocky bottom, and across this I propose to run a low flat dam, so as to give a sufficiency of water below Island Portage, at the shoals just mentioned. The southern outlet is smaller, but would also require a dam, and for these works I have included in the estimate a sum of four thousand dollars.

PORTAGE BETWEEN NEQUAQUON AND NAMEUKAN.

This Portage leads from the smooth water, at the western end of Nequaquon Lake, to a bay of the Nameukan Lake—its length is two miles, and the descent from one lake to the other about seventy-two feet. The ground is rough and difficult, but in the estimate I have included it with other portages, and taken a general average for the whole. From this Portage a reach of ten miles of navigable water ends at

BARE PORTAGE.

This is the last carrying place to Rainy Lake. The descent is $8\frac{66}{100}$ feet, and the length of the portage—eleven chains—can be much reduced by a little excavation.

LAKE OF THE WOODS DIVISION.

This comprises the navigable reach extending from Fort Frances to the north-west angle of the Lake of the Woods, a distance of one hundred and twenty miles.

At Fort Frances, there is a complete and sudden change in the appearance of the country, and an evident improvement in the climate. The ever-recurring rocks and hills of the lake region disappear, and in contrast to these are commodious buildings, a farm of some extent, and cattle grazing in the fields, with a broad river sweeping westward between banks of deep alluvial soil.

Rainy River is, here, a stream of great volume, nearly a quarter of a mile in width. The falls ($22\frac{88}{100}$ feet in height) are just opposite the Fort, and from this point to the north-west angle of the Lake of the Woods (a distance of one hundred and twenty miles as stated), the navigation is uninterrupted.

There are, however, two little rapids on Rainy River, the Manitou and the Long Rapids, occurring about half way to the Lake of the Woods, as set down on the accompanying map. The first, with a fall of $2\frac{60}{100}$ feet, has great depth of water, and could easily be stemmed by a steamer of moderate power. The Long

Rapid may have a fall of $3\frac{1}{2}$ to 4 feet, distributed over a distance of some thirty chains. In this rapid the water glides smoothly, but is in some places shallow. I think, however, that even at the lowest stage of water, a vessel drawing four feet could pass. In any case, the bottom is of a nature to be easily deepened, if required. The strength of the current presents no serious obstacle, as canoes can be paddled up, requiring the use of the setting poles at only two points. At the Manitou the tow line has generally to be used.

Any impediment in these rapids, therefore, would be so easily overcome, that it is hardly worth estimating, and to all practical purposes, the navigation in this long reach may be regarded as uninterrupted.

In my preliminary report, as already said, before the later explorations were made, in the country westward of the Lake of the Woods, Lac Plat was suggested as the starting point of a road to Fort Garry, chiefly because it was supposed to be the point which would involve the making of the smallest extent of road. The western extremity of Lac Plat is, however, one hundred and fifty eight miles from Fort Frances, while the north-west angle, which is now adopted as the starting point, is but one hundred and twenty miles; a saving of thirty-eight miles is thus effected in navigating the Lake of the Woods.

Before concluding this part of the subject, I would draw attention to the fact that two locks at Fort Frances, where the fall is $22\frac{88}{100}$ feet, would have the effect of adding Rainy Lake to the navigable reach which I have just been describing, giving one hundred and sixty-six miles without a trans-shipment.

FORT GARRY SECTION.

As already explained, a good deal of difficulty was experienced in finding a line practicable for a road, by which to get through the marshy region intervening between the Lake of the Woods and the prairie eastward of the Red River Settlement.

This section of country presents to the eye, in its general character, the appearance of an undeviating flat. From the Lake of the Woods, for a distance of twenty-five or thirty miles westward, swamps of great extent, covered with moss and stunted evergreens, are of frequent occurrence. In other sections, considerable areas are occupied by marshes or shallow lakes, with bulrushes and other aquatic plants standing out of the water. In the latter cases, the bottom, after a certain depth is attained, is generally firm, while, in the swamps, in some instances, the surface covering is itself afloat, and heaves and undulates beneath the feet, presenting a quagmire or peat bog, on an extensive scale. This description applies more particularly to the section nearest to the Lake of the Woods. On approaching the prairie, the swamps are less extensive and the ground in general more favorable. In the swampy sections however, there are some areas of dry ground and good soil, and where the bogs are deepest, they are intersected by low gravelly ridges which rise but a few feet over the general level. These ridges are firm, and their direction can be traced by the heavy growth of wood which they carry. Flat and level as the country appears to be, it is susceptible of being drained. The section most swampy, although but slightly higher than the Lake of the Woods is at an elevation of over three hundred feet above the valley of Red River, and wherever a run of water is met with, except in the lake-like swamps, it is seen gliding on with a speed which indicates a sufficient fall for drainage.

The principal streams in the region are the Broken Head River the White Mouth River, and the Roseau or River of Roses.

The latter takes its rise in the United States Territory, and runs westward, at a short distance from, and nearly parallel to, the Boundary Line, till it joins the Red River, a little to the north of Pembina. This stream forms a link in the ancient war-path of the Saulteaux Indians to the country of their enemies—the Sioux The Broken Head runs north to Lake Winnipeg, while the White Mouth falls into the Winnipeg River, just above the Seven Portages The section which I have just been describing, except in the swamps and marshes, is densely wooded. Westward of this is the Prairie having a depth of thirty miles to the eastward of Red River. This Prairie does not meet the wooded region as might be supposed gradually merging from prairie to woodland, but abruptly and at once. It seems to be an ancient lake bottom, still nearly as level as a lake, and generally without wood. Bordering on this is the wooded region, with points stretching into the plain, like the head lands of a lake. Just where the prairie and woodland meet, there are, in some places, banks of gravel which will eventually become of importance, as material for forming roadways over the soft and yielding soil of the plains.

From Fort Garry to the north-west angle of the Lake of the Woods, a road line has been laid out, and its practicability proved by the fact that, for several years, it was used as a post road and the mails carried over it on horseback. Wheeled vehicles, except in very wet weather, can already travel over the Prairie, and, taking the line altogether, its average cost, to form a first class country road, will be rather under than over the general average of such works

To describe it more particularly, starting from the north-west angle of the Lake of the Woods, the ground, for a distance of fifteen miles, is low and swampy, requiring deep and extensive cuts for draining, added to which the roadway, for several miles, will require to be fascined—no large bridges on this section.

Proceeding westward, there is a marked improvement in the next ten miles, but the ground is still very swampy. Material for fascining and bridging abounds, and two small bridges have to be made, on tributaries of the White Mouth River. Taking the above as one section of twenty-five miles, reckoning from the Lake of the Woods, I set its average cost at sixteen hundred dollars per mile, equal to forty thousand dollars; still proceeding westward for thirty-five miles (which may be regarded as one section) the ground is much improved in character. For some four or five miles, near the White Mouth River, nothing better could be desired. Then follows a series of low gravelly ridges, over many portions of which little more has to be done than to grub out the trees. An occasional intrusion from an adjoining swamp has to be fascined, and bridges will be required over the Broken Head and White Mouth Rivers. For this section, I have set down one thousand dollars per mile; in all thirty-five thousand dollars.

The next section is over low prairie embracing a distance of about thirty miles, from a place where there are a few Indian huts, called "Oak Point Settlement," to Fort Garry. For this section I have set down four hundred dollars per mile, which may appear to be a low estimate for a road, but all that can be done for it, without going to a very great outlay, is to drain it thoroughly, and, if this were done, it would be as good as the roads at Red River generally are. A road on a prairie has this advantage, that when the turf cuts and the wheels begin to sink in one track, another is always available, the width being quite unlimited.

To render the section under consideration practicable in this way, one deep ditch is necessary, with a little fascining and raising of the roadway in the lower parts. Lateral cuts, of considerable length, will have to be made to drain the water from the main trench; all which can be accomplished at an average cost of four hundred dollars per mile, making in all, twelve thousand dollars for the Prairie Section.

TOTAL LENGTH OF ROUTE BY LAND AND WATER.

	Land Miles.	Chains.	Water Miles.
Dog Lake Road........................	25		
Dog Lake and River.................			35
Height of Land Portage	10		
Lac des Mille Lacs and *Savane* Riv'r			42
Baril Portage...........................		16	
Baril Lake...............................			8½
Brulé Portage		21	
Windegoostegoon			12
French Portage........................	2		
Kaogassikok			15
Deux Rivières	2		
Sturgeou Lake			27
Island Portage		13	
Nequaquon			17
Nequaquon Portage	2		
Nameukan Lake			10
Bare Portage...........................		11	
Rainy Lake			46
Fort Frances...........................		10	
Rainy River and Lake of the Woods			120
Fort Garry.........	90		
	131	71	332½
			131
			463½

ESTIMATE.

The probable cost of opening the communication, in the way I have proposed, from Jourdain's Rapid, at the head of the navigable water on Dog River, to Fort Garry, would be as follows :—

LAKE REGION.

Roads and improvements at Height of Land, between Dog River and Lac des Mille Lacs	$11,000	00
Dam, with flood-gates, at eastern end Great French Portage	1,600	00
Dam, thirty-five feet high, across Sturgeon River, at Island Portage....................	18,000	00
Two low flat dams, at Nequaquon Lake ...	4,000	00

Dam, at Little Falls (Two Falls Portage on the River Seine)............................	20,000	00
Six and a half miles road and tramway over portages, between Lac des Mille Lacs and Rainy Lake....................................	10,400	00
	$65,000	**00**

LAND ROADS (FORT GARRY SECTION.)

Ninety miles land road, between north-west angle of the Lake of the Woods and Fort Garry, would cost for twenty-five miles, Eastern Section, at $1,600 per mile...............	$40,000	00		
Thirty-five miles, Middle Section, at $1,000 per mile......	35,000	00		
Thirty miles, Western Section, over low prairie, at $400 per mile	12,000	00		
			87,000	00
			$152,000	**00**

OTHER WORKS (LAKE SUPERIOR SECTION.)

A pier required at the Depôt, Thunder Bay, Lake Superior.................	2,500	00		
Seven miles land road, to connect Fort William with Dog Lake Line.......	7,000	00		
			9,500	00
			$161,500	**00**
Superintendence and contingencies.................			5,000	00
			$166,500	**00**

The above does not include such of the works, in the Lake Superior section, as were provided for in the grant of fifty-five thousand nine hundred dollars made last year, except a road at the Height of Land, which is allowed for in the present estimate. This was necessary, inasmuch as the total grant of last year will be required to complete the road to Dog Lake, and finish the dam, which latter was found to involve a little more work than anticipated, on account of the necessity which has arisen of running an additional dam along a rocky ridge of low ground, south of the outlet of Dog Lake.

PROBABLE TRAFFIC.

Within the last few years, since the North-west Territories have begun to attract so much attention, many schemes have been advanced and many suggestions made, as to the best means of opening the communication. Without going, for the present, into the merits of these schemes, I would draw attention to the fact that the country between Lake Superior and the Red River Settlement is a wilderness, as yet in a state of nature ; that, except to the canoe of the Indian, or the voyager, it is quite inaccessible in its present state, and that until some way of getting through it is devised, there can be no means of taking even the initiatory steps in the construction of works of great magnitude, such as railways or canals. A line of communication such as I have proposed would render the country accessible, and, when it is completed, it will be time enough to entertain greater projects.

But, while taking this view of its utility, I must also draw attention to the fact that the opening of the communication, even in this simple way, would have the immediate effect of drawing the trade of the North-west Territories to Canada.

The people of Red River, at present, purchase their goods in St. Paul, and take them from thence full six hundred miles, *overland*, to the settlement ; sometimes, indeed, there is a small steamer which runs on Red River during high water, but, as a general rule, the goods which the settlers require are carted all the way through, and the cost of freight is generally reckoned at from four and a half to five dollars per 100 ℔s.

Now, from an estimate which I have made, I feel confident that if the communication were opened, even in the primitive way suggested, the cost of transport from Lake Superior to the Red River Settlement would not exceed $1.75 per 100 ℔s.; but, supposing that it should cost as much as two dollars, it would still be less, by over one-half, than the cost of freight from St. Paul; and when the vastly cheaper rate at which goods can be purchased in Canada, as compared to Minnesota, is considered, it is but reasonable to suppose that the trade must come this way.

I have only alluded, so far, to the trade of the settlement, or rather of the settlers, apart from that of the Hudson's Bay Company, but I think the latter might be looked for also ; for the able officers who manage that ancient and honorable corporation, as soon as they saw that they could get their supplies cheaper by Lake Superior than by Hudson's Bay or St. Paul, would at once adopt the route. It is clear, therefore, that by opening the communication in the manner proposed, a trade, amounting to several millions of dollars annually, would be at once transferred to Canada. Even as a matter of speculation, without reference to political considerations or the vast field which would be opened to colonization, it would be a safe enterprise to open the line.

It is a circumstance of no small importance, in recommending the expenditure of money on a public work, to be able to show that, when completed, 'it will at once begin to yield a return. In the present instance, the return would not, of course, be in the shape of tolls on the works, but in the way of increasing trade, and consequently increasing revenue, the laying open of extensive tracts of fertile territory for settlement, and the development of a district now known to be rich in mineral resources.

The State of Minnesota has, of late, being doing a good deal to facilitate intercourse and trade with the Red River Settlement. During the summer now approaching, a tri-weekly line of stages will be established, mails will be delivered every second day, and the people, cut off from Canada, will naturally draw closer to the only neighbors with whom they can hold intercourse, and, if this state of things continues long, they must become a community of the United States, rather than a British Colony.

Now, it is evident, that if the trade of the North-west Territories is of value to Minnesota, it ought to be of some importance to Canada; and, if the people of a new State see advantage in taxing their scanty resources, to make roads and keep up lines of stages to attract that trade, *overland*, surely the Dominion, with much greater facilities and more ample resources, might do a little to obtain it, when nearly two-thirds of the distance would be by navigable water.

THE MEANS OF TRANSPORT.

When the traffic of the Red River Settlement and the North-west Territories has once fairly begun to take the route by Lake Superior, private enterprise will soon fall upon the means by which transport can be most easily effected.

LAND CARRIAGE.

In the meantime, I may suggest the mode, which, in the first instance, must be resorted to. At Lake Superior, of course, when the communication is once completely opened, there will, no doubt, be ample competition for the conveyance of articles over the road to Dog Lake, as there probably will be at the Height of Land Portage also.

At three of the portages in the interior, however, namely, the French, Deux Rivières and Nequaquon Portages, averaging two miles each, horses and oxen will have to be maintained for a time. At the Baril, Brulé, Island and Bare Portages, tramways will be arranged for hand cars, the latter being short.

Between the North-west angle of the Lake of the Woods and Fort Garry, no provision would have to be made, as the means of conveyance are abundant at the Red River Settlement.

WATER CARRIAGE.

On the shorter reaches, boats, such as the Hudson's Bay Company use in the transport of goods from York Factory to the Red River Settlement, would be the best. They carry about five tons, and are easily drawn over a portage. Such boats would answer well between Lac des Mille Lacs and Fort Frances. Once the communication was fairly established, a relay of boats might be kept on each reach, and then much larger vessels might be employed.

In the longer reaches, steamers might be used to advantage, and would probably—most certainly, if the traffic became extensive—be more economical than boats.

There would be in all five reaches in which I think it would be desirable to have small steamers, namely :—

On Dog Lake and River..................	35	miles navigable.
Savane River and Lac des Mille Lacs...	42	"
Sturgeon Lake and River..................	27	"
Rainy Lake..................................	46	"
Fort Francis to North-west Angle........	120	"
	270 miles.	

Thus, in five reaches, amounting in the aggregate to two hundred and seventy miles, the shortest of which would be twenty-seven miles in length, small steamers, of a cheap class, might be used to advantage. Gradually, as improvement advanced, the reaches might be connected together by means of locks, and then, of course, larger vessels would come into play.

In the five shorter navigable reaches of the "Lake Region," boats such as I have suggested, or indeed scows or boats of any kind, might be used, as for instance, in

Baril Lake	8½	miles.
Windegoostegoon	12	"
Kaogassikok	15	"
Nequaquon Lake...................................	17	"
Nameukan	10	"
	62½ miles.	

Five reaches, giving sixty-two miles and a half for ordinary row boats and scows.

COST OF FREIGHT.

With these arrangements on the carrying places and navigable reaches, the cost of freight would be nearly as follows :—

25 miles land carriage, to Dog Lake..............	25	cents.
35 miles water carriage, through Dog River and Lake	8	"
10 miles land carriage, Height of Land	12	"
184 miles, to Fort Frances, land and water	60	"
120 miles, Fort Frances to Lake of Woods, in steamers or barges carrying say fifty to one hundred tons.......................	8	"
90 miles, North-west Angle to Fort Garry, by land	80	"

464 miles.	$1 93

or say even two dollars per 100 lbs.

This would be less than half the cost of freight from St. Paul, which is $4 50 per 100 lbs. and sometimes five dollars.

I have set down the cost of transport purposely high, although in some places it may appear low ; for example, between the North-west Angle and Fort Garry, I have put down eighty cents per one hundred pounds, as the cost, in a distance of ninety miles. In estimating the accuracy of this, it must, in the first place, be considered that horses and carts are abundant at Red River. Horses are very numerous, and there is but little employment for them, and the people make their own carts and harness, which, although very serviceable, are very cheap ; they besides bring articles six hundred miles from St. Paul for $4.50 per 100 pounds, which would be but equal to sixty-seven and a half cents on ninety miles, and I have set down eighty cents, a fair allowance in any country. Even in Lower Canada, on the St. Maurice, where there is a good deal of competition in winter, loads can be sent one hundred and twenty miles into the interior for from seventy-five to eighty cents per 100 pounds ; and between Three Rivers and Montreal, a distance of just ninety miles, sixty cents per 100 pounds, would be considered, at Three Rivers, a high rate.

In the long navigable reach of one hundred and twenty miles, between the North-west Angle and Fort Frances, I have put eight cents per 100 pounds, equal to $1.60 per ton of 2000 pounds ; one dollar per ton would be ample, as large vessels can be used.

In the reach of broken navigation, of one hundred and eighty-four miles, between the *Savane* or Height of Land Portage and Fort Frances, I have put sixty cents per 100 pounds, equal to twelve dollars per ton of 2,000 pounds. Now five men with a boat carrying five tons, can go in five days from the *Savane* to Fort Frances, and return in four days, taking the same boat with them all the way. Allowing one dollar per day for each man, their expenses would be, for nine days, forty-five dollars, whereas I have allowed sixty dollars ; but, if there were a relay of boats and scows capable of carrying fifty tons, on each reach, with horses and waggons on the three longer portages, it could be done for six dollars per ton, or say thirty cents per 100 pounds.

For the Height of Land carriage of ten miles, I have set down twelve cents per 100 pounds, or say $2.40 per ton of 2,000 pounds. It requires no explanation to show that this is a very ample estimate.

In the Dog Lake and River reach of thirty-five miles, I have put down eight cents, equal to $1.60 per ton, and for the land carriage of twenty-five miles, from Thunder Bay to Dog Lake, I estimate twenty-five cents per 100 lbs., or say five dollars per ton of 2,000 pounds.

These estimates will all be considered ample; but, supposing the communication to be well opened, and the appliances for transport in full operation, the following would be a fair estimate :—

25 miles land road, Thunder Bay to Dog Lake......	25	cents.
35 miles water carriage, Dog River and Lake......	6	"
10 miles land carriage, Height of Land	10	"
184 miles, Fort Frances, 6¼ being by land............	30	"
120 miles, Fort Frances to north-west angle in Batteaux, of 100 tons	6	"
90 miles land carriage, North-west Angle to Fort Garry	75	"
464 miles.	$1.52 per 100 lbs.	

That is, $30,$\frac{40}{100}$ per ton of 2,000 lbs., from Thunder Bay to Fort Garry. But, as I said before, making every allowance, and taking the cost at $2 per 100 lbs., equal to forty dollars per ton, at the outset. From York Factory to Red River, the contract price used to be twenty pounds sterling, or one hundred dollars per ton, while the present rate, by the Prairies and Red River, is ninety dollars per ton of 2,000 lbs.

Beyond this, it surely requires no argument to show that, if the communication were opened, the whole trade of the Red River settlement, both that of the Hudson's Bay Company and the settlers, would pass by Lake Superior. A saving of fifty dollars per ton on freight would certainly decide the matter. But this is not all, the price of such articles as the people of the Red River require, being chiefly dry goods and groceries, is much lower in Canada than in any of the remote western Towns of Minnesota. If Fort William were again made a free port, as it recently was, and always supposing the communication to be opened, the people of the Red River Settlement would be in position to supply the northern settlements of Minnesota with merchandize, instead of being dependent upon them, as at present.

RESOURCES—TIMBER, &c.

When the communication is opened, and settlement begins to advance in the prairies of the West, there will be a demand for wood for building and other purposes, increasing gradually until it has attained proportions commensurate with the means of transport. Westward of the Height of Land, on the streams flowing towards Rainy Lake, there is an abundance of timber, such as red and white pine, of a large size and good quality. This section would compare not unfavorably with some of the best lumber regions on the Upper Ottawa.

The prairies are nearly destitute of timber, and here is a supply which, to all practical purposes, may be said to be illimitable, and, looking to the future of the western territories, and having regard to the probable traffic which is to support a line of communication, there are, in the forests of the Winnipeg slope, the elements of a trade which should be kept in view.

Another article of economic value, which should be taken into account, is the vast quantity of peat which might be obtained in the swampy region near the Lake of the Woods; some of the swamps are very deep, and hold in store great quantities of fuel of this description, for a region further to the west where there is but little wood. In a very short time the people of Red River Settlement will find peat cheaper than wood, although, doubtless, they have for the present a considerable supply of the latter article.

The country has, however, other valuable resources, of which but little is as yet known, and no doubt, in the future, attention will be directed to its

MINERAL RESOURCES.

It is now well known that silver mines of surpassing richness were discovered at Lake Superior last summer, but it is not so generally understood that a formation, of the same age as that in which they occur, extends with more or less interruption to the Lake of the Woods, and that, for a great part of the way, the line which it is proposed to open will pass over Schists of the Lower Silurian period, such as yield silver at Lake Superior, and gold in Nova Scotia.

That part of line, however, extending from a little eastward of Dog Lake to the Nameukan Lake, will be almost wholly in Laurentian gneiss—Silurian rocks then show themselves, and the Schists on rainy Lake are plentifully intersected with lodes of quartz. While at Fort William, last summer, I was shown some very fine specimens of Gold quartz taken from Rainy Lake. I was also informed, on what I believed to be good authority, that alluvial Gold had been discovered, but that the fact was being kept as secret as possible.' These reports gain confirmation from the fact, that on Vermillion Lake, in Minnesota, which is tributary to Rainy Lake, and only at a short distance from it, Gold quartz has been already worked and various claims taken up. The communication which it is proposed to open might, therefore, be the means of developing an American as well as a Canadian Gold Field.*

At the Lake of the Woods, chloritic and talcose schists, of Silurian age, similar to those of the Gold districts of the Chaudiere, are frequent on the Islands, and they are traversed by what appear to be very promising quartz lodes.

Upon the whole, the indications and actual discoveries throughout the region are such as to warrant the expectation that there are mineral resources, as yet undeveloped, which will eventually lead to a trade which will greatly aid in sustaining a line of communication.

OTHER METHODS OF OPENING THE COMMUNICATION.

RAILWAYS.

It has been urged that a Railroad from Lake Superior to Red River would afford the best and easiest means of communication, and that it would form a link in the great Railway system which it is believed will, at no distant day, span the continent from the Atlantic to the Pacific, within British Territory.

Now, while admitting the great advantages which would result from a work of this kind, it must be borne in mind that the means for its construction cannot at present be obtained. There is no amount of argument, as to prospective advantages, which could procure the investment of twenty millions of dollars, which

* The following extract shows that the mines in the Vermillion district, near Rainy Lake, are beginning to attract attention :—
"THE LAKE SUPERIOR COUNTRY.—The *Gazette* (Superior, Wis.,) says:—' Col. Henry Tyndall arrived here from the Vermillion district late last evening, and started for St. Paul this morning. Tests have been made from several of the veins, all with the most favorable results. The quantity of rock tested in each case was not less than five hundred pounds. In every experiment so far, the yield has been largely over $100 per ton ; and some of them have gone up to thousands. A private letter informs us of one instance where one hundred and fifty pounds of rock yielded a pound and one-half of bullion. Colonel Tyndall pronounces the country rich, and in this statement he is borne out by the amount of bullion which he brings with him, amounting to between seven and eight pounds of gold and silver."

would be about its cost, in an undeveloped region, such as that through which it would pass. Theoretically, the idea may be a good one, but practically, it is at least premature.

Moreover, a railroad between the points indicated would be isolated as regards other railways, and being available only during the season of navigation, would be without one of the chief advantages of a railroad, which is that it can be kept in operation, independently of the navigation.

It has been suggested that, whatever objections might attach to the project of a railway all the way to Red River, a comparative short line would best overcome the rough and difficult section intervening between Lake Superior and Rainy Lake. But the same objections which present themselves in regard to the former, apply to the latter.

Its length, that is of a line from Lake Superior to Rainy Lake, allowing for deviations, would not be greatly less than two hundred miles, and its cost would far exceed any means which there is a probability of obtaining.

It would absorb an amount of capital more than sufficient to provide for the lockage required to connect the navigable reaches between Dog Lake and Lake Winnipeg, and form a canal, which, in the present state of the country, or any stage of development to which it can attain for a considerable period, would be of greater utility than a railroad.

Finally, before such a work was undertaken, the country would have to be rendered accessible, as I have already said, by some such means of communication as I have suggested.

It will not be understood, however, from what I have said, that a railway is impracticable. In fact, with exception of the section between Lake Superior and Rainy Lake, which is rough and broken and has never yet been explored with a view to a work of the kind, the ground is not unfavorable, but, as I have said, the idea of such a work is premature.

CANALS.

On reference to what I have already stated, it will be seen that, from Dog Lake north-westward, to the Lake of the Woods, long navigable reaches occur in continuous succession, separated by short intervals of rapid water or other impediments. From the Height of Land Portage, where it strikes the *Savane* River, to the North-west Angle of the Lake of the Woods, the distance is three hundred and four miles, and the total amount of lockage that would be required, four hundred and twenty-five feet, being somewhat less than that of the Rideau Canal. By means of lock and

dam, the whole of this distance might be rendered navigable without a break, at comparatively small cost, if wooden locks were
adopted. The river channels between the navigable sections, are
every where of rock, and generally favorable for the construction
of such works as would be required.

With this extent of navigation might be connected the navigable water, east of the Height of land, having a length, in Dog
Lake and River, of thirty-five miles.

When the dam now in progress at Dog Lake is completed, the
difference in level between the waters of Dog River and the
Savane will be about a hundred feet, and a Canal with locks, by
way of Muskaig Lake, might be constructed to connect the two.
Lac des Mille Lacs would be the summit level, and it has sufficient water for a Canal both ways.

This would give three hundred and fifty miles of unbroken
navigation, approaching at its eastern extremity to within twenty-
five miles of Lake Superior, and at its western to within ninety
miles of Fort Garry.

All the lockage required would cost less than would a railroad
of two hundred miles to Rainy Lake, and it would be of vastly
greater utility.

A short Railway of twenty-five miles, from Dog Lake to
Thunder Bay, would connect the navigation with Lake Superior;
while a similar work of ninety miles, from Fort Garry to the
North-west Angle of the Lake of the Woods, would join it to the
Red River Settlement. The latter Railway would be over very
even ground.

I have offered these suggestions, not with a view of conveying
the impression that they should be immediately acted upon, but to
show what is practicable, and what would be the true way of
opening a line adapted for heavy traffic, when the country has attained a stage of development to warrant the expenditure which
it would involve.

SYSTEM OF WORK BY CONTRACT OR OTHERWISE.

The work is of that nature, which from long experience in carrying on similar operations, in remote sections, I believe could be
better performed by engaging good workmen and competent over-
seers than by contract.

Contract work is all well enough in a settled country, where, if
one man fails in accomplishing an undertaking, others are always
ready to take it up; but, in such a region as that in which the

works under consideration would be carried on, the Government would be, in a measure, at the mercy of the contractor; as for instance, if he should not make provision for a particular work, or from any cause break off, it would throw the enterprise back for a full year. Contractors, as a general rule, would only undertake work in a region so remote in the hope of large profits, which the comparatively small sums set down for each particular section would not bear. They would, as usual, have endless bills for extras, where every little contingency could not be foreseen; and if it appeared to be a losing business, would delay and petition for increase in their rates, and might, indeed, abandon the works altogether. Morever, the Indians, in some of the sections, have to be very carefully dealt with. At such a distance from the restraints of law, none but men of good character should be brought among them, and spirituous liquors should be strictly prohibited.

Under a system of contract, the Government would have little to say as to the class of men to be employed, and the officers in charge of the works might be unable to prevent liquor from being smuggled in. The Indians sometimes assemble at Fort Frances, and on Rainy River, to the number of five or six hundred, and if a few barrels of whiskey were rolled amongst them the consequences might, undoubtedly would, be serious.

Moreover, contractors, or their employés, would not consider themselves in any way bound to refrain from interfering in the fur trade, and their doing so would irritate and render hostile the employés of the Hudson's Bay Company, who had been so friendly and obliging in the past, and whose good offices will, I have no doubt, be equally at the disposal of the country in the future, if they meet with the courtesy they are always ready to extend.

In my allusions to the contract system, I wish it to be clearly understood that I speak from my own experience of such a system in the wilderness, and, meaning no reflection on contractors in general, I would say that if such a system is adopted in the Rainy Lake Section of the country, a military force will be required to support it, and this would soon occasion a greater outlay than the full amount of my estimate for the work.

For the works on the Lake Superior Section, and the Lake Region, the head-quarters, from whence supplies are to be sent in, must be at Fort William or Thunder Bay; the latter, of course, after the Dog Lake road is completed.

For the road between the North-west Angle of the Lake of the Woods and Fort Garry, supplies and men must be obtained at the Red River Settlement. Workmen in sufficient numbers can be had there, and, from letters I have recently received, I am led to believe that provisions also will be abundant, such as flour, beef, etc.

13

THE INDIAN ELEMENT.

In opening the communication to Red River, the country will be brought, to some extent, into contact with the Indians, who have their hunting grounds on the line of route.

Hitherto, Canada has been fortunate in dealing with the Indian element; and, in the present case, I see no reason for anticipating greater difficulty than has arisen in the past.

The only localities were the Indians are at all numerous, are at the Lake of the Woods and Rainy River, but the entire population does not greatly exceed three thousand. They can, however, collect in summer in larger numbers than Indians usually do, from the fact that they have abundance of food. This is afforded by the wild rice of the country which they collect, and by the fish which literally swarm in the lakes and rivers ; some industry practised on their own part, too, in raising Indian corn, serves to supply them to a small extent. I have seen as many as five or six hundred of them collected at one time, at the rapids on Rainy River, engaged in catching sturgeon, the flesh of which they preserve by drying it like Pemican and then pounding it up and putting it, with a due mixture of oil, into bags made of sturgeon's skin.

They have a rude sort of Government, and the regulations made by their Chiefs are observed, it is said, better than laws usually are where there are no great means of enforcing them.

They are very intelligent, and are extremely jealous as to their right of soil and authority over the country which they occupy.

When the Red River Expedition first came in contact with them, they manifested some displeasure, and were not slow to express it, at parties being sent through their country, to explore and examine it, without their consent being first asked and obtained. On becoming better acquainted with them, we found it to our advantage to keep up a little friendly intercourse with the Chiefs, calling upon them as we passed, and interchanging a few presents of no great value. When we had adopted this course, all difficulties vanished, and, ere the explorations were brought to a close, they manifested and expressed an earnest wish to see the communication opened.

The chief danger which could arise of coming into unfriendly relations with the Indians, would be from having large parties of workmen in the vicinity of their encampments. Now, this is a contingency not likely to arise, from the fact that where the Indians are numerous the navigation is unimpeded and but little work required ; but, as a rule, extreme prudence will always have to be observed by the officers in charge of men to keep them from coming in contact with the Indians.

These Indians are all heathens, and never seem to have been in the slightest degree impressed by the Missionaries who have attempted their conversion. They are, however, very pious in their own way, and much of their time seems to be occupied in religious observances, which have their manifestation in long fasts and nights of watching, when they pretend to hold familiar intercourse with Spirits, whose presence, in the secret recesses of their lodges, is indicated by drum-beating, chanting, incantations and many unearthly noises besides. At stated intervals, the greatest and most solemn ceremony of the tribe, the Mystical Feast of the White Dog, is held at Fort Frances, and, at such times, the gravity and terrible earnestness of their demeanor would do no discredit to more civilized congregations.

In appearance these Indians are tall and well formed, and, in bearing, independent; sometimes, even a little saucy, but in their intercourse with strangers they are hospitable and kind. Their morality is said to be of a high order, as compared to that of the Indians of the Plains.

They are, in general, keen traders, and seem to know the value of what they get and give, as well as any people in the world. Some of those who assemble at Rainy River for the sturgeon fishing, in summer, come from Red Lake, in the neighboring State of Minnesota, where they possess hunting grounds; and, among these latter, are some who have been parties to treaties with the United States for relinquishing certain tracts for settlement, for which they are now in receipt of annual payments. The experience they have thus gained has rendered them expert diplomatists, as compared to Indians who have never had such advantages, and they have not failed to impress on their kindred and tribe, on Rainy River, the value of the lands which they hold on the line of route to Red River.

Any one who, in negotiating with these Indians, should suppose he had mere children to deal with, would find himself mistaken. In their manner of expressing themselves, indeed, they make use of a great deal of allegory, and their illustrations may at times appear childish enough, but, in their actual dealings, they are shrewd and sufficiently awake to their own interests, and, if the matter should be one of importance, affecting the general interests of the tribe, they neither reply to a proposition, nor make one themselves, until it is fully discussed and deliberated upon in Council of all the Chiefs.

The Chiefs are fond of asking any travellers, whom they believe to be of importance, to attend a Grand Council, as it affords them an opportunity of making speeches, which are meant quite as much to swell their importance in the eyes of their own people as to impress the stranger; and with their people these meetings are popular, as it affords them an excuse for making a holiday, and coming out in all the varieties of colour which paint, unsparingly applied, can produce.

At these gatherings it is necessary to observe extreme caution in what is said, as, although they have no means of writing, there are always those present who are charged to keep every word in mind. As an instance of the manner in which records are in this way kept, without writing, I may mention that, on one occasion, at Fort Frances, the principal Chief of the tribe commenced an oration by repeating, almost verbatim, what I had said to him two years previously.

All this goes to show a certain stability of character, and a degree of importance attached to what they say, on such occasions, themselves, as well as to what they hear from others. The word of the Chiefs once passed, too, seems to be quite reliable, and this augurs well for the observance of any treaty that may be made with them.

For my own part, I would have the fullest reliance as to these Indians observing a treaty and adhering most strictly to all its provisions, if, in the first place, it were concluded *after full discussion, and after all its provisions were thoroughly understood by the Indians,* and if, in the next, it were never infringed upon by the whites, who are generally the first to break through Indian treaties.

THE TREATY.

From what I have said, I trust it will be seen that some sort of a treaty should be arrived at with the Indians. They are, as I have stated, desirous of seeing the communication opened, believing that it will conduce to their advantage, and I think a treaty with them should, in the first instance, be confined to this one point, namely, RIGHT OF WAY. This they expressed their willingness to accord many years ago, but the question of relinquishing land for settlement was always taken by them *en délibére.* In this latter respect, what they are afraid of is, that settlers would interfere with the fisheries, from which they derive their chief means of subsistence, and I think it would, in the first instance, be imprudent to introduce settlement in the particular section which they occupy. The first great point is to get the communication opened, and the first treaty should be confined, as I have said, simply to *right of way.* By combining it with the land question, surveys of townships for settlement, reserves for the Indians, and so forth, complications might arise which would prove embarrassing.

There is but one point more, in relation to this subject, to which I would invite attention; it is the necessity of adopting the most rigorous and strict measures to prevent the conveyance of ardent liquors to the Indian country. This the officer in charge of the works can easily see to, if he is armed with the proper authority. There is no likelihood of any of the employés of the works taking spirits, in any quantity, with them, unless contractors are employed ; but there are private traders who would follow in their wake, and would not be slow to bring liquor, if through it they could drive a trade for furs ; and such persons should, if they made the attempt, be at once arrested.

The Indians at Rainy River and the Lake of the Woods are, as a general rule, in happy ignorance of what ardent liquor is. On the American side, the penalties against its introduction are so severe that it rarely makes it appearance, while on the British side its use is prohibited by the Hudson's Bay Company.

To these fortunate circumstances, I believe, are due the well-being and orderly demeanor of the Indians, and the rapid increase in the population which, in this section, is, in contrast to the general rule, said to be taking place.

The precautions which I have recommended will appear not to be unnecessary, when it is considered that these Indians, notwithstanding their many good qualities, are still but savages ; that they, in common with all the untutored tribes of their race, are keen to resent an injury, real or supposed ; that a quarrel with one prominent individual would be a quarrel with the tribe, and that the sole arbiters of a dispute with them are the scalping knife and tomahawk, to the use of which they are well practised in their unceasing wars with the Sioux; and when, along with all this, it is considered that they can muster five hundred fighting men, accustomed to the woods, the rivers, and every defile in the country, the expediency as well as the justice of keeping from them that first prolific source of Indian quarrels and Indian demoralization, " Fire Water," will be apparent.

I have only further to say, that, with ordinary prudence, there need be no risk of getting into difficulty with the Indians. They will extend a warm welcome, in the first instance, to the parties sent in by the Government, and it will be for the latter to see that nothing occurs to interrupt a continuance of friendly intercourse.

(See Notices of Indians, in my printed Report, pages 14 and 26.)

AGRICULTURAL RESOURCES.

LAKE SUPERIOR SECTION.

In this section the cultivable areas are of limited extent, and confined chiefly to the valleys of the streams. There are, however, occasional plateaux at a considerable elevation, showing a moderate depth of loam. In the vicinity of the line of route, the best locations will be found in the valley of the Kaministaquia, and on the shores of Thunder Bay. The climate of the country bordering on the lake shore is favorable to the growth of cereals, and all kinds of vegetables which are usually raised in other parts of Canada. When the mines at Thunder Bay, and on the north shore of Lake Superior generally, become developed, they will create a market for all kinds of agricultural produce, and this must render of great value such lands as are susceptible of cultivation.

Around the shores of Dog Lake, there are occasional patches of fair land, but the elevation of the country is such as to render the climate rather cold. On Dog River, and at the plateaux at the Height of Land, there is any amount of pasturage, and oats, potatoes, &c., might easily be raised.

THE LAKE REGION.

The eastern section of this region is cold, on account of its great elevation, but on descending to the westward the climate rapidly improves, and by the time Sturgeon Lake is reached, the summers are as long as at Lake Superior, and I think somewhat warmer.

Eastward of Sturgeon Lake, the rock formation is Laurentian, and, as usual in regions occupied by that series, the cultivable areas are limited in extent, although, where they do occur, the soil is often very rich. It is such a country as that now being settled on the Gatineau or Upper Ottawa, with this difference, that whereas on the Gatineau and Ottawa the valleys present rivers bordered with alluvial soil, the valleys in this region are occupied by lakes. There are, nevertheless, occasional spots occurring at intervals throughout the whole region, where the soil is good, and of sufficient extent for farms ; but, as a rule, speaking generally, the country never can become an agricultural district.

There are those, however, who would prefer a mountainous and diversified region of this kind, to the level areas which are spread out like oceans, a little further to the west. Among the Laurentian hills, and on the borders of lakes studded with wooded islands, there are situations of surpassing beauty and magnificence. The forests abound in game, and the rivers and lakes are teeming with fish, water power is unlimited, and timber, which will yet find a market in the prairies of the West, is abundant.

A farmer who should establish himself on any of the carrying places with horses and waggons, would soon realize an independence, as many have done in similar situations on the Ottawa. The first to locate themselves would have the advantage, and might hope soon to see villages growing up around them. No more advantageous situations could be desired than Jourdain's Rapids, the Prairie Portage, where there is an abundance of grass, or the French or Deux Rivières Portages, all of which, until a canal is made, must be places of land carriage and trans-shipment. Here, then, in the event of the communication being opened, would be a field for enterprise, to steady and industrious farmers, who could combine the cultivation of the land with the profitable employment of carrying freight over the portages.

In such situations, too, the growing wants of a new settlement would soon create a demand for various branches of industry. Boat-builders, blacksmiths and carpenters, would find ready employment where small craft had to be provided for such a length of inland navigation, and saw mills would be required to supply them with material.

But, to proceed in regard to the capacity of the country for agriculture, on getting to Sturgeon Lake, the climate is improved, but the ground is rough and broken, as it is also at Nequaquon and Nameukan Lakes. Rainy Lake is so much indented with bays, that in passing through it only headlands and islands can be seen, and these are often rocky ; but I have heard it reported by the Indians that there are areas of very fine land about Rainy Lake.

LAKE OF THE WOODS AND FORT GARRY SECTIONS.

Arrived at Fort Frances, one hundred and ninety miles in an air line from Thunder Bay, the mountainous region is passed, and, commencing here, a beautiful tract of land extends along the bank of Rainy River to the Lake of the Woods. This tract is of the very richest alluvial soil, and in the whole distance there is not apparently an acre unsusceptible of cultivation. Old Indian gardens, growing vetches and wild grass, are met with at intervals on the banks, and the forests present basswood, oak and elm, with occasional white pines of gigantic proportions.

To this succeeds the Lake of the Woods, with fifty miles of navigation among islands varying in character, some fertile and others barren, but on some of which the Indians have grown maize from time immemorial. The section which comes next, that between the North-west Angle and the Prairie, as already described, is swampy. There are, nevertheless, occasional portions of it well adapted for settlement.

The wooded region ends with the section just referred to, and, from this point westward to the Rocky Mountains and north-westward to Peace River, the prevailing characteristic is prairie. These prairies are, for the most part, of rich alluvial loam, but they are in some places sandy, as on the upper portion of the South Branch of the Saskatchewan. So vast is the region, and the soil throughout the greater part of its extent so good, that it is no exaggeration to say the *cultivable areas may be reckoned by hundreds of millions of acres.*

The country is intersected with rivers, one of which, the Saskatchewan, drains an area greater than does the St. Lawrence, and is navigable for seven hundred miles of its course. From the South Branch of this great river, north-west to Peace River, the climate is adapted to the growth of wheat. Coal, salt, iron, gold and bitumen, are among the minerals to be found. Over the untilled fields which nature has spread out, the wild cattle of the plains roam in countless herds, and for hundreds of miles together may be seen grazing like domestic cattle in a field of pasture. A region which thus, in a state of nature, supports animal life in profusion, must be naturally rich, as regards its soil and climate. It is, in fact, fitted to sustain as dense an agricultural population as any area of equal extent on the face of the globe.

Such, in a brief view, is the country with which it is proposed to open communication ; but to describe it further would be beyond the scope of this Report.

THE WORK OF LAST SUMMER.

In the month of May, last year, at the request of the Hon. Alex. Campbell, the then Commissioner of Crown Lands of Canada, I submitted an estimate of the probable cost of the works I had proposed in the Lake Superior Section, and an appropriation of $55,900 having been made, on the same, from the Upper Canada Colonization Road Fund, as my time was greatly occupied by other engagements, it was eventually arranged that Mr. Bridgland, who had charge of the Upper Canada Colonization Roads, should undertake the road from Thunder Bay to Dog Lake, while, in regard to the dam, as he had no experience in works of the kind, I undertook to provide for its construction, and was accordingly instructed to lay out the work and place over it a competent superintendent, who should see to its management during my absence.

Under these arrangements, considering the lateness of the period of the season at which operations were commenced, a fair amount of work was accomplished. Six miles of the road were completed, under the able management of Mr. Snow, who had immediate charge of the working parties, and, at Dog Lake, under the direction of Mr. Joseph Samson, a considerable quantity of timber was got out for the dam. Boats and scows were built for the conveyance of stone and material to the work, and a suitable building erected for the accommodation of the workmen.

Much of the necessary material and tools for the road and dam, besides a small quantity of provisions, are now on hand, and it is greatly to be desired that the operations, so auspiciously commenced, should be proceeded with as early as possible in the spring, inasmuch as these works, as well as being of paramount and permanent necessity to the line of communication, will, when completed, be of great advantage in the first instance, in facilitating the conveyance of materials and supplies to works of similar character farther in the interior.

MR. J. W. BRIDGLAND'S REPORT.

I notice this document to correct an error into which Mr. Bridgland seems, inadvertently, to have fallen. He has projected, on a map, a line of Railway from Lake Superior to Rainy Lake, and, from the information gleaned from a mere preliminary report of mine, represents the country through which it would pass as being imperfectly examined, or wholly unexplored. Now, the fact is, that the region to which he refers, although not examined exactly with the view to a railway, has been explored to such an extent as to afford, at least, a fair knowledge of its topography. Messrs. Wells, Russell and Gaudet, Provincial Land Surveyors, crossed and recrossed it in various directions, as I, myself, also did, making surveys and determining levels over extensive sections, and should Mr. Bridgland ever visit the country, which he has not as yet done, I feel confident that he will perceive the accuracy of the description contained in my reports, and reproduced in an abridged form in this document, under the heads of " Lake Superior Section " and " Lake Region."

As regards the railroad, I have, in various reports submitted to the Government, explained that when the circumstances of the country would admit of works of such magnitude, and when the North-west Territories had attained a certain degree of development, a short line, of some twenty-five miles, from Thunder Bay to Dog Lake, would be of advantage, as would also a line from the North-west angle of the Lake of the Woods to Fort Garry, combining with these great works the improvement of the intermediate navigation, by means of lock and dam, from Dog Lake to the Lake of the Woods.

Mr. Bridgland has adopted the same idea, with this difference, that he proposes a railroad of no less than *two hundred miles at the outset*, with *one lock* at Fort Frances. In either case, it will be observed that there must be intermediate navigation. Then, why not bring the navigation as close as possible to Lake Superior, so as to have a shorter railroad ? A canal, supposing the lockage to average as much as that of the Rideau has done, would not cost half as much as a railroad of 200 miles in length, which latter, supposing it to involve no greater outlay than similar works in this country have averaged, would cost at least *eight millions of dollars*.

Such vast projects are as yet premature. In regard to Mr. Bridgland's scheme, as he professes no personal knowledge of the country, and merely submits it as a suggestion, I shall offer no further comment than to say that it would be useless to expend further sums of money in exploration of the route which he proposes, with the view to a railroad. His line, at the summit of the water-shed, would be at an elevation of some 1,500 feet above the level of Lake Superior, and that not in one gradual rise, but over successive hills and valleys. Further to the westward it would be on a sort of dividing ridge, between "long and irregular watercourses." Its course would be transverse to the strike of the gneiss which, over a considerable part of the route, is heaved up in mountain chains, or depressed in sharp valleys filled with lakes as already described, in this report, under the head of "Lake Region." Moreover, a railway of such considerable length should be so placed as to be available, at some future period, as a link in the extension of Canadian Railways to the vast prairies of the West, and, in this regard, Mr. Bridgland's proposed line would be quite out of the way.

I fully concur with him in his views as to the expediency of immediate and energetic action in opening such communication as would attract the trade of the western territories to this country, and I believe the plan which I have proposed would have the desired effect.

Respectfully submitted,
S. J. DAWSON.

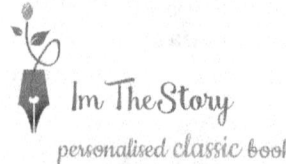

CPSIA information can be obtained
at www.ICGtesting.com
Printed in the USA
BVHW040943270819
556819BV00015B/3684/P